COOKSOURCE

ISABELLE TOURNEAU

COOKSOURCE

Doubleday

New York   London   Toronto   Sydney   Auckland

ACKNOWLEDGMENTS

Many thanks to Connie Clausen Associates, especially Susan Lipson for her enthusiasm for this project from the beginning. Thanks also to the terrific staff at Doubleday, including Judy Kern, Kara Leverte, John Duff, and Barry Zwieg for editorial direction, to Katheryn Tebbel, Susan Higginbotham, and Chaucy Bennetts for their helpful copy editing, and to Patrice Fodero for the design of *CookSource*.

I am grateful to the many companies who along with their catalogs sent helpful tips and inspiration for the book. Warm thanks go to those individuals who supplied the wonderful recipes, many of them family favorites, from which the recipes in *CookSource* were chosen.

Finally, thanks to my friends who so generously shared their ideas and sources for *CookSource*. Love and special thanks go to Don and Jason for their support and for their tastings and comments around the kitchen table.

PUBLISHED BY DOUBLEDAY
a division of Bantam Doubleday Dell Publishing Group, Inc.
666 Fifth Avenue, New York, New York 10103

DOUBLEDAY and the portrayal of an anchor
with a dolphin are trademarks of Doubleday,
a division of Bantam Doubleday Dell
Publishing Group, Inc.

LIBRARY OF CONGRESS CATALOGING-IN-PUBLICATION DATA

Tourneau, Isabelle.
    CookSource : an indispensable guide to the best mail-
order sources for specialty foods, ethnic and regional
ingredients, and other kitchen supplies / Isabelle Tourneau.
— 1st ed.
        p.   cm.
        1. Food—Catalogs.   2. Grocery trade—United States—
Catalogs.   3. Cookery—Equipment and supplies—
Catalogs.   I. Title.
    II. Title: CookSource.
    TX354.5.T68   1990
    641.3'0029'473—dc20   89-77788
                                                                          CIP

ISBN 0-385-41092-1

BOOK DESIGN AND ILLUSTRATION BY PATRICE FODERO

Copyright © 1990 by Isabelle Tourneau

All Rights Reserved
Printed in the United States of America
August 1990
First Edition
CUR

CONTENTS

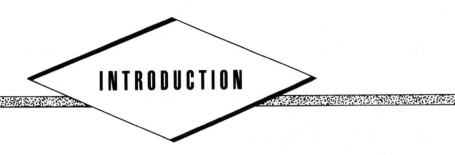

INTRODUCTION

Why Mail Order Foods?

Why mail order foods, you may ask, when supermarkets are already meeting consumer demands for more variety? There are quite a few reasons, some quite practical and others more esoteric. Let's consider the practical advantages first.

Mail order is convenient . . .

Most of us are busier than ever and have precious little time for scouting around shops looking for special foods and ingredients. Ordering by phone or mail saves countless hours in traffic, parking lots, and checkout lines—time you can spend at home planning, preparing, and enjoying wonderful food with family and friends.

Mail order brings you more choices . . .

Browsing through ethnic and regional cookbooks is great fun, but unfamiliar or hard-to-find ingredients can cool any cook's enthusiasm. (Those tiny footnotes, "Available in specialty food stores," aren't at all helpful when your only resource is an ordinary chain grocery store.) Mail ordering literally brings a world of ingredients to your door and makes delving into new cuisines an adventure. It lets you enjoy foods you're unlikely to find locally—handmade farmstead cheese, exotic tropical fruits, freshly picked hazelnuts, and many more.

Mail order gives you better value . . .

Mail ordering foods provides opportunities to save money by buying staples like rice, nuts, and dried fruit in bulk. You may pay more for specialty items, such as naturally raised lamb, flours stone-ground from organic grains, hand-made pasta, or wild berry preserves. But in these instances the higher prices purchase quality and taste you won't find in supermarket products.

About those esoteric advantages . . .

Good food nourishes the spirit, too. Ordering food directly from its source will put you in touch with families who are restoring gristmills to make quality flour, with New England maple farmers who send you newsletters about their sugaring season, beekeepers who still make old-fashioned crystallized honey, and cheese makers who send a personal note and photo of a pretty Nubian doe along with the cheese. You'll get to know companies who care so much about quality and service that they search the world to offer you the finest provisions. Your awareness and appreciation of the abundance and diversity of America's regional foods will deepen. Believe me, it's a fine restorative after the neon-lit super-market.

Using and Enjoying CookSource

I hope everyone who appreciates good food will use and enjoy CookSource. One hears so many pronouncements these days—everything from "No one's cooking anymore" to "Everyone's getting back to the kitchen." I think for most of us the reality is somewhere in between. Many days, especially weekdays, we are too busy to spend much time cooking, so we put together quick meals with the help of the microwave. But on more leisurely weekends and holidays we enjoy spending time in the kitchen preparing special meals for family or friends.

CookSource will help you on busy days and on leisurely days. For quick dinners, stock up on quality basics that will make simple meals outstanding— the best pasta, oils, and vinegars for the pantry, sourdough baguettes and easy-to-prepare meat and fish for the freezer. Select a variety of provisions from Chapter 6, "Condiments and Savory Sauces"—they'll make the simplest broiled chicken into something fantastic. For occasions when you have more time to cook, order stone-ground flours for hearty and aromatic home-baked breads, or get in everything you need to share a Southwestern or Cajun feast with friends.

Although there are probably dozens of ways to organize material in a source book like this, CookSource follows a system I have developed over the years for filing mail order information for my own use. It lets you browse through an alphabetical listing of provisions or regional and ethnic suppliers as interest moves you. Of course, CookSource has the advantage of an index to help you find specific ingredients, too. You'll discover that some suppliers appear in more than one chapter because they provide a variety of foods and ingredients. This seemed a better choice than putting in a complex system of cross-referencing.

With the convenience of toll-free numbers and credit card ordering, you'll be able to access many of these sources immediately just from reading the descriptions in CookSource. I suggest you also take the time to gather a collection of catalogs for foods and ingredients that interest you or that are difficult to find in your area. They will be a great resource on your cookbook shelf and soon you'll know right where to turn to order unusual items quickly.

Part III of CookSource is a potpourri of additional food-related sources you may enjoy—books, equipment, food gifts, where to order supplies to grow your own fresh produce and herbs, and, if the fancy strikes you, where to get supplies to make wine or beer.

How was CookSource compiled?

As the mail order industry exploded, several fine books about mail order foods appeared, but none quite met the needs of cooks who want to know where to get things like sourdough starters, balsamic vinegar, lemon grass, fresh quail, and dried wild mushrooms. I knew there was a need for CookSource, so I began combining my own sources with suggestions from fellow cooks and the recommendations I found in cooking magazines. In addition, I have contacted suppliers to professional chefs to see if they would also be interested in servicing the home cook; many happily agreed and are included here.

Of course, compiling a source book is a never ending process. There are always new suppliers, and things do change, even with well-established firms. I hope the omissions are few and that the suppliers in COOKSOURCE continue to thrive and delight their customers. If one of your favorite suppliers is missing, it may be for one of several reasons. Some suppliers who don't advertise and who are known almost exclusively to their customers may have been overlooked; some companies failed to respond to several requests for information (perhaps they are small suppliers doing all they can to keep up with current customer demand); information from some suppliers simply came too late to be included. (Only a few companies were intentionally excluded: those operating food clubs with a required regular purchase, and, in one case, a company that responded to a simple request for information with an avalanche of junklike mail for months.)

I'd be glad to hear about sources discovered by fellow cooks. Please write to me c/o Bantam Doubleday Dell, 666 Fifth Avenue, New York, NY 10103, and we'll try to include your suggestions in the next edition of COOKSOURCE. In the meantime, *bon appétit!*

Some Hints About Mail Ordering

Mail ordering is a popular and timesaving way to shop for many things. Here are a few guidelines to help make sure all your armchair shopping adventures are happy ones.

Some basic information . . .

The goal in COOKSOURCE was to keep symbols and abbreviations to a minimum. Only credit cards are abbreviated as follows:

AMEX: American Express
CB: Carte Blanche
DC: Diners Club
DISC: Discover
MC: MasterCard

All companies will accept money orders or checks with orders, although some will wait to ship until checks clear. (Of course, never send cash in the mail.) You may be baffled to see that some companies in COOKSOURCE accept phone orders but don't take credit cards. There are two reasons for this: first, they may ship UPS C.O.D.; second, believe it or not, there are still some companies that send you a bill.

Shop carefully . . .

Read catalog descriptions closely to make sure you're getting what you want. Be certain to figure in any shipping charges and be sure you understand when your order will arrive (especially if it is perishable, so someone will be home to receive it). Phone when possible, so that you can inquire directly about anything you don't understand.

Keep records . . .

Keep a copy of a written order and write down details of a phoned order; keep orders and the catalog until you receive your shipment.

Don't be reluctant to order perishables . . .

Suppliers of meat, fish, cheese, and other perishables take every precaution to make sure their products reach you in excellent condition. Insulated containers, gel and/or dry ice, and overnight shipping do an excellent job. However, in the hottest months, some suppliers do curtail shipment of certain products.

If things aren't right, let the supplier know . . .

Most companies are anxious to please customers; some even enclose postpaid postcards so you can let them know that everything arrived in good condition. If you aren't satisfied, please let them know and give them an opportunity to make it right.

There's help if you can't get satisfaction . . .

I hope it doesn't happen, but if you have a problem you can't resolve with a supplier, you can contact the Direct Marketing Association (6 East 43rd Street, New York, NY 10017) for free help in settling complaints.

PART ONE

QUALITY PROVISIONS

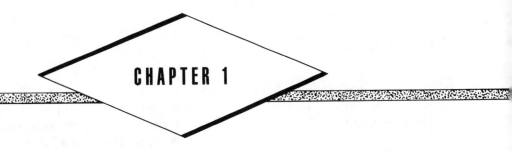

CHAPTER 1

BAKING SUPPLIES: CHOCOLATE, EXTRACTS, AND MISCELLANEOUS INGREDIENTS

All cooks will agree that the best baked goods start with top-quality ingredients. Here are some purveyors of excellent extracts, flavorings, and baking chocolate, as well as some very special things such as candied flowers to give your baked creations a glorious finishing touch.

How to choose from the riches offered here—especially the array of domestic and imported chocolate? Get together with some of your baking colleagues who also care about quality ingredients, order a sampling of the different brands, and then have a gala chocolate-tasting party. Even if you still can't decide, you'll all have had a wonderfully sweet time!

Flavors from almond to vanilla—

Bickford Flavors
282 South Main Street
Akron, OH 44308

800-283-8322
216-762-4666

The Bickford name has been associated with natural flavors for almost a hundred years. Their extensive list of flavors begins with almond and ends with white vanilla. The vanillas are available in half a dozen different-size bottles from one ounce to one gallon. The Bickford product line also includes flavored oils, carob syrup, and a new line of nonalcoholic liqueur flavors.

Free price list
Mail orders
No credit cards

Dessert shells and cordial cups—

Karl Bissinger French Confections
3983 Gratiot
St. Louis, MO 63110

800-325-8881 (orders only)
314-534-2408

The Chocolate Catalogue from Karl Bissinger French Confections contains a lavish selection of confections that changes with the seasons. This is also the place to order fine chocolate dessert shells and cordial cups.

Free color catalog
Phone and mail orders, gift orders
CB, DC, MC, VISA

Imported baking supplies in quantity—

The Chef's Pantry
P. O. Box 3
Post Mills, VT 05058

800-666-9940
802-333-4141

You can buy Callebaut chocolate in money-saving 11-pound bars in bitter, semi-sweet, milk, mocha, unsweetened, white, or gianduia. (Try it in the following recipe for elegant Sacher Torte from The Chef's Pantry.) This fine

Belgian chocolate is also available in 1.1-pound bars (bitter or milk) and batons for baking into croissants, cookies, and pastries. The Chef's Pantry also stocks vanilla beans, extract, and essence, candied orange and lemon peel, crystallized flowers (violets, mint leaves, lilacs, and whole roses), and orange blossom water.

Free illustrated catalog
Phone and mail orders, gift orders
MC, VISA

Sacher Torte

from The Chef's Pantry

Mary Spata calls this "an easy recipe with a grand result." You can make it in advance and it freezes well (freeze unwrapped first to set the icing, then wrap well).

Cake:
 8 ounces bitter or semi-sweet Callebaut chocolate
 8 ounces unsalted butter, softened
 ¾ teaspoon salt
 2 teaspoons vanilla extract
 1 cup sugar
 ⅓ cup flour
 8 ounces walnuts or hazelnuts, very finely chopped
 8 egg yolks
 8 egg whites
 ⅔ cup apricot preserve (or other fruit preserve, if you prefer)

Icing:
 ½ cup heavy cream
 2 teaspoons powdered instant coffee
 6 ounces bitter or semi-sweet Callebaut chocolate, chopped

Butter and flour a round 9-inch by 2½-inch-deep cake pan with a removable bottom, or a springform pan. Preheat the oven to 350 degrees. Melt the chocolate and cool until lukewarm. Cream the butter with the salt, vanilla, and sugar. Combine the flour and nuts. Add the egg yolks one by one to the butter-sugar mixture. Stir in the chocolate and nuts. Beat the egg whites to soft peaks and stir a quarter of them into the chocolate mixture to lighten the batter. Fold in the remaining whites. Pour the batter into the prepared pan and bake 1 hour. Cool in the pan 20 minutes and push down the puffed-up sides so that they are flush with the middle. Remove the sides of the pan and invert the cake onto a cooling rack set over waxed paper. (The bottom has now become the top of the cake.) Cool completely. Heat the preserve, push it through a sieve, and brush it over the top and sides of the cooled cake. Let the glaze set for about half an hour before icing the cake.

Icing (also makes a great warm chocolate sauce for any dessert):
In a metal mixing bowl or saucepan, scald the cream. Whisk in the coffee and add the chocolate. Stir one minute over the heat, then remove and continue to stir until the chocolate has completely melted. Cool to lukewarm and pour over the cake. Rotate the cake while spreading the icing evenly with a spatula. Chill the cake on its rack until the icing is completely set. Transfer to a serving plate and refrigerate. Bring to room temperature before serving.

Variations and serving suggestions:
Whatever you do for a garnish, keep it simple. A few candied violets around the perimeter seem appropriate, and at Christmastime sprigs of fresh holly are lovely. Whipped cream can be served alongside, although the cake is perfect alone.

Cranberry Sacher Torte:
Add 1½ cups coarsely chopped fresh cranberries and 1 tablespoon grated orange rind or chopped candied orange peel to the batter when you add the chocolate and nuts.

Baking chocolate plus tempting treats—

Confetti
Embarcadero Center 4
San Francisco, CA 94111

415-362-1706

Belgian Callebaut milk chocolate and bittersweet baking chocolates are available from Confetti, as well as a complete line from Ghirardelli, San Francisco's oldest and most famous chocolate company. You'll also be tempted by the assortment of imported and American chocolate treats. Although Confetti's emphasis is on chocolate, dried fruits and nuts, coffee and teas are also featured.

Free price list
Phone and mail orders, gift orders
AMEX, MC, VISA

Unusual extracts, vanilla powder, and special cookie vanilla—

Cook Flavoring Company
P. O. Box 890
1103 A Street, Suite 352
Tacoma, WA 98401

206-627-5499

Many years of owning an ice cream company in California taught Kenneth Cook how vital vanilla is as a flavoring agent. To produce a top-quality vanilla for the home cook, he founded Cook Flavoring Company in 1982. In addition to pure vanilla extract and powder, the company has formulated a vanilla especially for cookie baking. Cook's list of extracts includes all the basics and some unusual varieties—blackberry, cinnamon, Kona coffee, hazelnut, lime, and red raspberry. "Cook's Classic Collection," available for $2.00 or free with large orders, contains recipes for using some of these unusual extracts.

Free price list
Mail orders
No credit cards

Coffee syrup—

Eclipse Food Products
P. O. Box 7590
Warwick, RI 02887

401-739-3600

This Rhode Island company has made extracts and flavors since 1914, and if you like old-fashioned coffee syrup as an ice cream topping or for making flavored drinks, this is the place to find it. For a refreshing Coffee Frappe, try the following recipe from the Eclipse booklet, which also has recipes for coffee cream caramel custard, coffee spice cake, and coffee gelatin.

Free information
Mail orders
No credit cards

Vanilla and additional baking supplies—

KCJ Vanilla Company
RD 1, Box 184
Pittston, PA 18643

Contact by mail

KCJ Vanilla stocks vanilla extracts from Tahiti, Madagascar, and Mexico in both single and double strength; vanilla beans are available from the same three sources. More than twenty additional flavors are offered, including black walnut, butterscotch, coconut, and raspberry. KCJ Vanilla also stocks other baking ingredients, including dried wild blueberries, pistachios, and maple granules.

Brochure, $1.00 (refundable with order)
Mail orders
No credit cards

Coffee Frappe
from Eclipse Food Products

Combine 1 tablespoon Eclipse Coffee Syrup, 1 scoop of ice cream, and ¾ cup milk in a blender. Blend until smooth. Pour and enjoy.

How to Make a Baking Glaze
from KCJ Vanilla

Combine ¾ cup sugar and ½ teaspoon KCJ flavoring of choice. Heat over low heat until sugar melts and turns golden brown. Remove from heat and immediately spoon or drizzle over baked and cooled pastries, cakes, pies, or cookies.

For cake and candy makers—

Kitchen Krafts
P. O. Box 805
Mount Laurel, NJ 08054

609-778-4960

Baking chocolate, specialty sugars, flavorings, and extracts are included in this catalog for cake and candy makers. Baking supplies range from novelty cake pans to parchment paper, and from a tool for making homemade sugar cones to mini muffin pans. A list of cookbooks completes the selection.

Free illustrated price list
Mail orders
No credit cards

Hard-to-find baking supplies—

La Cuisine
323 Cameron Street
Alexandria, VA 22314

800-521-1176
703-836-4435 (in VA, call collect)

La Cuisine stocks high-quality baking ingredients such as French essences, Tahitian vanilla beans and extract, and imported baking chocolate, as well as very special and difficult-to-find items such as sheet gelatin used to create windowpanes in gingerbread houses.

Call the toll-free number for prices and availability of items you are seeking, since prices fluctuate on many imported items. When you order the La Cuisine catalog you will also receive regularly published catalog newsletters called "The Cook's Advocate," which supplement catalog information.

Catalog and supplements, $3.00
Phone and mail orders
MC, VISA

Flavors, extracts, and essential oils—

Charles Loeb
615 Palmer Road
Yonkers, NY 10701

914-961-7776

This company stocks Virginia Dare brand extracts in more than 20 flavors, Messina brand essential oils (anise, almond, lemon) and flavors for making cordials and liquers. Also fruit syrups, toppings, and a wide choice of herbs and teas.

Illustrated catalog, $1.00 (refundable with order)
Phone and mail orders
MC, VISA

A complete line of baking supplies—

Maid of Scandinavia
3244 Raleigh Avenue
Minneapolis, MN 55416

800-328-6722
800-851-1121 (in MN)
925-9256 (Twin Cities metro area)

In this very complete catalog for the baker and candy maker, the chocolate list includes Nestlé, Ambrosia, Callebaut, and Lindt brands. There are also carob and dietetic products, candy ingredients, and molds. Vanilla products include colorless vanilla, bourbon vanilla, vanilla sugar, powdered vanilla, and pure vanilla extract. You'll also find numerous specialty flavoring extracts and oils, and hard-candy flavors. A partial list of the dozens of baking supplies includes almond paste, macaroon paste, egg white powder, specialty sugars, and cake decorating supplies galore. Maid of Scandinavia, in business for more than forty years, also publishes *Mailbox News*, a monthly magazine for candy makers and bakers.

Color catalog, $1.00
Phone and mail orders
DISC, MC, VISA

Double-duty flavorings and extracts—

Northwestern Coffee Mills
217 North Broadway
Milwaukee, WI 53202

414-276-1031

This Milwaukee coffee mill bottles flavors and extracts for flavoring coffee, but they are equally suitable for cooking and baking. They are described as a commercial grade that is a bit more concentrated than commonly available

flavors. You can also order pure vanilla extract that is cold-pressed from Madagascar Bourbon vanilla beans as well as the beans, either singly or in packages up to one pound.

Free illustrated catalog (but they'll appreciate it if you send 50¢)
Phone and mail orders, gift orders, and gift certificates
MC, VISA

Imported baking ingredients—

Paprikas Weiss
1546 Second Avenue
New York, NY 10028

212-288-6117

In addition to dozens of Hungarian specialties, you'll discover Danish marzipan, French orange or rose water, imported vanilla sugar, crystallized flowers, candied angelica, vanilla beans, almond paste, chestnut puree, and crème de marrons. Of course, there's also everything you need to make an authentic Hungarian strudel.

Seasonal catalogs, $3.00 annual subscription
Phone and mail orders, gift orders and certificates
AMEX, MC, VISA

Domestic and imported chocolate—

Paradigm Foodworks, Inc.
5775 S.W. Jean Road, #106A
Lake Oswego, OR 97035

800-234-0250
503-636-4880

A source for Guittard chocolate, a high-quality domestic chocolate, in a variety of products: chips, slabs, coatings, and baking ingredients. Paradigm also

Tempering Chocolate

from Maid of Scandinavia

When chocolate is to be used for molding or dipping, rather than as an ingredient in baking, it must be tempered. When cocoa butter, the fat of chocolate, is cooled from a liquid to a solid state, it can crystallize into several forms. Tempering is important because it controls the type of crystal that is formed and ensures that the chocolate will be firm and glossy. If too many of the wrong type of crystals form, the chocolate will be soft and dull and may be streaked with white. There are many methods of tempering chocolate; this one requires less time than most.

The room should be 65 to 70 degrees, free from drafts and odors, with low humidity and good ventilation. It is advisable to have an accurate candy thermometer with a range of 80 to 130 degrees.

1. Preheat oven to 250 degrees and then turn off heat. Place 80 percent of the chocolate in a bowl in the oven for 5 minutes.
2. Remove the chocolate from the oven and stir, then return it to the oven for another 5 minutes. Repeat this step until the chocolate is between 115 and 120 degrees. Do not exceed 125 degrees.
3. Add a chunk of chocolate (from the remaining 20 percent) and stir well to lower the temperature. (Reserve remaining chocolate for retempering, if necessary, or for another use.)
4. When the chocolate reaches the appropriate temperature (86 to 90 degrees for dark chocolate; 83 to 88 degrees for milk chocolate), remove what's left of the chunk you added.
5. Test the temper of the chocolate by spreading a dab of chocolate on waxed paper and allowing it to set for 3 minutes. If the chocolate doesn't set up (hard and shiny), the whole procedure must be repeated from Step 1.
6. Maintain the temperature of the chocolate by placing the bowl of chocolate in a warm-water bath of the appropriate chocolate temperature. Avoid getting water into the chocolate. You are ready to dip.

After dipping and molding, pour the leftover chocolate onto waxed paper to set up. Store tempered chocolate in a cool, dry, odor-free room.

carries Swiss Lindt chocolate as well as its own chocolate, liqueur and caramel sauces, compotes, and jellies. The Sweet Tooth Samplers would make welcome gifts.

Free catalog
Phone and mail orders, gift orders
MC, VISA

Crystallized flowers and other special things—

G. B. Ratto & Company
821 Washington Street
Oakland, CA 94607

800-325-3483
800-228-3515 (in CA)
Fax: 415-836-2250

As well as the basics such as fine baking chocolate, vanilla extract and beans, flavored extracts and syrups, G. B. Ratto sells crystallized flowers from France (rose and violet petals, yellow mimosa and mint leaves) and French praline pastes, candied angelica, colored coarse sugar, orange and rose flower water.

Free illustrated catalog
Phone, fax, and mail orders, gift orders and certificates
MC, VISA

Lorann oils and tips for their use—

Rosemary House
120 South Market Street
Mechanicsburg, PA 17055

717-697-5111
717-766-6581

Rosemary House specializes in herbs and also carries a selection of Lorann oils in 1-dram bottles: over thirty flavors from anise to wintergreen. They also have a compendium of recipes, hints, and tips for using these oils.

Illustrated catalog, $2.00
Mail orders, gift orders
No credit cards

Falernum flavoring and Peychaud's bitters—

Sazerac Company, Inc.
803 Jefferson Highway
New Orleans, LA 70121

504-831-9450

Falernum is a sweet lemony-almond Caribbean syrup; Peychaud's is a premium brand of aromatic bitters. Not limited just to making drinks, these flavorings can be used to add new flavor to favorite dishes such as baked beans and to create some new appealing ones. Recipes are supplied with the products.

Free price list
Mail orders
No credit cards

Ready-to-use vanilla sugar—

Select Origins, Inc.
Box N
Southampton, NY 11968

800-822-2092
516-924-5447
Fax: 516-924-5892

Select Origins has created its own Turbinado Vanilla Sugar with a whole Madagascar vanilla bean in the jar. Cooking suggestions include adding it to sugar cookies, spiced breads, whipped cream, and chocolate mousse. Or simply use it on fresh fruit or berries and in coffee and iced tea. You can buy plain turbinado (a pure, unrefined sugar) to replenish the jar. The company also sells vanilla beans and pure vanilla extract.

Free illustrated catalog
Phone, fax, and mail orders, gift orders
AMEX, MC, VISA

Vanilla with a bean in every bottle—

The Spice House
P. O. Box 1633
Milwaukee, WI 53201

414-768-8799

The Penzey family, proprietors of The Spice House, like to follow a custom of vanilla trade that dates back many years: they put a whole vanilla bean in every bottle of pure vanilla that they sell. Why? Because it helps explain to children and grown-ups alike where vanilla comes from, and it gives customers the bonus of a fragrant bean when the vanilla is used up. Spice House customers find different uses for the bean: drop it in a quart of milk to make vanilla-flavored milk; dry it out

and wrap it in gauze for the handkerchief or lingerie drawer; cut it in pieces and mix it with sugar to make vanilla sugar. The Spice House vanilla is made from Madagascar Bourbon beans and comes in single and double strength; vanilla beans from French Polynesia, Mexico, the Bourbon Isles, and Tahiti are also available.

Illustrated catalog, $1.00
Phone and mail orders, gift orders
No credit cards

Vanilla beans and extract—

Vanilla, Saffron Imports
949 Valencia Street
San Francisco, CA 94110

415-648-8990
Fax: 415-648-2240

This restaurant supplier also offers a mail order service for home cooks. It carries Golden Gate brand pure vanilla extract (in a pantry-stocking and money-saving 1-quart size) and vacuum-packed vanilla beans.

Single- and Double-Strength Vanilla Extract

by Bill Penzey of The Spice House

It takes about a hundred genuine vanilla beans to make a gallon of single-strength vanilla extract. The Spice House vanilla, made from premium Madagascar Bourbon beans, is about the same strength level as cooks have purchased in America for years and about 10 percent richer than most brands of pure vanilla in supermarkets. Double-strength vanilla requires about two hundred beans to make a gallon of extract. This is the thick, rich, heavy grade of premium pure vanilla that is known to the bakery trade as "twofold" vanilla extract. Use exactly half as much as single strength; when making expensive, luxurious desserts, cakes, and pastries, you might like to add a little more.

Additional extracts include almond, lemon, peppermint, orange, black walnut, and more.

Free price list
Mail orders only
No credit cards

For more sources, check these chapters:

For more sweet and natural flavorings to enliven cooking and baking, see Chapter 14, "Maple Syrup and Maple Products."

For nuts, see Chapter 17, "Nuts, Seeds, and Nut Butters."

For dried fruit, see Chapter 11, "Fruit, Fresh and Dried."

BREADS, CRACKERS, AND SPECIALTY BAKED GOODS

As small neighborhood bakeries have been replaced over the years by large bread factories, much of the tradition of quality bread making has been lost. Fortunately, some wonderful old-fashioned bakers still exist, especially in ethnic neighborhoods, and it's encouraging to see new bakeries dedicated to quality products becoming established in many cities. If you're not fortunate enough to have one close by, here are some good sources for wholesome, delicious products to order by mail from bakers who are continuing fine bakery traditions.

Wild rice bread and other treats—

American Spoon Foods, Inc.
P. O. Box 566
1668 Clarion Avenue
Petoskey, MI 49770-0566

800-222-5886
616-347-9030
Fax: 616-347-2512

Breads from the French Meadow Bakery are featured by American Spoon Foods, which claims the bakery is "setting baking back two centuries" with its traditional sugar-free and yeast-free breads. Order Summer Bread (French sourdough), Minnesota wild rice bread, and whole rye in a sampler selection or a huge loaf of their hearty Bountiful Bread.

Free seasonal catalogs
Phone, fax, and mail orders, gift orders
DISC, MC, VISA

Sourdough-leavened breads—

Baldwin Hill Bakery
Baldwin Hill Road
Phillipston, MA 01331

508-249-4691

Hy Lerner and Paul Petrofsky established Baldwin Hill Bakery in 1974, inspired by a bakery in Belgium where they had discovered bread made from simple and pure ingredients, which was the most delicious they had ever eaten. Baldwin Hill Bakery bread is made with organic stone-ground flour, pure well water, and natural sourdough leavening. It is baked over a wood fire in a traditional brick oven. Varieties include whole wheat, sesame wheat, rye, salt-free whole wheat, raisin, and French bread. There is a minimum order of 12 loaves but prices are very reasonable, so you can take the opportunity to stock your freezer with quality breads.

Free price list
Mail orders
No credit cards

Traditional common crackers and water crackers—

G. H. Bent Company
7 Pleasant Street
Milton, MA 02186

617-698-5945

Josiah Bent's cold water crackers have been made for almost two hundred years and were first enjoyed by whalers, tea traders, trappers, and fur traders. Definitely a New England tradition, these crackers are indispensable for chowders, special soups, and as an accompaniment to fine cheese. In the fall the company's production of common crackers increases fivefold to satisfy the demand

of customers making turkey stuffing. (A stuffing recipe is available.) Try them in Bent's Traditional Fish Chowder, a recipe that proves there are some old-fashioned dishes that just can't be improved.

Free price list
Mail orders
No credit cards

Traditional San Francisco sourdough bread—

Boudin Bakery
132 Hawthorne Street
San Francisco, CA 94107

415-882-1800
Fax: 415-882-1821

Sourdough French bread from Boudin is made only from flour, salt, water, and the original "mother" dough that dates back to the company's first loaf baked

Bent's Traditional Fish Chowder

from G. H. Bent Company

  3 thin slices salt pork
  1 medium onion, chopped
1½ pounds haddock, scrod, or other firm white fish
 12 Bent's Common Crackers
  1 quart milk
  1 teaspoon butter
  6 boiled potatoes, diced
Salt and pepper to taste

Fry salt pork and chopped onion together. Simmer fish until tender. Break crackers into large pieces. Heat milk and butter in a double boiler and add crackers. Add pork, onion, potatoes, fish, salt, and pepper and heat thoroughly. Serves 4.

in 1849. Order loaves, sandwich rolls, or fruit-studded panettone. Croissants, breadsticks, croutons, cookies, and biscotti are also available, and you can choose gift selections that include California cheese and salami.

Free color catalog
Phone, fax, and mail orders, gift orders
AMEX, MC, VISA

Canapé and ragout shells—

The Chef's Pantry
P. O. Box 3
Post Mills, VT 05058

800-666-9940
802-333-4141

Order bite-size canapé shells or larger ragout shells from The Chef's Pantry (the larger shells are imported from Holland). Filled with your choice of savory fillings, they're ideal for hors d'oeuvres and appetizers.

Free illustrated catalog
Phone and mail orders, gift orders
MC, VISA

Whole wheat crackers from Wisconsin—

Croft's Crackers
W8368 Highway 33 East
Portage, WI 53901

608-742-4465

It seems that where you find fine cheese you'll also discover great little crackers. In Wisconsin, John and Nancy Croft bake crispy whole wheat crackers that are good with cheese or all by themselves. They also make a version of this cracker that's sweetened with fruit juice and dusted with cinnamon and sugar.

Free price list
Mail orders
No credit cards

Traditional Italian baked goods—

DiCamillo Bakery
811 Linwood Avenue
Niagara Falls, NY 14305

716-282-2341

This bakery started in the 1920s when their crusty loaves were delivered around Niagara Falls neighborhoods by horse and wagon. Still run by the DiCamillo family, the bakery ships an array of breads, cakes, and biscotti. Highlights include focaccia (Italian flatbreads flavored with pesto, cheese, oregano, and chives), celery dill stick bread, wine biscotti, and torta di cioccolata (chocolate date and nut cake). You can also order plain and seasoned bread crumbs. Assortments in pretty ribbon-tied bags or decorative canisters present a selection of products.

Free illustrated catalog
Phone and mail orders, gift orders
AMEX, MC, VISA

New Orleans French bread—

Gazin's
2910 Toulouse Street
P. O. Box 19221
New Orleans, LA 70179

800-262-6410
504-482-0302

Enjoy the same crisp, crusty bread served in New Orleans restaurants. If you like, Gazin's will deliver a regular order to you monthly. Store loaves in the freezer and just pop them in the oven for 10 minutes before serving.

(Gazin's catalog also contains a great selection of Cajun/Creole items; see details in Chapter 24, "American Regional Foods.")

Color catalog, $1.00 (credited on first order)
Phone and mail orders
AMEX, MC, VISA

Middle Eastern baked products—

Ghossain's Mid-East Bakery
2935 Market Street
Youngstown, OH 44507

800-544-2415
216-782-9473

The ovens at Ghossain's Mid-East Bakery turn out a variety of specialties: thin, flat breads; pita, or pocket, bread; spinach, cheese, and meat pies; and baklava. The bakery also stocks a complete range of ingredients for Middle Eastern cuisine; these are listed in Chapter 25, "The International Pantry."

Free price list
Mail and phone orders
MC, VISA

A bakery with its own stone mill—

Hawthorne Valley Farm
RD 2, Box 225A
Ghent, NY 12075

518-672-7500

This bakery specializes in sourdough breads baked in the traditional northern European way. Home-grown rye and wheat berries are freshly ground in the bakery's own stone mill just before baking to ensure that all the valuable vitamins and enzymes are preserved. Choose from rye, wheat, or fruited rye.

Hawthorne Valley Farm also mail orders its own granola and cheese and maintains a well-stocked farm store for those who live close by.

Free price list
Mail orders
MC, VISA

Dutch treats—

Jaarsma Bakery
727 Franklin Street
Pella, IA 50219

515-628-2940

This Iowa bakery will send you a taste of Holland in its bread, buns, rolls, doughnuts, quick breads, pies, cakes, and cookies. Several special boxes offer an assortment of Dutch pastries and cookies, including treats such as spice cookies, almond butter cake, and fruitcake.

Free price list
Mail orders
No credit cards

Muffins baked with good health in mind—

Joyce's Gourmet English Muffin Company
4 Lake Street
Arlington, MA 02174

800-234-6836
617-641-1900

This family bakery makes English muffins that are low in sodium and contain no cholesterol. They're baked with nonfat milk and without eggs, butter, or oil. Flavors are plain, onion, cinnamon raisin, honey wheat raisin, oat bran, and cheese, and you can order assortments and gift baskets.

Free price list
Phone and mail orders, gift orders
MC, VISA

Genuine New York bagels—

The Manhattan Bagel Company
P. O. Box 580
New York, NY 10014

800-635-3691
212-691-3041

You can order New York bagels in eight varieties: plain, poppy seed, sesame, onion, cinnamon raisin, pumpernickel, whole wheat, egg, and oat bran raisin. They're vacuum-packed to ensure fresh delivery.

Free price list
Phone and mail orders
MC, VISA

San Francisco sourdough—

San Luis Sourdough
845 Capitolio Way
San Luis Obispo, CA 93401

805-543-6142

San Luis Sourdough bread is baked in the old San Francisco tradition, using only water, flour, salt, and natural yeast from generations-old sourdough starter. Order loaves, sticks, or baguettes of basic sourdough, cracked wheat, wheat walnut, and cracked wheat raisin.

Free price list
Mail orders
MC, VISA

Sunberry Baking Company
757 Kohn Street
Norristown, PA 19401

800-833-4090

Cholesterol-free sourdough breads from the Morabito family's Sunberry Baking Company have been made for almost sixty years without sugar, shortening, baker's yeast, or artificial preservatives. You can order several assortments that include baguettes, batons, round loaves, demibatons, dinner rolls, and sliced loaves. All are ready to brown and serve or to freeze for later use.

Free price list
Phone and mail orders
MC, VISA

Traditional Armenian cracker bread—

Valley Bakery
502 M Street
Fresno, CA 93721

209-485-2700

Lahvosh is Armenian cracker bread, and Janet Saghatelian continues the baking tradition started by her father in Fresno in 1922, when the bakery was at the center of an Armenian neighborhood. This versatile flatbread comes in 15-inch, 5-inch, and 3-inch rounds as well as heart-shaped, bite-sized crackers. Some wine experts find lahvosh an ideal palate cleanser to nibble at tastings.

Free price list
Mail orders, gift orders
MC, VISA

common crackers from

The Vermont Country Store
P. O. Box 3000
Manchester Center, VT 05255-3000

802-362-2400

Common crackers have been a Vermont tradition since 1828 when no rural store was without a cracker barrel near the cheese counter. The Vermont Country Store makes its own crackers in the regular 2-inch size as well as a 1-inch bite size. They also make a salt-free version and a cheese cracker with—naturally—Vermont cheese added. If you like, you can order crackers packed in charming nineteenth-century-style tins; refills are always available. This old-fashioned catalog is packed with lots of surprises.

Free illustrated brochure
Phone and mail orders
MC, VISA

English muffins in more flavors than you thought possible—

Wolferman's
One Muffin Lane
P. O. Box 15913
Lenexa, KS 66215-5916

800-999-0169

If you're a fan of English muffins, you'll love Wolferman's tempting selection of 12 varieties that include Cheddar cheese, blueberry, sour cream and onion, jalapeño cheese, as well as the traditional favorites. You can mix and match varieties in various size assortments and choose attractive selections for gift giving.

Free color catalog
Mail and phone orders, gift orders
AMEX, DISC, MC, VISA

CHAPTER 3

CAVIAR

Although caviar is considered a rare delicacy, it is available in a surprising range of prices. If you're new to the delights of caviar, read through the "Caviar Glossary" and "Suggestions for Serving Caviar" provided by some of the experts especially for this chapter—then enjoy!

Caviars including Chinese imports—

California Sunshine Fine Foods, Inc.
144 King Street
San Francisco, CA 94107

415-543-3007

Since 1985, California Sunshine Fine Foods has processed sturgeon roe from northern China's beluga and osetra sturgeons. According to California Sunshine Fine Foods, these less expensive Mandarin malossol (reduced salt) caviars are in every way comparable in taste, appearance, and quality to the caviars from the Caspian Sea. This company also offers Caspian Sea and domestic caviars as well as smoked fish and specialty sausage.

Free brochures
Phone and mail orders
AMEX, MC, VISA

Imported and domestic caviars—

Caspian Caviars
Highland Mill
P. O. Box 876
Camden, ME 04843

800-332-4436
207-236-4436
Fax: 207-236-2740

Caspian Caviars' specialty is malossol (reduced salt), and orders are hand-packed and kept temperature-controlled until they are shipped in insulated containers. Choose from imported caviars (Caspian, beluga, osetra, sevruga) or from the domestic varieties (American sturgeon, salmon, golden whitefish). Fresh seafood includes North Atlantic salmon, Maine lobsters, scallops, halibut, and oysters; smoked salmon, sturgeon, and tuna are also offered.

Free catalog
Phone, fax, and mail orders
AMEX, MC, VISA

Order from Caviarteria, or stop by to sample—

Caviarteria, Inc.
29 East 60th Street
New York, NY 10022

800-4-CAVIAR
212-759-7410
Fax: 718-482-8985

Caviarteria provides a wide selection of imported and domestic caviars, gift assortments, and additional special food items such as foie gras, smoked salmon, and truffles. Caviar enthusiasts visiting New York City may enjoy a visit to the caviar bar at Caviarteria at Petrouchka, a restaurant on East 86th Street.

Free brochure
Mail, phone, and fax orders, gift orders
AMEX, MC, VISA

Fresh caviars and seafood specialties—

Hansen Caviar Company, Inc.
93D South Railroad Avenue
Bergenfield, NJ 07621

201-385-6221
Fax: 201-385-9882

Arnold H. Hansen-Sturm, president of Hansen Caviar Company, is the fifth

Caviar Glossary and Storage Tips

from Arnold H. Hansen-Sturm, President
of Hansen Caviar Company, Inc.

Caviar is made from the roe (eggs) of the sturgeon, but the roe of many fish—salmon, lumpfish, whitefish, and others—can be prepared as caviar. If not of the sturgeon variety, the proper name (e.g., salmon) must identify clearly the type of caviar on the label. The delicate eggs are made into caviar with the great skill of a caviar maker. The roe is separated from the skein (membrane) and the eggs are washed and then most carefully cured by the addition of the finest-quality salt for the United States market. The process takes up to twenty minutes and longer on nonsturgeon varieties. No. 1 grade fresh malossol caviar receives from 2.5 to 3.5 percent salt, whereas the No. 2 grade vacuum-packed and pasteurized caviar may have double or more this level. The word "malossol" is Russian for lightly salted, and fresh malossol is considered the best grade and quality.

Never freeze caviar. With the exception of golden whitefish caviar, which can be stored frozen, all other types of caviar will be damaged if the temperature dips below 26 degrees F., the temperature at which caviar will freeze. The eggs will break down and the caviar will lose its single-egg appearance by becoming soft and wet. Ideal storage temperature is 28 degrees F. to 32 degrees F. In the home refrigerator, caviar will keep unopened up to two weeks. An open container should be used within several days.

generation of his family to be involved in the caviar business. His company offers a selection of imported and domestic fresh caviars, smoked salmon, a wide variety of smoked fish, pâtés, and an attractive array of imported, handcrafted caviar spoons. Special gift selections and executive samplers are also available.

Free price list
Phone, fax, and mail orders, gift orders
MC, VISA

Caviar from the Canadian north—

Merchant Adventurers Tea & Spice Company
70 Hollins Drive
Santa Cruz, CA 95060

408-426-6211

Merchant Adventurers' golden caviar is the roe of the Canadian lake whitefish, harvested just before freeze-over from the clear lakes of northern Canada. The eggs are naturally gold in color and are packed with no additives, just a hint of salt.

Free price list
Mail orders
MC, VISA

Fresh and pasteurized domestic and imported caviars—

Poriloff Caviar
Caviar King Division of Purepak Foods, Inc.
47-39 49th Street
Woodside, NY 11377

800-654-7264
718-784-3344
Fax: 718-784-4028

Caspian Sea, Chinese, and American caviars, both fresh and pasteurized, are offered, as well as kosher caviars and a selection of items including smoked

Suggestions for Serving Caviar
from Poriloff Caviar

• Spread a little caviar over broiled or baked fish steaks such as salmon, halibut, and swordfish after they are cooked.
• Add caviar to an omelet that is firm and has been left in the pan a few seconds.
• Place a dollop of sour cream on a baked potato and spoon caviar on top.

For appetizers and hors d'oeuvres:
• Mix salmon caviar with whipped cream cheese and serve with onion bagel crisps.
• Stuff artichoke bottoms and mushroom caps with natural-color caviars such as golden whitefish, salmon, and American sturgeon for color variation.
• Fill the cavities of pitted ripe avocado halves with caviar.
• Serve caviar surrounded with crispbread and toast points.

Scotch salmon, tuna fillets, and dried wild mushrooms. Try some of the suggestions above for serving caviar provided by Poriloff.

Free catalog
Phone, fax, and mail orders, gift orders
AMEX, VISA

If you'd like to try a variety of caviars, samplers are available from:

Balducci's
Mail Order Division
11-02 Queens Plaza South
Long Island City, NY 11101-4908

800-822-1444
800-247-2450 (in NY State)
718-786-9690 (special requests)

and

S. E. Rykoff & Company
P. O. Box 21467
Market Street Station
Los Angeles, CA 90021

800-421-9873 (orders)
213-624-6094 (product inquiries)

CHAPTER 4

CHEESE AND DAIRY PRODUCTS

The story of American cheese making would make a fascinating book, and in that volume one of the most interesting chapters would describe the recent renaissance of cottage-industry cheese makers. Many small farms across the country are producing very fine products. After sampling two-year-old farm-aged Cheddar or creamy fresh chèvre, it may be impossible to go back to the supermarket's selection of cheese. Best of all, direct from the supplier, prices are often much more reasonable than you'd find locally for specialty cheese.

This chapter begins with small producers of specialty cheese, continues with medium-size farm-based businesses and cooperatives that offer a variety of products, and concludes with a few large companies that provide a broad selection of domestic and imported cheese.

Small Companies and Farms Making Specialty Cheese

Browse through this section and see what some of America's most innovative cheesemakers are up to, then sample some of their fine products. You'll also find several sources for crème fraîche and fromage blanc here.

American Camembert—

Craigston Cheese Company
45 Dodges Row
Box 267
Wenham, MA 01984

800-365-6299
508-468-7497
Fax: 508-468-6338

Craigston Cheese Company makes American Camembert in small batches from fresh New England milk. Each step is done by hand under the watchful eye of master cheese maker Tom Gilbert. In addition to traditional Camembert, you can also order Craigston's Green Peppercorn Camembert. Try the Camembert serving suggestions from Susan Hollander of Craigston Cheese Company.

Free price list
Phone, fax, and mail orders, gift orders
MC, VISA

French-inspired fresh cheeses—

The Guilford Cheese Company
RD 2, Box 182
Guilford, VT 05301

802-254-9182
Fax: 802-254-4282

Camembert Serving Suggestions

from Susan Hollander of Craigston Cheese Company

Allow Camembert to reach room temperature and unwrap at least 15 minutes before it is served to allow it to breathe. Serve a wedge of Craigston Camembert with fresh fruit such as apples or grapes. It's also delicious as an accompaniment to poached pears in port, baked apples, and fresh strawberries.

Easy Camembert Fondue: melt Craigston Camembert in microwave or double boiler, remove rind. Add kirsch, champagne, or wine of your choice. Place in fondue pot and keep warm over Sterno. Accompany with skewered squares of crusty French bread. Fun on a blustery cold evening around the fire!

Brie, Camembert, fromage blanc and crème fraîche are the specialties of the Dixon family, who run the Guilford Cheese Company. Verde-mont, the brand name for their spreadable fromage blanc, comes plain or with herbs or green peppercorns. Guilford recommends its crème fraîche, which does not separate in cooking, for reductions, sauces, soups, and marinades.

Free price list
Mail orders
No credit cards

Raw-milk Swiss-style cheese—

Hawthorne Valley Farm
RD 2, Box 225A
Ghent, NY 12075

518-672-7500

Hawthorne Valley Farm describes its cheese as reminiscent of the mountain cheese made in Switzerland and France: very mild when young, becoming more assertive and complex as they mature. Varieties include plain, aged, caraway, and raclette. You can also order the Farm's sourdough breads and granola (for more information, see Chapter 2, "Breads, Crackers, and Specialty Baked Goods").

Free price list
Mail orders
MC, VISA

Sheep's milk cheese—

Hollow Road Farms
Stuyvesant, NY 12173

518-758-7214

Sheep's milk products, part of the culinary heritage of many countries (France's Roquefort, Italy's Romano, and Greece's feta, for example) are becoming a part of America's growing array of specialty farmstead cheese. Hollow Road Farms produces several kinds of fresh curd cheese, some dusted with herbs; soft-ripened cheese; ricotta;

a spreadable fresh cheese; and several types of fresh cheese packed in herbed oil. (Several varieties of fresh cheese are limited to seasonal availability.) You can find these products in specialty shops in the Northeast or order directly from the farm.

Free brochure
Mail orders
No credit cards

Crème fraîche and chèvre—

Kendall Cheese Company
P. O. Box 686
Atascardo, CA 93423

805-466-7252

The signature cheese of Sadie Kendall's cheese company is Chèvrefeuille, a soft-ripening goat's milk cheese that matures into a complex, full-flavored product. Drier and more pungent than Chèvrefeuille is Petit-Chèvre, similar to the French Crottin. Chèvre Frais comes in plain and a choice of herbs: poivre, fines herbes, romarin, poivre vert, and herbes de Provence. Crème fraîche is made from minimum 40 percent butterfat cow cream and, although made without stabilizers or preservatives, has a refrigerated shelf life of six weeks.

Free price list
Mail orders, gift orders
No credit cards

Cheese from the Ozark Hills—

Morningland Dairy
Route 1, Box 188B
Mountain View, MO 65548

417-469-3817/4163

Jim and Margie Reiners produce cheese on their Ozark Hills farm from the fresh milk of their 50-cow Holstein herd. They make a variety of raw-milk

Pizza with Pesto and Chèvre

from Sadie Kendall of Kendall Cheese Company

One pizza crust (the pre-made deli crusts are fine)
Pesto
    4 ounces Chèvre Frais
2–3 cloves garlic, minced
    3 tablespoons fine-flavored olive oil
Black olives
Pine nuts

Smear pesto over crust. Mash cheese with garlic and 2 tablespoons olive oil. Spread over crust. Distribute pine nuts and olives over crust. Drizzle remaining oil over all. Bake on top shelf of a very hot oven (400–450 degrees) until crust is crispy.

cheese, including plain and flavored varieties of Jack, Colby, and Cheddar. Jim and Margie's brochure shows their family at work on the farm and describes their agricultural methods and commitment to all-organic production.

Free price list and brochure
Mail orders
No credit cards

Goat's milk cheese, butter, and whey—

Mount Capra Cheese
279 S.W. 9th Street
Chehalis, WA 98532

206-748-4224

This small company produces five varieties of goat's milk cheese: Alpine white (English-farm style), Olympic (white Greek style), Alpine Herb with five fresh herbs, Olympic Pepper (with jalapeño and chilies), and Caraway (Alpine White seeded with caraway). This is one of the few sources for goat butter and dehydrated goat whey, which is available as powder or capsules.

Free price list
Mail orders, gift orders
No credit cards

Cheddar from a historic Vermont farm—

Shelburne Farms
Shelburne, VT 05482

802-985-8686

Shelburne Farms is an independent, nonprofit educational institution dedicated to teaching and demonstrating the stewardship of natural and agricultural resources to thousands of visitors, teachers, and schoolchildren each year. It is also a historic 1000-acre working farm with a herd of Brown Swiss cows whose milk is made into Cheddar cheese under the supervision of master cheese maker Bill Clapp.

Select medium, sharp, extra-sharp, or smoked Cheddar, or ham, garlic, or green peppercorn Cheddar spreads. Sampler packs of cheese, as well as sourdough bread, honey, maple syrup, and raspberry jam are available. Shelburne Farms also runs an inn at the restored country manor house on the shores of Lake Champlain—a perfect spot to relax and enjoy Vermont's beautiful lake and mountain scenery.

Free color catalog
Phone and mail orders, gift orders
AMEX, MC, VISA

Massachusetts farm Gouda—

Smith's Country Cheese
20 Otter River Road
Winchendon, MA 01475

508-939-5738

Smith's Country Cheese specializes in Gouda and makes plain, smoked, and caraway cheese as well as Gouda spreads. They advise that their Gouda freezes well, so you can order a 5- or 10-pound wheel and cut it into 1-pound pieces to store in the freezer. (Thaw in the refrigerator to preserve the texture of the cheese.) Holiday gift baskets are packed with Massachusetts maple syrup, honey, and preserves.

Free price list
Mail order, gift orders, and
gift certificates
MC, VISA

Chèvre from Maine innkeepers—

The Squire Tarbox Inn
RR 2
Box 620
Wiscasset, ME 04578

207-882-7693

At their circa 1763 inn, Karen and Bill Mitman keep a herd of purebred Nubian goats to supply milk for their small cheese plant. They produce Farmstead Chèvre, a spreadable cheese with chives and garlic; Tellicherry Crottin, aged for several days and rolled in cracked pepper; and Caerphilly, an aged, waxed cheese. Two sampler packs are offered to let you try all three. Guests at the Squire Tarbox Inn enjoy breakfasts and leisurely five-course dinners that feature the Mitmans' specialties, including homemade breads and cheese. Karen Mitman supplied the following recipe for Chicken Chèvre Patisserie—it's simple to prepare and spectacular to serve.

Free price list
Mail orders, gift orders
MC, VISA

Chèvre, fromage blanc, crème fraîche, and mascarpone—

Vermont Butter and Cheese Company, Inc.
P. O. Box 95
Pitman Road
Websterville, VT 05678

802-479-9371
Fax: 802-479-3674

Chicken Chèvre Patisserie
from Karen Mitman, The Squire Tarbox Inn

2 boneless, skinless chicken breasts, cut in half
Puff pastry dough, either sheets or patties, defrosted
Salt and pepper to taste
8 tablespoons Farmstead Chèvre (add additional seasonings if you wish)
1 egg yolk, slightly beaten

Wash and drain chicken breasts. Pat dry. Roll out puff pastry dough into 4 circles approximately 8 inches in diameter. Salt and pepper chicken breasts and place on dough. Top with 2 tablespoons seasoned chèvre. Roll pastry around chicken, coating edges of pastry with warm water and pinching together to seal. From extra dough, make attractive cutouts with a cookie cutter to garnish the patisserie; place garnishes on top, using a little warm water to hold them in place. Poke 4 holes in the top of each pastry and brush with egg yolk. Bake on a greased cookie sheet for 25 minutes at 425 degrees. Let stand for 10 minutes before serving. Serves 4.

Crème Fraîche, Fromage Blanc, and Mascarpone: Tips and Serving Suggestions

from Don Hooper, Vermont Butter and Cheese Company, Inc.

What Is Crème Fraîche (pronounced "cremme fresh")?

Crème fraîche is a cultured fresh cream that has been the trademark of French cooking for centuries. A natural product that contains no additives, it is the ideal ingredient for both novice and expert cooks who like elegant, instant results in the kitchen. Even an inexperienced cook can make a sumptuous, worry-free sauce in minutes because Vermont crème fraîche will never separate or curdle when heated. (Refrigerated shelf life is sixty days.)

Serving Suggestions for Crème Fraîche:

• Use it as a base for your favorite dip or salad dressing.
• Splash a dollop over a burrito or a baked potato.
• Mix it with lemon and herbs for a special treat over lightly steamed vegetables.
• Create master sauces by adding crème fraîche to pan juices and cooking gently over low heat to desired consistency.
• Add crème fraîche to strawberries and sprinkle with a hint of brown sugar.

What Is Fromage Blanc?

Fromage blanc, a wonderful-tasting light cheese that contains no fat and no salt, is made from fresh skimmed cow's milk according to finest French tradition. Health-conscious cheese lovers are enthusiastic over Vermont fromage blanc because it has virtually no cholesterol, nothing artificial, high protein value, and only 20 calories per ounce. Enjoy this spreadable tangy cheese many ways. (Refrigerated shelf life is five weeks.)

Serving Suggestions for Fromage Blanc:

• Mix it with your favorite salsa or herbs for a zesty dip.
• Use it in lasagne, manicotti, or other pasta dishes as the main ingredient.
• Make a smoked salmon pâté by combining fromage blanc with chopped onion, capers, dill, and salmon; season with a little salt, pepper, and lemon juice.
• Create a low-calorie dessert by adding fruit juice or maple syrup, then freeze and *voilà!*

What Is Mascarpone (pronounced "mass cahr po-nay")?

This sinfully delectable staple of Italian cookery is a rich, creamy fresh cheese used in pastas, pastries, tortas, and desserts—or on its own. Each region of Italy has its own favorite use for mascarpone, and it's indispensable for making tirami su. Many Italian recipes call for mascarpone and it is hard to find in the United States, so Vermont Butter and Cheese decided to make it in Vermont. (Refrigerated shelf life is five weeks.)

Mascarpone Cups

from Vermont Butter and Cheese Company, Inc.

In a bowl stir 1 cup mascarpone with a wooden spoon; add 4 tablespoons powdered sugar and 2 egg yolks, one at a time. Slowly pour in 2 to 3 tablespoons rum or brandy, then, always stirring, delicately fold in 2 stiffly beaten egg whites. Pour the blend into four cups and refrigerate a few hours. Before serving, decorate with maraschino cherries, chocolate shavings, or amaretti crumbs. For chocolate-flavored mascarpone cups, you may add 2 tablespoons cocoa powder to the recipe. Makes 4 servings.

Vermont Butter and Cheese Company makes chèvre, crème fraîche, and fromage blanc using traditional French methods. The newest product is Allison's Vermont Mascarpone, a rich fresh cheese introduced as a fifth birthday present to the company and its customers. Look for these products in specialty shops or order directly from the company. Don Hooper of Vermont Butter and Cheese Company provided the accompanying tips and serving suggestions for crème fraîche, fromage blanc, and mascarpone. Try the simple and delicious recipe for Mascarpone Cups.

Free price list
Phone, fax, and mail orders
MC, VISA

European-style goat cheeses—

Westfield Farm Capri Cheese
28 Worcester Road
Route 68
Hubbardston, MA 01452

508-928-5110

Bob and Letty Kilmoyer raise Nubian and Saanen goats on their 20-acre farm in central Massachusetts. From the fresh goat's milk they make cheese, using European farmstead cheese-making methods combined with their own special techniques, which have resulted in some innovative products such as their prize-winning Hubbardston Blue, a surface-ripened cheese that has the mold on the outside of the cheese rather than streaked through it. They also produce plain, pepper, and herb garlic goat cheese, an award-winning Camembert, and a classic blue.

Free brochure
Mail orders
No credit cards

Fresh and aged goat cheese—

York Hill Farm
York Hill Road
New Sharon, ME 04955

207-778-9741

Because they believe it's important for people to see how and where their food is produced, Penny and John Duncan invite you to visit their 10-acre farm in central Maine. Their herd of dairy goats produces milk for three kinds of aged cheese and three types of fresh cheese;

the latter include an award-winning Pepper Roule, a jelly-roll-shaped cheese with a hint of garlic rolled with fresh-cracked peppercorns. The York Hill Farm Sampler is a perfect way to discover a variety of cheese.

Free illustrated brochure
Mail orders, gift orders
MC, VISA

Larger Companies Offering a Variety of Cheese

These companies, which provide several kinds of cheese, also often supply a variety of other farm products, such as maple syrup, honey, and preserves.

From a Vermont cooperative—

Cabot Creamery
Main Street
Box 128
Cabot, VT 05647

802-563-2650

Cabot Creamery is owned and operated by 450 farm families in Vermont. For more than seventy years Cabot has been crafting Cheddar by hand, with no chemicals or preservatives. In addition to mild, sharp, and extra-sharp Cheddar bricks and wheels, Cabot makes smoked and sage Cheddar, as well as Vitalait, a new product that has half the fat and cholesterol and 30 percent fewer calories than Cheddar. Try their sampler or variety packs to taste-test a little of each. Gift packs add other Vermont specialties to Cabot Creamery Cheddar. Since Cabot has a busy holiday season, all orders received prior to November 15 receive a 5 percent discount.

Free color catalog
Mail orders, gift orders
MC, VISA

"Snappy" Cheddar—

Calef's Country Store
Route 9, P. O. Box 57
Barrington, NH 03825

603-664-2231

Perhaps patriarch Austin L. Calef should be allowed to describe his own Cheddar cheese: "It's snappy. Makes a man sit up and take notice. All you have to do is give a customer a sample on a cracker from the barrel and he's sold." It must be true, because Calef sells up to 75,000 pounds a year of regular, extra-sharp, and smoked Cheddar, both in the United States and in Europe. Calef's stocks other New Hampshire specialties, including maple syrup and candy, their own jams and jellies, New England dried beans, and smoked hams and bacons.

Free illustrated price list
Mail orders, gift orders
MC, VISA

A Vermont tradition since 1882—

Crowley Cheese
Healdville, VT 05758

802-259-2340

The method for making Crowley Cheese has remained unchanged for over a hundred years. The original cheese factory, now a National Historic Place, is a traditional post-and-beam building situated next to a small mountain brook. You can order mild, medium, or sharp Crowley Cheddar, or ask for flavored Cheddar: garlic, caraway, hot pepper, sage, dill, or smoked.

Free color brochure
Phone and mail orders, gift orders
MC, VISA

European-style cheese from Minnesota—

Eichten's Hidden Acres Cheese Farm
16705 310th Street
Center City, MN 55012

612-257-4752

Joe and Mary Eichten and their family have been in the cheese business since 1976. Their products include Dutch Gouda, Danish Tilsit, baby Swiss, Colby, Muenster, and many more. If you're in the neighborhood, stop and visit. The children will enjoy Grampa Joe's Barnyard, where they'll get a close look at buffalo, llama, and yak. The Eichtens also stock other Minnesota products, including honey, maple syrup, and wild rice.

Free color brochure and price list
Mail orders, gift orders
No credit cards

From a treasured monastery recipe—

Gethsemani Farms
Highway 2479
Trappist, KY 40051

Fax: 502-549-8021

Trappist monks at Gethsemani Farms make a Port Salut-type cheese from a formula handed down from one generation of monks to another. They also offer salt-reduced versions of Colby, Cheddar, and Monterey Jack, as well as a "lite" Swiss. The monks also

bake a bourbon-laced fruitcake developed by one of their members who was a professional baker before joining the monastery.

Free color brochure and price list
Fax and mail orders
MC, VISA

Several varieties of Vermont Cheddar—

Grafton Village Cheese Company, Inc.
P. O. Box 87
Townshen Road
Grafton, VT 05146

802-843-2221

Grafton specializes in natural Vermont Cheddars. The premium Cheddar is aged one year; the classic reserve is aged two years. Grafton also makes smoked and sage Cheddar. All varieties are available in bars, small wheels, and blocks of various sizes (up to 40 pounds for Cryovac-packed Cheddar). Their brochure illustrates the step-by-step process of creating Grafton Village Cheese. You're welcome to visit this cheese company in the historic village of Grafton, known for its quaint shops and resident artisans.

Free color brochure
Mail orders, gift orders
No credit cards

From a Massachusetts country store—

The Granville Country Store
Granby Road Cut Off
P. O. Box 141
Granville, MA 01034

800-356-3141
413-357-8555

The recipe and aging process for Granville Cheddar was developed in

1851. It's made in medium, sharp, extra-sharp, and super-sharp. (Owner Rowland Entwistle advises that super-sharp Granville "is for gamblers only.") Granville's gift selections tuck regional food treats together with cheese into attractive baskets and wooden boxes.

Free color brochure
Phone and mail orders, gift orders, and gift certificates
MC, VISA

Aged Cheddar and New Hampshire specialties—

Harman's Cheese & Country Store
Sugar Hill, NH 03585

603-823-8000

Maxine Aldrich continues this country business that was begun in 1954. She stocks a popular "Really-Aged" Cheddar cheese, which has been aged well over two years. She also stocks her shop and mail order brochure with treats rarely found in markets or specialty food shops, including regional maple products, beans, honey, and crackers.

Free brochure
Mail orders
No credit cards

Chutter and cheese from New York State—

Herkimer Family Treasure House
Upper Otsego Street, Route 51
Ilion, NY 13357

315-895-7832

Chutter, for those of you unfamiliar with this special product, is a blend of

New York State Cheddar and fresh cream—a spreadable cheese suitable for snacking and cooking. Herkimer's makes chutter in the original flavor; pesto flavor (speckled with fresh basil and a touch of garlic); and Cajun flavor (with bold and spicy seasonings). You can also buy aged Cheddar, cheese spreads in assorted flavors, cheese balls, or choose from the ten gift packages that provide a selection of products. At the shop near Utica, you can buy cheese and browse through Norma Basloe's antiques shop.

Free price list
Mail orders
No credit cards

Blue cheese produced for five decades—

Maytag Dairy Farms
RR 1, Box 806
Newton, IA 50208

800-247-2458
800-BLU-CHES (in IA)

In 1919, E. H. Maytag, son of the founder of the famous appliance firm, established a prize-winning herd of Holstein cattle. The farm, still operated by the Maytag family, has produced blue cheese since 1941 by the time-consuming method of hand-making cheese in small batches using fresh milk from their own cows. Although renowned for blue cheese, Maytag also manufactures natural Cheddar, baby Swiss, brick cheese, and Edam.

Free color catalog
Phone and mail orders, gift orders
AMEX, MC, VISA

Award-winning blue cheese—

Nauvoo Blue Cheese Company
P. O. Box 188
Nauvoo, IL 62354

800-358-9143
217-453-2213

The Nauvoo Blue Cheese Company's award-winning blue cheese is available in wheels, squares, wedges, and also crumbled. If you've ever wondered about the difference between blue cheese and Roquefort, the Nauvoo brochure supplies the answer: "Only cheese made from sheep's milk and cured in the limestone caves in the Roquefort area of France can be called Roquefort. Blue cheese, however, is made from whole cow's milk. Italy and England also produce blue-marbled cheese. The Italian version is called Gorgonzola; the English is known as Stilton."

Free brochure and price list
Phone and mail orders, gift orders
MC, VISA

Traditional Vermont curd cheese—

The Plymouth Cheese Corporation
P. O. Box 1
Plymouth, VT 05056-001

802-672-3650

The primary product of this company is a true, old-fashioned granular curd cheese made in the original Vermont tradition. Sage, pimiento, and caraway flavors are available in addition to plain, and you can order 3- or 5-pound wheels. Plymouth also offers an array of New England food gift packages that include such items as baked beans, brown bread, Indian pudding, and watermelon pickle.

Free price list
Mail orders, gift orders
No credit cards

Blue Cheese Serving Suggestions
from Nauvoo Blue Cheese Company

- Stuff raw celery stalks with a mixture of equal parts Nauvoo Blue Cheese and cream cheese.
- Add crumbled Nauvoo Blue Cheese to deviled eggs.
- Top bacon, lettuce, and tomato sandwiches with crumbled Nauvoo Blue Cheese.
- Mix crumbles of Nauvoo Blue Cheese with breadcrumbs and use to top vegetable casseroles.
- Add 2 tablespoons Nauvoo Blue Cheese to pastry when making crust for pies.
- A slice of Nauvoo Blue Cheese on top of hot apple pie is a wonderful dessert.

Oregon blue, Cheddar, Jack, and
Colby—

Rogue River Valley Creamery
311 North Front Street
P. O. Box 3606
Central Point, OR 97502

503-664-2233

From Rogue River Valley Creamery you
can order 2½- or 5-pound wheels of
Oregon blue. Other kinds of cheese—
Cheddar, Jack, and Colby—are
available in 5-pound blocks. Flavored
Jacks include garlic, jalapeño, and
caraway; there is also a low-fat, low-salt
Cheddar.

Free price list
Mail orders
No credit cards

Cheddar and Jack cheese from
California—

Sonoma Cheese Factory
2 Spain Street
Sonoma, CA 95476

800-535-2855

Sonoma Cheese Factory visitors can
watch cheese being made or have lunch
in the deli at the company's historic
Sonoma Plaza location, where it has
been in business for almost 60 years.
Mail order customers can order
Cheddar or the traditional Jack or
choose from flavored Jack cheese in
garlic, onion, caraway, and hot pepper.
Gift selections are packed with recipe
booklets, and for gifts sent to California
locations you may include wine.

Free color brochure
Phone and mail orders, gift orders
AMEX, MC, VISA

All of Wisconsin's favorite cheese—

Stallman's Cheese Factory
35990 Mapleton Road
Oconomowoc, WI 53066

414-474-7142

You can place orders for bulk quantities
of all your Wisconsin favorites—brick,
Muenster, Cheddar, Swiss, Monterey
Jack, Colby, domestic blue, Gouda,
Edam, and Provolone. There's also
Limburger, several cheese spreads, as
well as a selection of low-cholesterol,
low-salt cheese, including Cheddar,
farmer cheese, and Swiss. Numerous
gift selections are available; many
include summer sausage.

Free color catalog
Phone and mail orders, gift orders
MC, VISA

Cheddars and flavored cheeses—

State of Maine Cheese Company
75 Front Street
Rockland, ME 04841

207-596-6601

State of Maine cheese is available in
stores throughout the New England
area. Cheese enthusiasts in the rest of
the country can order from a selection
that includes two Cheddars, smoked
Cheddar, Aroostook Jack, Allagash
Caraway, Kennebec Dill, and Saco
Jalapeño. President Taylor Mudge
invites you to tour the cheese-making
facilities on Tuesdays and Thursdays.

Free illustrated brochure
Phone and mail orders, gift orders
MC, VISA

From a Vermont family farm—

Sugarbush Farm
RFD 1, Box 568C
Woodstock, VT 05091

802-457-1757

Sugarbush Farm makes a variety of natural cheese: sharp and mellow Cheddar, sage, maple-hickory smoked, Green Mountain Jack, and Green Mountain Bleu. This family business, which now spans three generations, sends its customers a newsletter that keeps them up to date on activities at the hundred-year-old farm—last winter/spring's newsletter included a diary of the company's sugar-making activities.

Maple products and gift selections are available. Betsy Luce invites you to visit next time you're in New England.

Free color brochure
Phone and mail orders, gift orders
AMEX, DC, MC, VISA

Not just Swiss—

The Swiss Cheese Shop
Highway 69N, P. O. Box 429
Monroe, WI 53566-0429

608-325-3493

More than Swiss cheese is available from this Wisconsin cheese shop—it also offers Cheddar, blue cheese,

Tillamook Cheese Jalapeño Cheddar Muffins
(courtesy of Ron Paul Catering & Charcuterie, Portland, Oregon)

    1 cup flour
    1 tablespoon baking powder
    1 teaspoon salt
    1½ teaspoons sugar
    1½ cups grated Tillamook sharp Cheddar
    ¼ cup minced onion
    2 small minced jalapeño peppers
    ½ teaspoon crushed chilies
    4 strips diced cooked bacon (reserve drippings)
    2 eggs
    ½ cup melted butter
    1 cup buttermilk
    1 teaspoon Dijon mustard

Combine dry ingredients. Add grated cheese. Sauté onion, jalapeños, and chilies in bacon drippings. Whisk together eggs, butter, buttermilk, and mustard. Add sautéed onions and peppers and diced bacon to wet ingredients. Combine wet and dry ingredients. Do not overmix. Scoop into buttered or paper-lined 2½-inch muffin tins, filling each cup ⅔ full with batter. Bake at 350 degrees for 20 to 25 minutes. Makes 1 dozen.

Muenster, Colby, and Port Salut. The shop offers bulk quantities of cheese that are ideal for cooking and snacking, as well as a selection of gift assortments.

Free price list
Mail orders
No credit cards

A selection of Oregon cheeses—

Tillamook Cheese
P. O. Box 313
Tillamook, OR 97141

800-542-7290
503-842-4481

The Tillamook County Creamery Association was organized in 1909 by ten cheese factories operating in Tillamook County, Oregon. Today the creamery has grown to over 200 member dairies and produces Cheddar, Monterey Jack, low-salt cheese, and whey powder. Their attractive catalog includes additional Oregon specialties, cookbooks, and a nice selection of recipes. The Tillamook Cheese Jalapeño Cheddar Muffins (recipe on page 39) are excellent!

Free color catalog
Phone and mail orders
MC, VISA

From the Sonoma Valley—

Vella Cheese of California
315 Second Street East
P. O. Box 191
Sonoma, CA 95476-0191

800-848-0505
707-938-3232

For over fifty years the Vella Cheese company has been making Dry

Monterey Jack with natural ingredients. In addition to six varieties of Jack, they produce blue cheese and Cheddar and put together variety packages. Include a visit to the cheese factory when you're touring the wine country; Mr. Vella is usually there to answer your questions.

Free brochure
Phone and mail orders, gift orders
MC, VISA

From a university creamery—

WSU Creamery
Washington State University
Troy Hall 101
Pullman, WA 99164-4410

509-335-4014

Cougar cheese is manufactured and marketed by the university's Creamery which is run by the food science department. The varieties are WSU Cheddar; Cougar Gold (Swisslike); Viking (a mild, white cheese); and varieties of flavored cheese that include smoked, jalapeño, caraway, sweet basil, and Mediterranean (with pimientos and olives). Order early for the holidays— they usually run out of cheese because of high demand in the month of December.

Free brochure
Mail orders
No credit cards

If you are particularly interested in cheese from the state of Washington, you might want to order the informational brochure put out by the Dairy Farmers of Washington. Write to The Dairy Farmers of Washington, 1107 N.E. 45th Street, Suite 205, Seattle, WA 98105

Larger Companies Providing a Wide Variety of Domestic and/or Imported Cheese:

Cheese in bulk quantities—

Antone's Import Company
P. O. Box 3352
Houston, TX 77253

713-526-1046

Antone's is an excellent source for bulk cheese from around the world. If the minimum quantities are too large for you, combine your order with family or friends: Antone's prices make it worth while. Write for the extensive list of cheese and other foods.

Free price list
Mail orders
No credit cards

Italian specialties—

Balducci's
Mail Order Division
11-02 Queens Plaza South
Long Island City, NY 11101-4908

800-822-1444
800-247-2450 (in NY state)
718-786-9690 (special requests)

The Balducci family specializes in Italian cheese. Fresh, whole milk mozzarella, made every day, is used to create Bocconcini (small balls of their mozzarella marinated in olive oil, garlic, red pepper, and oregano) and Burrini with Gorgonzola (fresh mozzarella filled with Gorgonzola and fresh butter and aged until an edible rind forms). They also have other Italian specialties, as well as imported English Stilton and French Camembert.

Free seasonal catalogs
Phone and mail orders, gift orders
AMEX, MC, VISA

More than 1000 kinds of cheese—

Cheese of All Nations
153 Chambers Street
New York, NY 10007

212-732-0752

Phil Alpert has an enviable job: traveling the world, sampling and selecting cheese to include in his encyclopedic catalog of more than 1000 varieties. Gifts and a good selection of imported crackers are also included. The catalog contains recipes, interesting and historic facts about cheese, and even a cheese quiz to test your knowledge! When in New York, plan a visit to Mr. Alpert's Cheese 'n Wine Restaurant at the same address.

Catalog, $1.00
Phone and mail orders, gift orders, and gift certificates
AMEX, MC, VISA

Cheese from around the world—

Cheese Junction
One West Ridgewood Avenue
Ridgewood, NJ 07450

201-445-9211

Cheese Junction brings you more than 100 varieties of cheese from around the world, each with a brief catalog description. Price reductions are offered for quantity orders. Cheese gift selections and various monthly gift plans are available.

Free illustrated catalog
Phone and mail orders, gift orders, and gift certificates
AMEX, MC, VISA

Specially selected Italian cheese—

Dean & DeLuca, Inc.
Mail Order Department
560 Broadway
New York, NY 10012

800-221-7714
212-431-1691

Dean & DeLuca's New York store carries over 300 types of cheese; the catalog features almost 20 classics, including Parmigiano-Reggiano, which they describe as "nothing less than the taste of Italy"; Gorgonzola Dolce, a soft, blue-veined cheese from Lombardy; and Fontina Val d'Aosta from the Italian Alps.

Color catalog, $2.00
Phone and mail orders, gift orders, and gift certificates
AMEX, MC, VISA

Wisconsin cheese with an international flavor—

Kolb-Lena Cheese Company
3990 North Sunnyside Road
Lena, IL 61048

815-369-4577

Kolb-Lena makes cheese daily, using milk from a local dairy farm and employing the talents of fully apprenticed Swiss, French, Greek, and American cheese makers. Their products include Cheddar, American Brie, Feta, baby Swiss, and Camembert. Gift selections are available.

Free color brochure
Phone and mail orders, gift orders
AMEX, MC, VISA

Looking for Clarified Butter?

Clarified butter, essential for sautéeing, imparts a wonderful butter flavor but won't burn. It's available from:

Dean & DeLuca, Inc.
Mail Order Department
560 Broadway
New York, NY 10012

800-221-7714
212-431-1691

and

Select Origins, Inc.
Box N
Southampton, NY 11968

800-822-2092
516-924-5447
Fax: 516-924-5892

If you'd like to try your hand at cheese making, see Chapter 7, "Dairy Cultures," for suppliers and equipment.

CHAPTER 5

COFFEE AND TEA

What's more welcome than a steaming mug of coffee or a fortifying cup of tea —as an eye-opener first thing in the morning, an afternoon energizer, or the final touch to a wonderful dinner? Here are some sources for some very special coffees and teas from specialists who take pride in their products. Most will grind coffee to your specification, or just tell them your type of coffee maker and they will select the proper grind. Many of these companies also carry a line of top-quality coffee- and tea-making equipment.

Single-estate Darjeeling and specialty teas—

Barrows Tea Company
142 Arnold Street
New Beford, MA 02740

508-990-2745

Although most Darjeeling teas are blended from several plantations, Sam Barrows's Darjeeling has the distinction of being imported from a single estate in northern India. Currently, Barrows offers two other products—American Breakfast (a blend of Assam and Ceylon teas) and Japanese Green Sencha (a low-caffeine tea). You'll find Barrows teas in some specialty stores, and you can also order directly from the company.

Free price list
Mail orders, gift orders
No credit cards

Swiss-roasted coffee—

Café La Semeuse
P. O. Box 429
Brooklyn, NY 11222

800-242-6333

Café La Semeuse coffee is a blend of Central and South American arabica beans roasted at high altitudes in the Swiss Alps, where reduced air pressure lets the coffee develop its flavor at lower roasting temperatures. Whole-bean Café La Semeuse, shipped in 250- or 500-gram quantities and available decaffeinated by the Swiss water process, can be prepared as both American coffee and as espresso.

Free price list
Phone and mail orders, gift orders
AMEX, MC, VISA

Coffee, tea, and coffee club—

Coffee Drop Shop
12 North 3rd Street
St. Charles, IL 60174

312-584-7989

A wide variety of coffees, including some flavored, are available, as well as a selection of samplers that consist of quarter-pound quantities of your choice. For coffee lovers on your gift list, Coffee Drop Shop operates a "gourmet year-round club" that sends the lucky recipient a pound of different coffee each month. A nice selection of teas is featured, including some unusual flavors such as clove, ginger, and elderberry.

Free price list
Mail orders, gift orders
No credit cards

Traditional Louisiana blends—

Community Kitchens
P. O. Box 2311
Baton Rouge, LA 70821-2311

800-535-9901

Community Kitchens has perfected its coffee blends over three generations. So that you can try several of these special blends, the company has put together sampler packs, and the Gourmet Coffee Club offers members discounted prices and regular deliveries. Imported French chicory is also available. An array of regional foods, recipes, and kitchenware completes the catalog.

Free color catalog
Phone and mail orders, gift orders
AMEX, MC, VISA

Fine coffees from around the world—

Fairwinds Gourmet Coffee Company
P. O. Box 1294
Concord, NH 03302-9860

800-448-7359

Choose from over a dozen coffees from some of the world's most famous growing regions, including Jamaican Blue Mountain, Kenya AA, and Colombian Supremo. The Fairwinds Coffee Collection includes 2-ounce vacuum-sealed packages of 14 different coffees. A coffee club is also available.

Free color brochure
Phone and mail orders
AMEX, MC, VISA

Coffee and tea from America's oldest coffee merchant—

Gillies Coffee Company
160 Bleecker Street
New York, NY 10012

212-614-0900

Gillies Coffee Company, which was established before the Civil War, is proud of its distinction as the oldest coffee merchant in the United States. Gillies offers a wide selection of varietal, flavored, and espresso coffees, as well as its own blends; each is carefully described in the catalog, and many are also available naturally decaffeinated. Teas, loose or in tea bags, include Darjeeling, Earl Grey's Blend, and English Breakfast. You may also order Melitta coffee makers and filters from Gillies Coffee.

Free price list
Mail orders, gift orders
AMEX, MC, VISA

A tea supplier for a quarter century—

Grace Tea Company, Ltd.

50 West 17th Street
New York, NY 10011

212-255-2935

Grace Tea Company has supplied black teas, oolong teas, and pouching tea for more than twenty-five years. Loose tea and teapot-size tea bags come in attractive black metal canisters, for which you can order refills. A sampler package of five varieties is available.

Free color brochure
Mail orders, gift orders
No credit cards

Fast service from New England—

Green Mountain Coffee Roasters
33 Coffee Lane
Waterbury, VT 05676

800-223-6768
800-622-4240 (in VT)

Green Mountain Coffee Roasters have several stores in New England and ship their products all over the country. Speedy service is their hallmark—if you order before 11 A.M., they'll ship your coffee the same day. The brochure gives explicit instructions for making the ultimate cup of coffee, and varieties are grouped into suggested choices for morning, afternoon, and evening enjoyment. A line of coffee-making accessories includes unbleached coffee filters. Try Spicy Mexican Coffee with Green Mountain Coffee Roasters' Viennese Spiced coffee.

Free brochure
Phone and mail orders, gift orders
AMEX, MC, VISA

Spicy Mexican Coffee

from Green Mountain Coffee Roasters

  4 teaspoons chocolate syrup
½ cup heavy cream
¼ teaspoon cinnamon
¼ teaspoon nutmeg
  1 tablespoon sugar
  1 pot brewed Viennese Spiced coffee

Put 1 teaspoon chocolate syrup into each mug. Combine the cream, cinnamon, nutmeg, and sugar in a large bowl. Whip until stiff. Pour the coffee into the mugs and stir to mix the coffee and chocolate syrup. Top with the whipped cream mixture and sprinkle with nutmeg, cinnamon, or cocoa powder. Makes 4 servings.

Time for tea—

Harney & Sons, Ltd.
Village Green
P. O. Box 676
Salisbury, CT 06068

800-TEA-TIME
203-435-9218

When you stop in for afternoon tea at some of America's most famous hotels, chances are you may be enjoying a pot of Harney & Sons tea. This company supplies hotels, restaurants, and clubs, and mail orders its products to tea enthusiasts across the country. Choose loose tea or tea bags in over a dozen varieties, including Hot Cinnamon Spiced, Flowery Jasmine, English Breakfast, and several low-caffeine and caffeine-free teas.

Free price list
Mail orders
No credit cards

From a coffee house on Chicago's North Shore—

Harvest Blend Coffees
1029 Davis Street
Evanston, IL 60201

708-475-1121

The mail order business at this coffee house began as a way for the shop's customers to simplify their holiday shopping. Now Harvest Blend's coffees are shipped across the country all year round. There are over two dozen coffees and blends, each well described, plus almost ten decaf coffees (Swiss water process), and over twenty flavored coffees (highlights: raspberry/chocolate, coconut cream, macadamia, and Southern pecan). Coffee can be ground for your coffee maker, or order

whole beans and store them in the freezer for long-term freshness.

Free price list
Phone and mail orders, gift orders
MC, VISA

Coffee with the personal touch—

The Kobos Company
5620 S.W. Kelly Avenue
Portland, OR 97201

503-222-5226

Since 1973, when David Kobos and his wife opened their first store, the business has grown to six retail locations and thriving wholesale and mail order divisions. They personally select and roast all of their coffees, which include a particularly nice selection of decaffeinated types. Black, green, blended and flavored teas, including Kobos's own iced tea blend, are featured. The product line also includes culinary herbs and spices.

Free price list
Phone and mail orders
AMEX, MC, VISA

Real New Orleans coffee—

Luzianne Blue Plate Foods
Box 60296
New Orleans, LA 70160

800-692-7895

Since 1903, when William B. Reily founded the Luzianne Coffee Company, this New Orleans establishment has been satisfying Cajun/Creole taste buds. This company claims that "nobody loves a good meal and a good cup of coffee more than Louisianians." You can order from a selection of coffee, coffee and chicory blends (also available as instant coffee), and teas. Luzianne also stocks a line of Cajun/Creole dinners, which are featured in Chapter 24, "American Regional Foods."

Free catalog
Phone and mail orders, gift orders
MC, VISA

From N.Y.C.'s Greenwich Village—

McNulty's Tea & Coffee Company
109 Christopher Street
New York, NY 10014

800-356-5200
212-242-5351

McNulty's fragrant and old-fashioned tea and coffee shop is located in the heart of Greenwich Village. This company, a purveyor of coffees and teas since 1895, provides a mail order service that offers dozens of coffees from around the world, as well as flavored coffees and its own blends. The tea selection includes black, oolong, and green teas, McNulty's own blends, and a variety of flavored, decaffeinated, and herbal teas. You can also order popular imported teas through McNulty, including Jacksons of Piccadilly, Twinings, Fortnum and Mason, and McGrath's of Ireland.

Free brochure
Phone and mail orders
AMEX

Chinese teas and tea accessories—

Madame Chung's Finest Teas
P. O. Box 597871
Chicago, IL 60659

312-743-5545

Margaret Chung imports high-quality teas from China and Taiwan and provides an informative catalog that is also a guide to the history and varieties of Chinese teas and an introduction to the thousand-year-old tea-serving tradition known as *gongfu*. You can order from a list of almost a dozen teas, including Dingdong Oolong, Keemun, Lichee Black, and China Jasmine. A *gongfu* tea set and a selection of beautiful traditional and modern teapots are also offered.

Illustrated catalog, $1.00
Phone and mail orders, gift orders
MC, VISA

Coffee and biscotti, anyone?—

Maria's
111 South Stratford Road
Winston-Salem, NC 27104

919-722-7271

Maria's advises that coffees are roasted "daily in the shop, allowing the beans to develop a slightly darker, fuller bloom than that of most commercial roasting houses." There is a nice selection of coffee gifts, including a combination of Maria's house blend with Italian almond biscotti and cognac chocolate cordials.

Free price list
Phone and mail orders, gift orders
AMEX, CHOICE, MC, VISA

Kona coffee from Hawaii—

Mauna Kea Coffee Company
P. O. Box 829
Captain Cook, HI 96704-9989

800-367-8047, ext. 150
Fax: 808-329-7110

Mauna Kea's Royal Kona Coffee Mill and Museum in Hawaii offers a wide selection of Kona coffee, including pure Kona, blends, decaffeinated, flavors (such as macadamia nut and Dutch chocolate), and convenient freeze-dried Kona. Other Hawaiian specialties from this company include jams, jellies, nut butters, and confections.

Free color brochure
Phone, fax, and mail orders, gift orders
AMEX, MC, VISA

From a landmark Midwestern coffee mill—

Northwestern Coffee Mills
217 North Broadway
Milwaukee, WI 53202

414-276-1031

This Milwaukee coffee mill was established in 1875, and the present owners have been roasting coffee since 1969. To supply their customers nationwide they roast about 60,000 pounds of coffee and blend or process about 5000 pounds of tea and spices each year, still using much of the original mill equipment. The catalog helpfully describes the flavor, aroma, and body of each of the numerous coffees, which include blends, fancy and rare straights, dark roasts, and decaffeinated coffees. Northwestern teas include black, oolong, and green teas, several rare varieties, and flavored and herbal teas. Coffee-making supplies and coffee flavorings are available, as well as herbs, spices, seasonings, vanilla, and other extracts.

Free illustrated catalog (but they'll appreciate your sending 50¢)
Phone and mail orders, gift orders, and gift certificates
MC, VISA

From the company that wakes up San Diego—

Pannikin Coffee & Tea
675 G Street
San Diego, CA 92101

800-232-6482
619-239-1257 (in CA)

Pannikin is proud to have been "wakin' up San Diego" since 1968. It now has several local retail shops in San Diego County, some combined with sidewalk cafes, craft shops, and bookstores. The company also mail orders coffee, tea, and spices all over the country. The coffee selection includes full city roasts, blends, dark roasts, and decaffeinated varieties, as well as chicory. Three different coffee samplers each offer eight varieties in 2-ounce bags—a great way to find your favorites. Green, oolong, black, decaffeinated, and fruit and herbal teas are offered. Three tea samplers—connoisseur's, traditional, and herbal—let you compare flavors. The equipment line includes stainless-steel-lined unbreakable carafes, mugs, coffee makers, and elegant imported kettles. There are also culinary herbs and spices.

Free illustrated catalog
Phone and mail orders, gift orders
AMEX, MC, VISA

Freshly roasted coffee from New York—

Schapira Coffee Company
117 West 10th Street
New York, NY 10011

212-675-3733

Schapira has been roasting coffees and blending teas since 1903 and will ship your coffee order the same day it's roasted. There's a great selection of favorites and special imports, sampler gift selections, and flavors to add to coffee. The tea selection features many varieties both loose and in bags. The descriptive Schapira pamphlet helps you get a sense of the flavor and aroma of teas you may be unfamiliar with. There are also tea sampler gift selections and a selection of coffee- and tea-making accessories.

Free price list
Mail orders, gift orders
MC, VISA

Coffee, tea, and English tea things—

Simpson & Vail
P. O. Box 309
38 Clinton Street
Pleasantville, NY 10570

914-747-1336

In business since 1929, Simpson & Vail offer a selection of more than forty high-grown, hard-bean coffees, including flavored and decaffeinated varieties. There's also a selection of black, green, and oolong teas, and many different blends. Their choice of tea accessories is especially nice and includes charming English-style tea cozies. Coffee-making supplies and specialty foods complete the Simpson & Vail catalog.

Free illustrated catalog
Phone and mail orders
MC, VISA

Seattle's famous coffee—

Starbucks Coffee
2010 Airport Way South
Seattle, WA 98134-1633

800-445-3428

Choose from Starbucks' varietal coffees from the Americas, the Pacific, and Africa, as well as blends, decaffeinated, and dark roasts in your choice of eight grinds. Samplers and special holiday blends are also available. Coffee-making equipment includes grinders, coffee makers, espresso machines, Swiss Gold filters, carafes, and a selection of mugs. A variety of French Press coffee makers, including an economical Bistro model, are recommended by Starbucks for making the most flavorful cup of coffee because the grounds are fully immersed in water for the full brewing time.

Free color catalog
Phone and mail orders, gift orders
AMEX, MC, VISA

In-house blends from Zabar's—

Zabar's
2245 Broadway
New York, NY 10024

212-496-1234
Fax: 212-580-4477

This famous New York City food emporium roasts and blends its own coffee to create over ten blends, including Kenya AA, Jamaica Style, and light and dark espresso blends. Two of Zabar's most popular coffees, Colombian Blend and Gourmet Decaffeinated, are offered in all-method drip grind in 1-pound vacuum-packed cans. Coffee makers and grinders and espresso/cappuccino machines are also available.

Free color catalog
Phone, fax, and mail orders, gift orders
AMEX

If you'd like to order unbleached coffee filters, they're available to fit all sizes of coffee makers from Natural Brew. Ask for the retail price list:

Natural Brew
P. O. Box 1007
Sheboygan, WI 53082-1007
800-558-7790

For more sources of herbal teas, see Chapter 12, "Herbs and Spices." Many of these suppliers blend their own herbal teas.

If you're particularly fond of oriental teas, many of the suppliers listed in the "Asian Cuisines" section of Chapter 25, "The International Pantry," also import teas.

CHAPTER 6

CONDIMENTS AND SAVORY SAUCES

Mustards, Chutneys, Marinades and Dressings, Olives, Pickles, and More ...

Browse through this chapter for appealing condiments and sauces that will elevate even the simplest meal to a special occasion. Stock up on these marinades and dressings as inspiration for creating your own very delicious dishes. You'll also find unusual items such as jalapeño-stuffed olives, chutneys made from regional fruits, and special things like pepper jelly that you haven't seen since you were last in Grandma's kitchen.

American Spoon Foods, Inc.
P. O. Box 566
1668 Clarion Avenue
Petoskey, MI 49770-0566

800-222-5886
616-347-9030
Fax: 616-347-2512

American Spoon Foods has chosen American regional condiments for its catalog: olives from California; dried tomatoes from Ohio; pickled vegetables from Washington State; and Cowboy Caviar, a California family recipe that blends fresh vegetables, garlic, and spices to make a vegetable pâté. American Spoon Foods has added its own specialties too: cranberry catsup, plum catsup, tomato apple relish. Larry Forgione (of An American Place

restaurant in New York City) has contributed peanut sauce, barbecue sauce, and corn relish. You can order a Cook's Collection that assembles a selection of these products in a pretty birch-bark basket.

Free seasonal catalogs
Phone, fax, and mail orders, gift orders
DISC, MC, VISA

Italian specialties—

Balducci's
Mail Order Division
11-02 Queens Plaza South
Long Island City, NY 11101-4908

800-822-1444
800-247-2450 (in NY State)
718-786-9690 (special requests)

Balducci's makes its own pasta sauces and imports a number of Italian specialty items: antipasti, sun-dried tomatoes, whole tomatoes packed with basil, marinated porcini mushrooms. You'll also find an assortment of English relishes as well as some unusual condiments like pickled quail eggs.

Free seasonal catalogs
Phone and mail orders, gift orders
AMEX, MC, VISA

Herb jellies, fruit catsups, chutneys, and more—

Bear Meadow Farm
Route 2
Moore Road
Florida, MA 01247

413-663-9241

Hilary and George Garivaltis's product list includes unusual items like herb jellies, apple catsup, cranberry catsup, rhubarb chutney, and beet relish. They also offer four kinds of mustard, honey mint sauce, tomato olive pasta sauce, hot pepper jelly, and spiced wild blueberries.

Free price list
Mail orders
No credit cards

From a company that started with horseradish—

Beaverton Foods, Inc.
P. O. Box 687
Beaverton, OR 97075

503-646-8138

Rose Biggi began this company in a small way in 1929, growing and selling horseradish for Portland customers.

Today the company, still run by the Biggi family, produces mustards, sauces, dressings, and condiments— and still sells its original product. Although the products are available in some specialty shops, you can order a variety of sampler packs that will let you stock up on your favorites from among the ten horseradish products, over twenty mustards, and twelve sauces and condiments.

Free price list with recipes
Mail orders, gift orders
AMEX, MC, VISA

Tasty treats from Vermont—

Blanchard & Blanchard, Ltd.
P. O. Box 1080
Norwich, VT 05055

802-295-9200

The Blanchard & Blanchard product line offers almost a dozen salad dressings (including Sesame Seed Dressing and Honey-Mustard Dressing with Tarragon), as well as marinades and glazes, catsups, a cocktail sauce, and dessert sauces. These products are stocked nationally by many specialty stores, and Blanchard & Blanchard will be pleased to mail order products for customers who can't find them locally— just ask for the retail price list.

Free price list
Mail orders
No credit cards

Real Old World mustard—

Boetje Foods, Inc.
2736 12th Street
Rock Island, IL 61201

309-788-4352

This business was founded in 1889 when the Boetje family delivered their Dutch-style mustard door to door in Rock Island, filling buyers' containers for a nickel. It's still made from the same Old World recipe with the same all-natural ingredients. You can order very reasonably priced six- or twelve-packs of Boetje mustard.

Free price list
Mail orders
No credit cards

Imported mustards and condiments—

The Chef's Pantry
P. O. Box 3
Post Mills, VT 05058

800-666-9940
802-333-4141

The Chef's Pantry imports mustards from a variety of French producers. The Marcel Recorbet line includes such treats as black olive, lime, shallot, and chervil mustards. You can also order an economical, restaurant-pack 9-pound tin of Bornier Dijon or Whole Grain mustard. Condiments include capers, cornichons, sun-dried tomatoes, and some hard-to-find items like olive paste (black and green), sorrel puree, and pâtissons (baby squash melons packed in vinegar and herbs).

Free illustrated catalog
Phone and mail orders, gift orders
MC, VISA

A selection of Vermont products—

Cherry Hill Cooperative Cannery, Inc.
MR 1, Barre-Montpelier Road
Barre, VT 05641

800-468-3020
802-479-2558

Cherry Hill Cooperative Cannery offers foods made by small, independently owned companies in Vermont. In addition to maple syrup and preserves, the Cannery sells mustards, salad dressings, barbecue and seafood sauces, pickles, and specialties like salsas and marinara pasta sauce.

Free price list
Phone and mail orders
No credit cards

Condiments from Grandmother's recipes—

Clearview Farms
RD 1, Box 5070
Enosburg Falls, VT 05450

802-933-2537

Caroline Longe relies on her grandmother's recipes to produce old-fashioned relishes that include Piccalilli, Maple Cran-Orange, Farmstead Zucchini, and Honied Carrot. She also make chutneys, mustards, barbecue sauces, and preserves, and ships a selection of traditional maple products. Recipes and tips are included in the catalog.

Free illustrated catalog
Phone and mail orders, gift orders
MC, VISA

California condiments—

Cuisine Perel
P. O. Box 1064
Tiburon, CA 94920

415-435-1282

Silvia and Leonardo Perel create ready-to-serve dressings, sauces, mustards, butters, and toppings by combining the fresh produce of California with Napa,

Brazilian Shrimp Salad
from Cuisine Perel

1 pound fresh shrimp
4 stalks celery, finely chopped
1 avocado, cut in small pieces
3 scallions, finely chopped
⅓ cup shredded coconut
Cuisine Perel Thai Peanut Dressing

Sauté, broil, or boil shrimp. Add celery, avocado, and scallions. Garnish with coconut and serve. Accompany with a pitcher of Peanut Dressing to pour over the salad. Serves 2 as a main course, 4 as a first course.

Monterey, and Sonoma wines. Highlights from the product list of almost thirty items include Tomato Zinfandel Dressing, Champagne Mustard with Jalapeño Pepper, Pear Cabernet Topping, California Raspberry Vinegar, and Apricot Chutney. Try Cuisine Perel Thai Peanut Dressing to make a quick and tasty shrimp salad.

Free price list
Mail orders
No credit cards

Italian and international specialties—

Dean & DeLuca, Inc.
Mail Order Department
560 Broadway
New York, NY 10012

800-221-7714
212-431-1691 (in NY state)

Aïoli (garlic mayonnaise), ortilina (concentrated marinara sauce), Italian mint sauce, and roasted pimientos are a few of the unusual items you'll find in this catalog that also offers chutneys, mustards, olives, pesto, sun-dried tomatoes, tomato paste, and sauces.

Color catalog, $2.00
Phone and mail orders, gift orders, and gift certificates
AMEX, MC, VISA

Glazes and dressings made with Vermont maple syrup—

Dodd Enterprises, Inc.
East Fairfield, VT 05448

802-827-3739

The Vermont Fare brand of maple glazes, recommended for grilled, baked, or pan-fried meats, are available in mustard, sweet and sour, and sparerib blends. Two dressings, Apple Lemon or French, are also made by Linda Dodd, a home economist who combines her talents with those of her husband, a third-generation maple sugar maker. Baking mixes, maple syrup and sugar, and gift selections are also part of the Vermont Fare line of products.

Free illustrated brochure
Phone and mail orders, gift orders
MC, VISA

Maine chutneys and cranberry relish—

Downeast Delicacies
Cape Porpoise Chutneys, Ltd.
P. O. Box 1281
Kennebunkport, ME 04046

207-967-5327

In addition to serving her Downeast
Delicacies chutneys as condiments for
meat, poultry, and fish, Jane Lamont
has some interesting suggestions: try a
dollop of chutney on a cracker topped
with cheese for a wonderful canapé; use
a tablespoon or so of chutney to lend
extra zip to chicken or tuna salad; baste
chicken or fish with your favorite
chutney during baking or broiling.
Chutney flavors include peach,
gingered pear, and apple lime; there's
also a cranberry apple relish and two
fruit sauces. Jane includes a wise adage
of the tag of her chutneys: "They
improve with age—like most women."

Free illustrated brochure
Phone and mail orders, gift orders
MC, VISA

Pesto and herb products—

Drake's Ducks
RD 2
Box 810
Keene, NH 03431

800-533-8257
603-357-5858

Marie and Chris Drake, once farmers
themselves, use their knowledge to
purchase farm-fresh ingredients for
their line of herb products and fruit
butters, which are sold in specialty
shops. For mail order customers they
ship sampler packs that contain six
products—herb cheese, herb butter,
pesto, and three fruit butters. The herb
products are ready to use for making
pesto salad and herb garlic bread, and
they can be incorporated into Marie
Drake's recipes, which are included
with all orders.

Free price list
Mail orders
No credit cards

Mustard made with balsamic vinegar—

Fox More Than a Mustard
Fox Hollow Farm
RFD 85
Lyme, NH 03768

603-643-6002

Phyllis Fox started experimenting with
mustard recipes about ten years ago,
when she moved to a Vermont farm.
Now she is marketing her favorite
product, which is living up to its name
as Phyllis and her customers develop
new ways to use this versatile product.
The addition of a few extra ingredients
transforms the mustard into a
marinade, a sauce for fish and seafood,
a glaze for ham, or a dressing for cold
salads.

Free price list
Mail orders, gift orders
No credit cards

Dried tomatoes—

Genovesi Food Company
P. O. Box 5668
Dayton, OH 45405

513-277-2173

Dried tomatoes are available plain or packed with herbs in olive oil or sunflower oil. For mail order customers, the company has thoughtfully put together several product selections that include recipe booklets. Custom combinations are also available.

Free price list
Phone and mail orders, gift orders
MC, VISA

Zesty sauces from Tennessee—

Gourmet Foods, Inc.
P. O. Box 419
Knoxville, TN 37901-0419

615-970-2982

This company produces the Peppervine line of sauces, which will appeal to cooks who like to add a little "zing." The Tiger Sauce, for example, blends 28 ingredients in a cayenne pepper base to accompany meats, seafood, and poultry. Eight additional products include Spicy Pepper Sauce, Worcestershire Sauce with wine and pepper, Steak and Burger Sauce, and Concentrated BBQ Sauce. You may select your favorites in an assortment pack.

Free price list
Phone and mail orders
MC, VISA

Hot products from Vermont—

Jasmine & Bread
RR 2, Box 256
South Royalton, VT 05068

802-763-7115

Sherrie Maurer's growing business, a natural extension of her catering career, began with Beyond Catsup, a blend of tomatoes, apples, vegetables, cider vinegar, and spices. Over the last few years she has added more zesty concoctions, including Beyond Belief (a tomato-pear-chili-pepper condiment), prepared horseradish, a horseradish mustard and jelly, barbecue sauce, and a sweet and sour plum sauce. Sampler packages are available.

Free price list
Mail orders
No credit cards

Here's help to make quick meals—

Judyth's Mountain
1737 Lorensen Drive
San Jose, CA 95124

408-264-3330

The culinary talents of Mona Palmer Onstead have produced a selection of products that can help you make a meal in minutes. Her imaginative creations include pasta sauces (examples: California Almond with Leeks and Capers, Pepper Olive with Walnuts); salad dressings/marinades (Tart Cumin Lime, Curried Ginger); garlic butters; ginger jelly; pepper jellies; and California olive oil and wine vinegars. Since Mona also distributes her products in quantity to wholesalers, specify that you'd like the retail price list when you write.

Free price list
Mail orders
No credit cards

Relishes and dressings from
Pennsylvania Dutch country—

Kitchen Kettle Village
Box 380
Intercourse, PA 17534

800-732-3538
717-768-8261

From Kitchen Kettle Village, a
community of shops in Lancaster
County, Pennsylvania, you can order
an array of old-fashioned relishes and
dressings. The selection includes apple
and pepper chutney, bean salad,
chowchow, pickled beets, spicy hot
piccalilli, a number of relishes,
dressings, and more than two dozen
jams and jellies.

Free price list
Mail and phone orders, gift orders
MC, VISA

A popular salad dressing and
chutneys—

La Casa Rosa
107 Third Street
San Juan Bautista, CA 95045

408-623-4563

La Casa Rosa is a San Juan restaurant
that has been in business since 1935.
The mail order business, begun thirty
years ago when customers repeatedly
asked for their French Herb French
Dressing, has expanded to include
chutneys, spiced watermelon rinds,
fruit preserves and butters,
marmalades, nuts, and dried fruits.
Chutney flavors include apricot with
curry, peach with ginger, pear with
almonds, and pineapple with almonds.

Free price list
Mail orders, gift orders
MC, VISA

Dried tomato products from Virginia
tomatoes—

L'Esprit de Campagne
P. O. Box 3130
Winchester, VA 22601

703-722-4224

Although the products of this quickly
growing company are increasingly
available in specialty shops nationally,
you can still order dried tomato
products directly from Carey and Joy
Lokey. Choose from locally grown
minced or halved dried tomatoes in oil
with herbs (in 8-ounce or pantry-
stocking 64-ounce size) or dried
tomatoes in 2-ounce or 10-ounce bags
The Lokeys also produce dried apples
from local York apples and dried sweet
cherries.

Free price list
Mail orders
No credit cards

Distinctive condiments, including a
pineapple mustard—

The Lollipop Tree
Box 518
Rye, NH 03870

800-842-6691
603-436-8196

Laurie and Bob Lynch of The Lollipop
Tree make a line of condiments
including a pepper jelly that combines
three kinds of peppers; mint jelly with
suspended spearmint leaves; cranberry
conserve with walnuts; and a tangy
meat and seafood sauce. Laurie and
Bob suggest trying their pineapple
mustard as a glaze for poultry, ham,
game, and lamb. Additional products
from The Lollipop Tree include baking
mixes for beer breads, scones, and

muffins; and preserves. Gift boxes that combine selections of products are available.

Free color catalog
Phone and mail orders, gift orders
MC, VISA

Pickled peppers, jellies, and chutneys, mild and hot—

Micks' Peppourri
1707 South 74th Avenue
P. O. Box 8324
Yakima, WA 98908

509-966-2328

After years of delighting friends and relatives with pepper jelly, Ginger and Walt Mick began to manufacture it commercially in 1982. Since then they've added pickled peppers and chutney to their product line. If you live in the West, you may find these products in local specialty shops; otherwise order from the source—you'll get some of Ginger's recipes as well.

Free price list
Mail orders
No credit cards

More than mustard from Mother's—

Mother's Mountain Mustard
110 Woodville Road
P. O. Box 6044
Falmouth, ME 04105

207-781-4658

Carol Tanner and Dennis Proctor pool their talents to produce all-natural products that include several mustards based on Carol's mother's homemade mustard recipe from the Depression days. In addition to this original mustard, you can order Country Dijon,

Zesty, and grainy Portland Beer mustards. Other products include catsup and an 1880 New England Chili Sauce (from another family recipe). Carol and Dennis promise there are more new products "on the back burner."

Free price list
Mail orders
No credit cards

Condiments from a New Jersey country restaurant—

Muirhead
Box 189, RD 1
Ringoes, NJ 08551

201-782-7803

Muirhead is a restaurant nestled in New Jersey's Hunterdon County, where proprietors Doris and Ed Simpson are known for delicious meals based on fresh, seasonal foods. Several of the kitchen specialties are available for mail order customers. These include mustards (Dijon, four-seeded, and horseradish) and salad dressings (balsamic vinaigrette and sweet and sour), as well as apricot jalapeño jelly, pecan pumpkin butter, garlic butter, and cooking sauces.

Free price list
Mail orders
No credit cards

Wine country mustards and catsup—

Napa Valley Mustard Company
P. O. Box 125
Oakville, CA 94562

800-288-1089
707-944-8330

This company was started by three entrepreneurial women who love to cook. Ann Grace, Ruthie Rydman, and Susan Simpson perfected their recipes in their own kitchens to produce three mustards: Herbs of the Valley, California Hot Sweet, and Green Chili and Garlic. Their catsup has been descriptively christened "Not Your Ordinary Catsup."

Free price list
Mail orders
No credit cards

Nectarine chutney and more unusual products—

Narsai's
350 Berkeley Park Boulevard
Berkeley, CA 94707

415-527-7900

Narsai's makes some out-of-the-ordinary dressings, including citronade and feta cheese, as well as a seafood sauce and an Assyrian marinade. Condiments include mustards (green peppercorn, tarragon, or dill) and an unusual nectarine chutney. You will find them in specialty stores, or mail order direct from Narsai's. This company also makes dessert sauces, jams, and fruit conserves.

Free price list
Mail orders
No credit cards

Condiments from a French restaurant in Wisconsin—

The Postilion
615 Old Pioneer Road
Fond du Lac, Wisconsin 54935

414-922-4170

Madame Liane Kuony established The Postilion in her Victorian homestead almost thirty years ago. She makes small batches of a few specialties of the house such as mango chutney, a mustard sauce, and several French vinaigrettes. Other items include fruit liqueur compotes and Christmas treats such as mincemeat, yule log cakes, and plum pudding with hard sauce.

Free illustrated brochure
Phone and mail orders, gift orders
No credit cards

Chutneys, mustards, and more—

Putney's Specialty Foods
2415 S.E. 10th Street
Portland, OR 97214

800-627-0657
503-236-1169

Cathy Farley, owner of Putney's Specialty Foods, has put together a selection of condiments especially for the discriminating cook. Chutney flavors include cranberry-tangerine, apple walnut, and spicy carrot lemon. Choose from champagne, creamy dill, whole grain, and curry mustards. Among more than 40 products, you'll also find English-style horseradish sauce, seafood rémoulade, plum basting and dipping sauce, oils and dressings, and salt-free seasoning mixes. Gift boxes and baskets are available.

Free illustrated catalog
Phone and mail orders, gift orders
MC, VISA

Mustards and unusual sauces—

G. B. Ratto & Company
821 Washington Street
Oakland, CA 94607

800-325-3483
800-228-3515 (in CA)
Fax: 415-836-2250

G. B. Ratto provides an array of domestic and imported mustards, including a salt-free Dijon and several flavors of imported French Maille. Ratto's buyers have shopped all over the world to bring home some unusual sauces from Hawaii, North Africa, Jamaica, India, and Mexico, as well as Escoffier sauce and shredded celery root from France. They've also stocked up on such American specialties as Louisiana hot sauce, picante sauce, and remoulade sauce. There are also anchovy paste, cornichons, olives, olive puree, pimientos, pesto, and sun-dried tomatoes. Don't overlook the garlic jelly, caponata (Italian eggplant appetizer), or tomato tapenade.

Free catalog
Phone, fax, and mail orders, gift orders and certificates
MC, VISA

From a Virginia jam and jelly factory—

Rowena's
758 West 22nd Street
Norfolk, VA 23517

800-627-8699
804-627-8699

Originally a jam and jelly factory, Rowena's has branched out to include imaginative cooking sauces in its product line. Highlights include Oriental Sweet and Sour Sauce, Mexican Mole, and Mariner's Sauce (recommended for a quick gazpacho). Also, flavored oils, conserves, pepper jelly, numerous jams, and regional fare such as peanuts, hams, and other specialties.

Free color catalog
Phone and mail orders, gift orders
MC, VISA

Pickled vegetables and stuffed olives—

S. E. Rykoff & Company
P. O. Box 21467
Market Street Station
Los Angeles, CA 90021

800-421-9873 (orders)
213-624-6094 (product inquiries)

Among Rykoff's pickled vegetables, which make quick and ready-to-serve appetizers, you'll find green beans, miniature corn, carrots, asparagus— even pickled cactus. Spanish olives are stuffed with anchovies or hot peppers. Also salad dressings, mustards, anchovy paste, pesto, sun-dried tomatoes, and fourteen varieties of bases for sauces, soups, stews, and casseroles.

Color catalog, $1.00
Phone and mail orders, gift orders
AMEX, MC, VISA

Mustards, including traditional whole-seed products—

San Francisco Mustard Company
P. O. Box 883962
San Francisco, CA 94188

415-435-5211

Robert Dickinson calls his products "the caviar of mustards." Popular in the San Francisco Bay area, they are requested by cooks all over the country who like the crunchy texture that whole-seed mustard imparts to a recipe. In addition to Traditional Whole Seed Mustard, Bob makes a Hot Garlic Mustard and a Hot Honey Mustard, available in jars or earthenware crocks. All products are free of salt and preservatives.

Free illustrated price list
Mail orders
No credit cards

More than thirty kinds of olives—

Santa Barbara Olive Company
1661 Mission Drive
Solvang, CA 93463-2631

800-624-4896
800-521-0475 (in CA)

This California company makes more than a dozen varieties of green spiced olives, as well as stuffed olives, hand-picked natural black olives, and pitted olives. They also offer imported capers, kalamata olives, olive paste, olive oil, specialty oils, and herb and fruit vinegars.

Free price list
Phone and mail orders
AMEX, MC, VISA

A peck of pickles—

Ralph Sechler & Son, Inc.
St. Joe, IN 46785-0152

219-337-5461

The Sechler family has been pickling their pickles since 1921 and now proffer more than forty varieties, many of which can be found throughout the Midwest. If they aren't available locally, order from a list that includes candied sweet, medium sweet, and fresh-pack pickles as well as miscellaneous items such as hot mixed pickles and dill pickle relish. The Sechlers' brochure extends an invitation to visit and includes a map so you can tour the pickle factory next time you're in the neighborhood.

Free price list and brochure
Mail orders, gift orders
No credit cards

An amazing selection of imported olives and more—

Select Origins, Inc.
Box N
Southampton, NY 11968

800-822-2092
516-924-5447
Fax: 516-924-5892

Tom and Kristi Siplon's catalog features a selection that olive enthusiasts won't be able to resist: brine-cured French olives, Niçoise and Picoline olives from France, four varieties of Moroccan olives, and Greek kalamata olives. If you can't decide, order an "olive tasting" pack of four varieties. Other items include olive spread, pesto, pasta sauce, sun-dried tomatoes, concentrated tomato paste in a tube, domestic and imported mustards, marinades and basting sauces, and a selection of relishes.

Free illustrated catalog
Phone, fax, and mail orders, gift orders
AMEX, MC, VISA

Unusual pickles, olives, and relishes—

Seyco Fine Foods, Inc.
25574 Rye Canyon Road, #E
Valencia, CA 91355-1109

800-423-2942

You'll find all your favorite olives at Seyco as well as some unusual varieties such as almond- or onion-stuffed olives and spiced green Spanish olives. From the many relishes, choose winter salad, corn, zucchini, or jalapeño. Also mustards, chutney, salsa, sun-dried tomatoes, and salad dressings.

Color catalog, $2.00; 10 percent off first order
Phone and mail orders, gift orders
AMEX, DC, MC, VISA

Condiments and sauces from creative cooks—

The Silver Palate
274 Columbus Avenue
New York, NY 10023

212-799-6340

Readers who enjoy the Silver Palate cookbooks may have already cooked with some of the many condiments and sauces created by Julee Rosso and Sheila Lukins. There are half a dozen mustards, several chutneys, salad dressings, a barbecue sauce, a duck sauce, and more.

Free price list
Phone and mail orders
AMEX, MC, VISA

Pestos with a Southwestern flavor—

Spagetti Western Foods
P. O. Box 658
Tesuque, NM 87574

505-753-6409

To concoct her special pestos, Julie Feldman adds extra ingredients to the classic combo of basil, cheese, garlic, pine nuts, and oil. To make the red pesto, she adds tomatoes and red chili peppers; for the green, she adds spinach and green chili peppers. Use them as you would regular pesto to give pasta, grilled meats, and other dishes a Southwestern spice. Julie also

makes red chili marinara sauce and spicy barbecue sauce. Spagetti Western Foods products are available in specialty stores in the Southwest, or you can order directly from the company.

Free price list
Mail orders
No credit cards

Blueberry products from home-grown blueberries—

Spruce Mountain Blueberries
Mount Pleasant Road
West Rockport, ME 04865

207-236-3538

Molly Sholes grows her own blueberries to make Spruce Mountain Blueberries chutney and conserve. The chutney, for which Molly roasts and grinds the spices, is an old North India recipe specially adapted for wild Maine blueberries; it comes plain or with raisins and almonds. The conserve is also spiced and goes well with meats and poultry. You can order individual 10-ounce jars of these products or a pack featuring one of each.

Free price list
Mail orders
No credit cards

Chutneys from Vermont harvests—

Stowe Hollow Kitchens
Box 6830 North Hollow Road
RD 3
Stowe, VT 05672

802-253-8248

To make her cranberry, apple, and peach chutneys, Patti Soper combines choice fruit with raisins, sugar/honey, vinegar, and a blend of seasonings. No

Chutney Chicken Pâté

from Stowe Hollow Kitchens

2 cups cubed cooked chicken
¼ cup minced onion
1 large sweet pickle, minced
½ cup minced parsley
1 teaspoon tarragon
1 teaspoon dried thyme
3 tablespoons chopped almonds
½ teaspoon salt
¼ teaspoon pepper
½ cup Stowe Hollow cranberry or peach chutney
¾ cup mayonnaise

Mince chicken in food processor. Combine remaining ingredients in a bowl and add minced chicken. Pack in crocks and chill overnight.

salt or preservatives are added. Each of the three varieties comes with a brochure of her kitchen-tested recipes. Although Patti does a large wholesale business, she will also mail a pack of three chutneys to retail customers.

Free price list
Mail orders
MC, VISA

Salt-free condiments with a Southwestern flavor—

Sugar's Kitchen
P. O. Box 41886
Tucson, Arizona 85717

602-624-3360

Arizona Champagne Sauces from Sugar's Kitchen are salt-free, with a piquant Southwestern flavor. There are three mustard sauces (hot, Cajun-style, and regular), jalapeño jellies (mild and hot), and a vegetable dip. Sugar's Kitchen also makes two salt-free and sugar-free herbal mixes. The Herbal Spice Mix is recommended for flavoring soups, salads, and omelets; suggestions for the Southwest Mix include creating salsa, vegetable dips, and making extra-tasty Spanish rice or Bloody Marys.

Free illustrated brochure
Mail orders, gift orders
No credit cards

A variety of dried tomato products—

Timber Crest Farms
4791 Dry Creek Road
Healdsburg, CA 95448

707-433-8251
Fax: 707-433-8255

You can order Timber Crest Farms's dried tomato products in small or large quantities—for example, order either 3

Mushroom Caps Filled with Dried Tomato Tapenade

from Timber Crest Farms

18 large mushrooms
 1 tablespoon capers, drained
 1 large garlic clove
 4 anchovy fillets
 ¼ cup fresh or 1½ teaspoons dried basil leaves
 1 tablespoon fresh lemon juice
 ⅓ cup pitted ripe olives
 ½ cup dried tomato bits
 ¼ cup olive oil
Black and cayenne peppers, to taste

Remove stems from mushrooms and set caps aside. In bowl of food processor fitted with steel blade, combine capers, garlic, anchovies, basil, and lemon juice; pulse on and off until coarsely chopped. Add mushroom stems and olives; process until finely minced, scraping sides as needed. Transfer to medium bowl. Mix in dried tomato bits, olive oil, and black and cayenne peppers. Stuff each mushroom cap with 1 rounded tablespoon tapenade mixture. Place on baking sheet and bake at 425 degrees for 4 to 5 minutes or until hot. Serve immediately. Makes 6 to 8 appetizer servings.

ounces or 5 pounds of tomato bits to sample an unfamiliar ingredient or stock up on a favorite. In addition to tomato bits, Timber Crest Farms ships dried tomato halves, marinated tomatoes, pasta sauce, and dried tomato chutney. A new product is dried tomato tapenade. Timber Crest Farms also sells dried fruits, nuts, and fruit butters.

Free color catalog
Phone, fax, and mail orders, gift orders
AMEX, MC, VISA

Old-fashioned treats from Vermont—

Vermont Epicurean
P. O. Box 59
Wolcott, VT 05680

800-232-3922
802-888-3922

The Vermont Epicurean product list sounds like an inventory of Grandma's pantry: jellies (pepper, onion, cucumber, mint pepper, and tomato with horseradish); mustards (tangy maple, maple with horseradish, green peppercorn); and Tangy Maple Salad Dressing.

Free price list
Mail orders
MC, VISA

Condiments sweetened with fruit concentrate—

Wax Orchards
22744 Wax Orchards Road S.W.
Vashon Island, WA 98070

800-634-6132
206-682-8251

Wax Orchards uses concentrated fruit juice to sweeten products that include gingered apricot and cranberry chutneys, sweet and sour sauce, and a tomato herb condiment. Wax Orchards also makes an all-fruit mincemeat, dessert toppings, preserves, fruit butters and syrups. All are low-calorie and contain very little salt.

Free price list and nutritional information (please send two 25¢ stamps)
Phone and mail orders, gift orders
MC, VISA

Barbecue sauces are the specialty here—

Wicker's Barbecue Sauce
Box 126
Hornersville, MO 63855

800-847-0032
314-737-2372

This company concentrates on barbecue, making just two products: Wicker's Barbecue Marinade and Baste and Wicker's Thicker Barbecue Sauce. They're made from the recipe of Peck Wicker, who had a barbecue pit that served customers from miles around. The sauce is based on vinegar—no tomato and no sugar—so it makes a good cooking sauce, base, or marinade.

Free price list
Phone and mail orders
MC, VISA

For more pickled vegetable sources, check Chapter 23, "Vegetables," for some interesting items, including pickled fiddleheads.

CHAPTER 7

DAIRY CULTURES

Many cooks have experimented with making yogurt at home. Now, if you'd like to be more adventurous, here are sources for cultures that will allow you to keep a supply of fresh homemade buttermilk, sour cream, and cheese in your refrigerator. You can even make European-style crème fraîche and fromage blanc easily and economically at home; these products are difficult to find and expensive to buy in specialty shops. Another bonus offered by homemade dairy products is the health advantage of low-fat and salt-free products.

Cultures for yogurt, sour cream, buttermilk—

DaisyFresh Dairy Cultures
P. O. Box 36
Santa Cruz, CA 95063

408-423-7852

DaisyFresh, suppliers of cultures to individuals and health food stores since 1963, offers cultures for Bulgarian yogurt, Swiss acidophilus, Irish buttermilk, and Danish sour cream. You may want to begin with one of the sampler or starter kits. John and Kerry Pennick, new owners of DaisyFresh, ship all orders within twenty-four hours. A 30-page yogurt manual and cookbook with over 160 recipes is available for $4.00. Mix up a batch of Swiss Apple Breakfast (recipe follows) from the *DaisyFresh Yogurt Manual and Cookbook* and have ready-to-go breakfasts all week long.

Free price list
Mail orders
No credit cards

A basic cheese-making kit—

Home Brew International, Inc.
1126 South Federal Highway, Suite 182
Fort Lauderdale, FL 33316

305-764-1527

Home Brew International, which sells a complete line of home wine- and beermaking supplies, has also assembled a basic cheese-making kit that contains everything you need to make a variety of cheese, including Cheddar, Monterey Jack, cottage cheese, ricotta, and fresh herbed cheese. You'll get a mold, rennet, a starter culture, an herb packet, cheesecloth, a thermometer, and a curd cutter in addition to a recipe booklet with easy-to-follow instructions.

Free illustrated catalog
Mail orders
No credit cards

Cultures and yogurt products—

International Yogurt Company
628 North Doheny Drive
Los Angeles, CA 90069

213-274-9917

Cultures are available from International Yogurt for yogurt, kefir, and acidophilus, as well as cheese, buttermilk, and sour cream. Money-saving selections of four or six cultures of your choice are offered. This company, in the yogurt business for over 45 years, also supplies an incubator, dairy thermometer, yogurt tablets, and an assortment of yogurt beauty products.

Free illustrated brochure
Mail orders
No credit cards

Everything for the home cheese maker—

New England Cheesemaking Supply Company
P. O. Box 85
Ashfield, MA 01330

413-628-3808

Bob and Ricki Carroll have been providing information and supplies to the home cheese maker and the small farmstead cheese maker for over twelve years. Their catalog is a complete source of supplies, including cultures, rennet, molds, and books. Unusual items include a gourmet soft cheese kit to make creamy and delicious soft cheese.

Illustrated catalog, $1.00
Phone and mail orders
MC, VISA

Swiss Apple Breakfast
from the DaisyFresh Yogurt Manual and Cookbook

    2 cups rolled oats
    2 cups yogurt
    ½ cup lemon juice
    1 cup raisins
    1 cup chopped nuts
    5 medium apples, peeled, cored, and grated

Combine all ingredients. Refrigerate until well chilled. If you like, add sliced bananas or other fresh fruit before serving. Keeps for about a week in the refrigerator and just gets better and better.

How to Make Crème Fraîche

from Bob Carroll, Home Dairy Specialist,
New England Cheesemaking Supply Company

Crème fraîche is a rich, creamy cheese to serve with fresh fruit or in place of sour cream.

1. Take 1 pint heavy cream and 1 pint light cream and heat to 175 degrees F. Cool quickly by placing pot of cream in sinkful of cold water. Cool to 72 degrees F.
2. Place contents of packet of Fromage Blanc Starter Culture in a bowl. Add cream. Stir and allow to set from 12 to 24 hours until the cream shows a thick set.
3. Pour the cream curd into a cheesecloth-lined colander. Hang the bag of curd to drain from 6 to 12 hours until the curd stops dripping. (Be sure to use a double thickness of very fine cheesecloth for this step.)
4. Place the cheese in a bowl and refrigerate immediately.

CHAPTER 8

ESCARGOTS

Now you and your guests don't have to wait to savor escargots in restaurants. Here are the sources for this epicurean delight—you supply the butter and garlic!

True French snails—

The Chef's Pantry
P. O. Box 3
Post Mills, VT 05058

800-666-9940
802-333-4141

The Chef's Pantry imports Menetrel brand helix snails hand-packed in tins of 6 and 8 dozen. You can also order escargot shells in quantities of 24 or 100.

Free illustrated catalog
Phone and mail orders, gift orders
MC, VISA

Escargots plus serving accessories—

G. B. Ratto & Company
821 Washington Street
Oakland, CA 94607

800-325-3483
800-228-3515 (in CA)
Fax: 415-836-2250

G. B. Ratto has everything you need to serve this delicacy at home: tins of escargots, escargot shells, and an herb mixture for escargot butter. The escargot accessories include ceramic or stainless steel escargotières (dishes designed to hold shells) with 6 or 12 holes; shell holder/pincers; and escargot forks. Here are G. B. Ratto's easy instructions for preparing escargots: "You simply drop one or two escargots in each shell, topped with a dab of butter and herb mixture. Put them in the oven for just a few minutes or until the escargots bubble slightly in the shell. Now comes that time to experience a superb gustatory delight!"

Free illustrated catalog
Phone, fax, and mail orders, gift orders and certificates
MC, VISA

Buy the snails, and you'll get the shells, too—

Seyco Fine Foods, Inc.
25574 Rye Canyon Road, #E
Valencia, CA 91355-1109

800-423-2942

These French snails are packed 24 to a tin. Shells are available at no extra charge.

Color catalog, $2.00; 10 percent off first order
Phone and mail orders, gift orders
AMEX, DC, MC, VISA

CHAPTER 9

FISH AND SEAFOOD

Thanks to some enterprising Northeastern companies, you can enjoy a fresh lobster boil or clambake anywhere in the country at any time of the year. Just pick up the phone, call one of these companies, and serve a spectacular meal to your family or guests within forty-eight hours. Insulated containers packed with gel ice and speedy UPS service bring these feasts to your door at the peak of freshness. What could be easier?

You'll also find a variety of delicious smoked fish and seafood in this chapter. Some are "hot" smoked and others are "cold" smoked. Here's the difference: with hot smoking, the fish is heated to 140 degrees or more and the result is a "cooked" taste and texture (hot smoking is frequently used for trout and coho salmon, for example); with cold smoking the temperature stays below 80 degrees and the fish remains translucent and firm textured (this process is frequently used for smoked Atlantic salmon).

Don't think of smoked fish and seafood only as appetizers—try the recipes in this chapter that incorporate smoked salmon, scallops, and catfish in deliciously different entrées.

An abundant lobster pot and imported specialties—

Balducci's
Mail Order Division
11-02 Queens Plaza South
Long Island City, NY 11101-4908

800-822-1444
800-247-2450 (in NY State)
718-786-9690 (special requests)

Balducci's New England lobster pot comes ready to cook, with live Maine lobsters, littleneck clams, mussels, potatoes, onions, and corn on the cob. Other seafood items include scalone steak (a combination of bay scallops and abalone); imported Swedish gravlax; and frutti di mare insalata, a Mediterranean specialty of assorted seafood in vinaigrette. Balducci's smoked seafood includes sides of smoked Scotch salmon; apple-smoked sturgeon; baby shark; shrimp; and a salmon log that combines smoked salmon with butter, cream cheese, and herbs.

Free seasonal catalogs
Phone and mail orders, gift orders, and gift certificates
AMEX, MC, VISA

Seasonally available Alaskan salmon—

Briggs Way Company
Main Street
Ugashik, AK 99613

Contact by mail

Roger and Emorene Briggs run a family operation that cans red and medium-red salmon in glass jars within a few hours of the catch. The canning operation runs from late June through the beginning of September; shipments begin the first of September and are usually completed by early November. Orders should reach the Briggses by mid-August. Since they can a limited quantity of salmon each year, Emorene Briggs says, her customers feel it is a rare privilege to receive it.

Free price list
Mail orders
No credit cards

Imported delicacies—

California Sunshine Fine Foods, Inc.
144 King Street
San Francisco, CA 94107

415-543-3007

Although caviar is the prime product of California Sunshine Fine Foods, the company also offers some interesting seafood: New Zealand green-lipped mussels (frozen) and smoked New Zealand eel, Norwegian salmon, smoked sturgeon, and mussels. Smoked game birds and specialty sausage are also carried.

Free brochure
Phone and mail orders
AMEX, MC, VISA

Specialties of the season—

Caspian Caviars
Highland Mill
P. O. Box 876
Camden, ME 04843

800-332-4436
207-236-4436
Fax: 207-236-2740

This caviar company also offers a selection of seafood. The list is extensive and some items are only seasonally available. Highlights include live Maine lobsters, including colossal ones (over 10 pounds); fresh sushi-grade tuna; fresh rainbow trout; smoked fish and shellfish; and a number of fish pâtés.

Free catalog
Phone, fax, and mail orders
AMEX, MC, VISA

Choose the best from Cape Cod—

The Clambake Company
P. O. Box 1677
5 Giddiah Hill Road
Orleans, MA 02653

800-423-4038
617-255-3289

This Cape Cod company packs up a feast for each diner that includes a lobster, soft-shelled clams and mussels, codfish, corn on the cob, new potatoes, onions, and sweet sausage. Extra lobsters and steamers can be added, or you can order just the lobsters and steamers if you do not want a complete clambake.

Free price list
Phone and mail orders, gift orders
AMEX, MC, VISA

Seasonally available fresh oysters and cherrystone clams—

The Cotuit Oyster Company
P. O. Box 563
Little River Road
Cotuit, MA 02635

508-428-6747

The Cotuit Oyster Company ships fresh oysters and fresh local cherrystone clams during the fall and winter. Contact the company for availability and price. Stainless steel oyster and clam knives are also available. Storage tips, shucking instructions, and recipes are included with each order.

Write or call for prices and availability
Gift orders
No credit cards

European delights—

Dean & DeLuca, Inc.
Mail Order Department
560 Broadway
New York, NY 10012

800-221-7714
212-431-1691

As part of its array of international foods, Dean & DeLuca stock Pinney's smoked seafood specialties (salmon, salmon pâté, trout, and eel) smoked over an oak fire in Dumfriesshire, Scotland. You'll also find imported anchovy fillets, sardines, and tuna fillets.

Color catalog, $2.00
Phone and mail orders, gift orders and certificates
AMEX, MC, VISA

Fresh Maine lobster, crab meat, scallops—

Downeast Seafood Express
Box 138
Route 176
Brooksville, ME 04617

800-556-2326
207-326-8246 (in ME, call collect)

These live Maine lobsters are packed in seaweed and guaranteed to arrive in perfect condition. (If any lobster does not arrive alive, Downeast Seafood Express will replace it with two lobsters by return mail.) You can also order fresh cooked lobster meat, crab meat, fresh sea scallops, and steamer clams (scallops and clams are seasonal), or combinations of these items.

Free illustrated brochure
Phone and mail orders, gift orders, and gift certificates
MC, VISA

Seafood smoked with Maine fruitwoods and hardwoods—

Ducktrap River Fish Farm, Inc.
RFD 2
Box 378
Lincolnville, ME 04849

207-763-3960

Des FitzGerald's Ducktrap River Fish Farm is located just two miles from the Maine coast, giving him an abundant supply of fresh fish and shellfish for his smoking operation. Choose from smoked trout, salmon, bluefish, monkfish, tuna loin, pollock, haddock, mussels, scallops, and shrimp. Or order a sampler that combines mussels, scallops, and salmon. There are also several pâtés: smoked salmon, trout, tuna, and bluefish.

Free price list
Phone and mail orders, gift orders, and gift certificates
MC, VISA

Fresh and smoked oysters—

Ekone Oyster Company
Star Route, Box 465
South Bend, WA 98586

206-875-5494

Ekone grows its oysters in the cool waters of Willapa Bay and smokes them over red alderwood. Vacuum-packed fresh smoked oysters are offered, as well as canned oysters in 3-ounce packs. Pints and half gallons of freshly shucked oysters are currently shipped to seafood lovers in the states of Oregon and Washington only.

Free price list
Mail orders
No credit cards

Smoked sockeye salmon from icy Alaskan waters—

Fisherman's Finest
3318 North 26th Street
Tacoma, WA 98407

206-759-7163

Fisherman's Finest owners Richard and Marguerite Lang are involved in every step of catching, processing, and packaging their product. Sockeye salmon is hand-trimmed, lightly brined, and cold-smoked overnight before being packed and processed in a gold foil

pouch that keeps the salmon indefinitely without refrigeration. The box is decorated with a commissioned drawing of a fishing scene, which makes it particularly nice for gift giving.

Free price list
Phone and mail orders, gift orders
MC, VISA

Fresh from Maine—

Bill Foster's Downeast Clambake
P. O. Box 486
York Harbor, ME 03911

207-363-3255

Live Maine lobsters and clams are packed with fresh-cut seaweed in refrigerated containers, complete with cooking instructions and eating utensils. These feasts are shipped Monday through Thursday for next-day delivery.

Free price list
Phone and mail orders, gift orders
MC, VISA

Fresh and smoked rainbow trout from northern Michigan—

Green River Trout Farm
Mancelona, MI 49659

616-584-3486

You can do your own fishing at this northern Michigan trout farm in one of three ponds—the kids' pond, the intermediate pond, or the trophy pond. But if you can't make it any time soon, order some of their smoked rainbow trout from a product list that also includes smoked mako shark, Hawaiian marlin, oysters, scallops, sable, and salmon. An extensive list of smoked and frozen meats is offered too.

Free price list
Mail orders, gift orders
MC, VISA

Smoked and fancy-packed seafoods—

Hegg & Hegg
801 Marine Drive
Port Angeles, WA 98362

800-435-3474
206-457-3344

Whole and half alder-smoked salmon
start off this seafood selection, followed
by Nova-style smoked salmon and
Puget Sound red sockeye steaks packed
in oval tins. You can order cases and
half cases of sockeye, pink, or smoked
red salmon, smoked sturgeon, tuna,
shrimp, and crab meat. (Several of
these items are packed without salt for
those on sodium-restricted diets.)
Variety packs give you a selection of
these products, and you may also

include smoked oysters, salmon pâté,
and steamed clams.

Free illustrated brochure
Phone and mail orders; gift orders
AMEX, DISC, MC, VISA

A well-researched smoking technique—

Horton's Smoked Seafoods
P. O. Box 430
Waterboro, ME 04087

800-346-6066
207-247-6900

This Maine smokehouse is run by Don
Horton, who researched Scottish,
Swedish, Irish, and Norwegian smoking
methods before settling on a
combination of brining solutions,
smoking times, and wood chips that
were just what he wanted for his own
company. His products include smoked
rainbow trout, salmon (Atlantic and
Western), sturgeon, sable, halibut,

Gingered Smoked Scallops
from Horton's Smoked Seafoods

¼ cup butter
1½ pounds Horton's smoked scallops
2 tablespoons finely sliced fresh ginger root
Salt to taste
Freshly ground black pepper
2 tablespoons fresh parsley, minced

Melt butter in a large skillet until sizzling. Add scallops and ginger root and
gently sauté 5 to 7 minutes until lightly browned. Transfer to serving dish, add
salt and pepper to taste, and sprinkle with parsley. Serves 4 to 6.

tuna, catfish, cod, finnan haddie, pollock, mackerel, and bluefish. Smoked shrimp, mussels, and scallops are also available, as well as smoked salmon, trout, and bluefish pâtés. Horton's will also prepare custom orders for dinners and parties.

Free price list
Phone and mail orders, gift orders
AMEX, MC, VISA

From a famous Portland restaurant—

Jake's Famous Products
4910 North Basin
Portland, OR 97217

503-220-1895

Jake's Restaurant, known for its fresh seafood and delicious soups and desserts, has been a Portland tradition

Smoked Salmon in Dijon Cream with Sautéed Vegetables Served Over Pasta
from Jake's Restaurant

Fresh fettuccine
2 7-ounce tins Jake's smoked salmon (save salmon juices)
½ cup butter
1 clove garlic, chopped
½ cup chopped onion
1 cup carrots, julienned
1 cup snow peas
2 cups heavy cream
2 tablespoons Dijon mustard
2 tablespoons pesto sauce

Boil fresh fettuccine al dente; rinse with cold water and set aside. Remove bones from salmon. In a large saucepan, melt butter and sauté garlic, onion, carrots, and snow peas until cooked yet still crisp. Add heavy cream, reserved salmon juice, mustard, and pesto sauce. Reduce heat to medium and stir until sauce is thick and smooth. Add salmon chunks to finished sauce and vegetables. Add cooked pasta and stir together over low heat. (Option: serve sauce over a bed of pasta.) Serves 4 to 6.

Variation: Use Jake's kippered salmon or Jake's smoked trout in place of the smoked salmon.

Serving suggestion: This entrée would be complemented nicely by a hearty Chardonnay.

since 1892. You can order these Jake's Famous Products to give you a taste of the restaurant at home: salmon and smoked salmon, salmon pâté, trout pâté, clam chowder, seafood sauces, and desserts. A gift basket combines a selection of these items. Senior Chef Bill King was selected Oregon Chef of the Year in 1988. Try his recipe for Smoked Salmon in Dijon Cream with Sautéed Vegetables Served Over Pasta.

Free price list
Phone and mail orders
AMEX, DISC, MC, VISA

Smoked, fresh, and pickled seafood plus seafood jerky—

Josephson's Smokehouse and Dock
106 Marine Drive
P. O. Box 412
Astoria, OR 97103

800-772-3474
800-828-3474 (in OR)

Michael and Linda Josephson carry on the smoking business begun by Grandfather Anton seventy years ago. They maintain a retail shop at the smokehouse site and ship products all over the world. They have an extensive list of smoked specialties, fresh, canned, and frozen items, and a concentrated homemade clam chowder. Unusual items include smoked salmon or shark jerky, smoked tuna strips, and pickled seafoods—tart or sweet and sour salmon and prawns.

Free color catalog
Phone and mail orders, gift orders
MC, VISA

Crab, and much more—

Nelson Crab
Tokeland, WA 98590

800-843-8370
800-262-0069 (in WA)

Nelson Crab has been shipping its Sea Treats brand products all across the country since 1941. The product list is long and includes Dungeness crab meat and crab legs, albacore tuna in oil and water, minced razor clams, tiny cold-water shrimp, Columbia River blueback and Chinook salmon. Smoked items include king and coho salmon, oysters, river shad, sturgeon, and crab legs. Variety and gift packs are available.

Free price list
Phone and mail orders, gift orders
MC, VISA

Smoked catfish from Tennessee—

Pickwick Catfish Farm
Highway 57
Counce, TN 38326

901-689-3805

Betty and Quentin Knussman smoke farm-raised catfish, sell them at the farm, and ship them to chefs and home cooks across the country. Discounts for orders of 10 or more fish. If you've never prepared a dish with smoked catfish, you may like the following recipe from Pickwick's for Lafitte's Cajun Salad with Creole Mustard Vinaigrette.

Free price list
Mail orders
MC, VISA

Lafitte's Cajun Salad with Creole Mustard Vinaigrette

created by Lafitte's Hampshire House, Washington, D.C.,
using Pickwick Smoked Catfish

Salad:
1 smoked catfish
Watercress or romaine lettuce for 4
A few pecans for garnish

Dressing:
1 large egg yolk (optional)
1 small jalapeño pepper, seeded and cut up
⅓ cup olive oil
1 tablespoon lemon juice
1 tablespoon Grey Poupon mustard
Freshly ground black pepper
Pinch of salt
Touch of honey to taste (after mixed)

Place all ingredients for dressing in a blender and blend until smooth. Taste and add honey. Dip lettuce or watercress in dressing and arrange on four individual plates. Arrange strips of Pickwick smoked catfish on greens. Drizzle a small amount of dressing on fish. Garnish with pecans. Serves 4.

Fresh and smoked brook trout—

Red-Wing Meadow Farm, Inc.
187 North Main Street
Sunderland, MA 01375

800-321-4118
413-549-4118

Red-Wing Meadow Farm, specializing in brook trout, sells it fresh in 8-, 10-, or 12-ounce portions, and will bone the trout for you if you wish. The farm's Trout Nouveau are 4- to 5-inch brook trout, suitable for appetizers or entrées, in which the bones just cook away. Fresh trout are shipped the day they are harvested, packed in insulated containers with gel ice. Smoked trout are available whole or boneless; the boneless trout are flavored with lemon and pepper.

Free price list
Phone and mail orders
MC, VISA

Seafood from around the world—

Seyco Fine Foods, Inc.
25574 Rye Canyon Road, #E
Valencia, CA 91355-1109

800-423-2942

Seyco offers seafood delicacies from around the world, including crab meat from Chile, lobster from Nova Scotia, Spanish tuna, Alaska Chinook salmon, and domestic smoked sturgeon and brook trout.

Color catalog, $2.00; 10 percent off first order
Phone and mail orders, gift orders
AMEX, DC, MC, VISA

Smoked salmon and oysters—

Specialty Seafoods
605 30th Street
Anacortes, WA 98221

800-645-3474
800-445-5426 (in WA)

North Pacific smoked salmon and oysters are offered individually or in combination packs. This company is geared to the gift business and offers discounts for multiple orders, which may make all the smoked seafood enthusiasts on your gift list very happy.

Free color brochure
Phone and mail orders, gift orders
AMEX, DC, MC, VISA

Crab meat and smoked fish—

Stone Harbor Seafood Company
8250 N.E. Underground Drive
Kansas City, MO 64161

800-821-6101
816-459-7244

Stone Harbor Seafood ships a variety of blue crab meat: jumbo lump, backfin lump, white, whole crab claws, and claw meat. Smoked salmon and sturgeon are also available. Gift packs provide a sampling of products. Order products by quarter, half, or whole

cases; discounts apply to half and whole cases.

Free price list
Phone and mail orders, gift orders
MC, VISA

Northwestern seafood from Pike Place Farmers' Market—

Totem Smokehouse
1906 Pike Place
Seattle, WA 98101

800-972-5666
206-443-1710

Totem products are shipped from Don Fleming's smokehouse store in Seattle's famous Pike Place Farmers' Market, where he has been doing business for more than ten years. For mail order customers, he has put together 18 combination packs of salmon, shrimp, crab, and smoked items (salmon, sturgeon, oysters, clams, salmon pâté). They make fine gifts—or choose one for yourself to stock the cupboard.

Free color brochure
Phone and mail orders, gift orders
AMEX, MC, VISA

A clambake, complete with utensils and bibs—

Weathervane Lobster Company
62 Badger's Island
Kittery, ME 03904

800-343-4000
207-439-0920

Weathervane's down east clambake comes with lobsters, steamers, fish chowder base (just add milk or cream), and even lobster crackers, picks, and bibs. You can also order just lobsters (live or cooked), lobster meat, crab meat and legs, clams, scallops, shrimp, and fresh fish by the pound. The shellfish accessories department sells seafood picks and lobster crackers, a lobster apron, and seafood sauces.

Free illustrated brochure
Phone and mail orders, gift orders, and gift certificates
MC, VISA

Fish, seafood, and ready-to-cook entrées—

Wisconsin Fishing Company
P. O. Box 965
Green Bay, WI 54305

800-527-3590
800-236-1457 (in WI)

Fresh frozen fish and seafood have been specialties of the Wisconsin Fishing Company for almost ninety years. A few unusual items on the extensive list include whole calamari (squid), polpo (octopus), salt cod, smoked eels, marlin steaks, and red snapper fillets. There's a full menu of ready-to-cook breaded fish and seafood, plus entrées such as flounder stuffed with crab meat, as well as coating mixes and spices for crab boils and blackened fish. A choice of caviar, smoked seafood, and Scandinavian-style herring products completes the selection.

Free color catalog
Mail and phone orders, gift orders
MC, VISA

CHAPTER 10

FLOUR, MEAL, AND BAKING MIXES

The gristmill was once an essential part of the life of every town in America. Even though we can buy our flour and meal in the supermarket now, some mills continue to operate, many of them restored through the hard work of their present owners. Their products, many from organically grown grains, are fresh and pure—and the best way to start a loaf of bread or a batch of muffins. And if you don't have time for baking "from scratch," many of these millers have put together mixes that combine the best of old-fashioned goodness with modern convenience. This chapter also contains sources for some difficult-to-find items like Italian cornmeal for polenta, and unusual grains like quinoa and amaranth.

Buckwheat products—

The Birkett Mills
P. O. Box 440
Penn Yan, NY 14527

315-536-3311

The Birkett Mills has produced buckwheat products since it was established in Penn Yan, New York, in 1797. The mill supplies buckwheat flour, buckwheat and buttermilk pancake mixes, roasted buckwheat kernels (kasha), stone-ground groats, cream of buckwheat, and sprouting buckwheat seed. In addition, there's wheat bran, wheat germ, whole wheat cereal and flour, unbleached pastry flour, and graham flour. *The Buckwheat Cookbook* (available for an extra dollar) contains over 40 recipes for cooking with buckwheat.

Free price list
Mail orders
No credit cards

Buckwheat flour and mixes for traditional "ployes"—

Bouchard Family Farm
Route 1
Fort Kent, ME 04743

207-834-3237

For years the Bouchard family has been growing Silver Skin Buckwheat to make a flour that has been used by generations of French Canadians to prepare "ployes." Ployes (rhymes with boys) are light buckwheat pancakes that have been enjoyed in Northern Maine since 1785. Made without additives or preservatives, Bouchard's ploye mixes (original and whole wheat) also make a low-calorie product: one ploye has less calories than a slice of bread. Their brochure tells the whole ploye story and provides recipes and serving suggestions.

Free brochure and price list
Mail orders
No credit cards

Products from Vermont's only steam-powered gristmill—

Brewster River Mill
Mill Street
Jeffersonville, VT 05464

802-644-2987

The Albright family has spent more than 12 years painstakingly restoring their historic gristmill, using cut nails, wooden pegs, and traditional methods. Their eventual goal is to convert their steam-powered mill to its original state when it was powered by the river's water. The mill grinds local organic products into flours and meals, and also sells baking mixes, maple syrup from Mrs. Albright's father's farm, and other Vermont products.

Free brochure
Mail and phone orders
MC, VISA

Bread, pastry, and cake flour—

Dean & DeLuca, Inc.
Mail Order Department
560 Broadway
New York, NY 10012

800-221-7714
212-431-1691

New Hope Flour Mills bread, pastry, and cake flours are stocked by Dean &

DeLuca, as well as mixes made from stone-ground flours for buttermilk and buckwheat pancakes. From Dean & DeLuca you can order Italian cornmeal with just the right texture for making authentic polenta.

Color catalog, $2.00
Phone and mail orders, gift orders, and certificates
AMEX, MC, VISA

Baking mixes flavored with Vermont maple sugar—

Dodd Enterprises, Inc.
East Fairfield, VT 05448

802-827-3739

Linda Dodd is a home economist and creative cook, and her husband is a third-generation maple sugar maker. Their combined talents have created Vermont Fare brand baking mixes, naturally sweetened with pure maple sugar. Choose Maple Nut or Maple Spice muffin mixes; Maple Apple, Cherry, or Blueberry Almond pancake and waffle mixes, or Maple Cornbread & Muffin Mix. Linda suggests that the pancakes make fine desserts when topped with a scoop of vanilla ice cream. Gift packs of assorted products are also available.

Free illustrated brochure
Phone and mail orders, gift orders
MC, VISA

Organic baking mixes and cereals from Maine—

Fiddler's Green Farm
RR 1
Box 656
Belfast, ME 04915

207-338-3568

Husband-and-wife team Richard Stander and Nancy Galland are devoted to organic farming on their 115-acre Fiddler's Green Farm. The baking mixes are made from their home-grown wheat, rye, and corn and from additional grains supplied by the area's organic farmers. All are stone-ground at the farm. Mixes include pancake and muffin mix, bread and biscuit mix, and buttermilk spice cake mix. All come with recipes that expand on the basic idea (the cake mix recipes, for example, include Shaker Apple-Gingerbread Cake, Banana Spice Cake, and Chocolate Chip Spice Cupcakes). Fiddler's Green cereal varieties are Penobscot Porridge and Toasted Oat Bran and Brown Rice.

Free brochure
Mail orders
MC, VISA

Sourdough starter and mixes—

G & H Frontier Company
P. O. Box 40803
Bakersfield, CA 93384

Contact by mail

Sourdough starter, crocks, and a cookbook are offered by G & H Frontier as well as dry sourdough mixes to make buttermilk pancakes and waffles, honey French bread, bran muffins, biscuits, cornbread, and oatmeal muffins and cookies. Some of these mixes are available packed in canisters in larger quantities.

Free price list
Mail orders
No credit cards

A Rhode Island tradition continues—

Gray's Grist Mill
P. O. Box 422
Adamsville, RI 02801

508-636-6075

Gray's Grist Mill dates back to 1675 and is currently run by Tim McTague, who spent two years learning the business from a miller who was the last of three generations of Grays to own the mill. Gray's products are johnnycake meal, wheat and rye flour, brown bread and muffin mix, pancake and waffle mix, and yellow cornmeal. All come in paper bags fastened with a traditional miller's knot. Tim is an avid cook and includes recipes in his brochure—try his Sweet Fennel Cornbread on the next page.

Free brochure
Mail orders
No credit cards

Adaptable mixes—

Hearty Mix
1231 Madison Hill Road
Rahway, NJ 07065

201-382-3010

Hearty Mix produces dozens of mixes for yeast breads, quick breads, doughnuts, cookies, and cakes. Recipe sheets are enclosed to help you adapt the mixes; you can, for example, make croissants, Danish pastry, panettone, and Swedish cardamom bread from the Buttermilk Bread Mix; and pita and pizza from the Italian Bread Mix. Special wheatless and low-sodium mixes may interest cooks who need to consider dietary restrictions.

Free price list
Mail orders
No credit cards

Sweet Fennel Cornbread

from Tim McTague, Gray's Grist Mill

1½ tablespoons fennel seeds
 1 cup Gray's johnnycake meal or white cornmeal
 1 cup all-purpose flour
 1 tablespoon baking powder
 1 teaspoon salt
 1 cup milk
 2 eggs, well beaten
 3 tablespoons honey
 3 tablespoons unsalted butter, melted and cooled slightly

Preheat oven to 400 degrees, with a rack at center level. Butter a 9-inch skillet or pie pan (or an 8-inch square baking pan) and set aside. In a small, dry skillet toast fennel seeds over medium heat, stirring often, until fragrant but not browned, 3 or 4 minutes. Remove from heat. In a mixing bowl combine the meal or cornmeal, flour, baking powder, salt, and fennel seeds. In a small bowl, stir together milk, eggs, honey, and melted butter. Make a well in the center of the dry ingredients and add the milk mixture, stirring just to combine. Pour into buttered pan. Bake until the cornbread is golden, 25 to 30 minutes. Serve hot in wedges, directly from the pan, with butter. Makes 8 to 10 servings.

Sourdough starter and bread mix—

Home Brew International, Inc.
1126 South Federal Highway, Suite 182
Fort Lauderdale, FL 33316

305-764-1527

Home Brew International, a supplier of home wine- and beer-making supplies, also sells sourdough starter with recipes that can be ordered with or without a storage crock. A sourdough bread mix is also available, and you can find supplies for making cheese and vinegar, too.

Free illustrated catalog
Mail orders
No credit cards

Organic grains and grain products—

Jaffe Bros. Inc.
P. O. Box 636
Valley Center, CA 92082

619-749-1133
Fax: 619-749-1282

Jaffe offers a long list of organic grains and grain products. Unusual, hard-to-find items include amaranth and amaranth flour and quinoa. The list also includes a multi-grain cereal, whole kernel corn, popcorn, and buckwheat groats. All grains can be ordered in 5- or 25-pound quantities. Jaffe also has a great selection of dried fruit, dates, nuts, seeds, peas, and beans.

Free catalog
Phone, fax, and mail orders, gift orders
MC, VISA

Baking supplies and mixes, including
clam cake and fritter mix—

Kenyon Corn Meal Company
Usquepaugh
West Kingston, RI 02892

401-783-4054

In addition to white and yellow
cornmeal, Kenyon Corn Meal grinds
wheat, graham, rye, oat, and
buckwheat flours. The baking mixes,
made from whole-grain flours, include
muffin/bread mixes, pancake mixes, and
clam cake and fritter mix. Assortments
of flours and mixes are available, and
you can also order a variety of New
England delicacies that includes
chowders, syrups, relishes, and
preserves.

Free price list
Mail orders
MC, VISA

Baking mixes for scones, muffins, and
beer breads—

The Lollipop Tree
Box 518
Rye, NH 03870

800-842-6691
603-436-8196

The Lollipop Tree baking mixes for beer
breads include Farmhouse White,
Hearty Cracked Wheat, Savory Garlic
Herb, Spring Onion Dill, and Epicurean
Oat Bran. (Just add a 12-ounce bottle of
beer and they're ready to bake.) There
are also two scone mixes: traditional
and lemon-poppy seed. An oat bran

mix makes it easy to have healthy
muffins on hand for breakfast. Gift
selections combine The Lollipop Tree's
bread mixes with selections of its
preserves and condiments.

Free color catalog
Phone and mail orders, gift orders
MC, VISA

Brown rice flour—

Lundberg Family Farms
P. O. Box 369
Richvale, CA 95974-0369

916-882-4551

Brown rice products are the specialty of
this family enterprise in California. You
can order premium or organic brown
rice flour in 12 individual 2-pound
packages or an economical 25-pound
package. In addition to rice, other
products are cereals, rice syrup, and
rice cakes.

Free price list
Mail orders
No credit cards

From a water-powered gristmill in
Maine—

Morgan's Mills
RD 2
Box 4602
Union, ME 04862

207-785-4900

In 1981 Richard and Helen Morgan
opened their newly restored mill,
originally established by one of the
area's first settlers in 1803. They offer
the following flours: bread, pastry,
whole wheat pastry and bread, oat,
barley, rye, corn, millet, buckwheat,
and brown rice. Baking mixes include

johnnycake mix and muffin mixes—
blueberry, maple corn, and orange
bran. A popular item is Morgan's
"griffles" (griddle-waffle mixes) in
buttermilk, buckwheat, blueberry, and a
combination of rice, corn, and oat
flours. Morgan's Mills also ships a
selection of specialty foods from Maine.

Free price list
Phone and mail orders
MC, VISA

A source for unusual flours—

G. B. Ratto & Company
821 Washington Street
Oakland, CA 94607

800-325-3483
800-228-3515 (in CA)
Fax: 415-836-2250

G. B. Ratto stocks Blue Corn brand
products, including blue cornmeal, blue
corn polenta, and blue cornmeal
pancake and waffle mix. The wide
variety of flours and meals includes
pizza flour, matzo meal, and unusual
items like chestnut flour and garbanzo
flour. Sourdough mixes are available to
make several kinds of baked items.

Free illustrated catalog
Phone, fax, and mail orders, gift orders
and certificates
MC, VISA

Stone-ground products from an historic
mill—

1788 Tuthilltown Grist Mill
Albany Post Road
Gardiner, NY 12525

914-255-5695

This gristmill is on both the National
and the New York State Register of

Historic Places, and has been in
constant operation for nearly two
centuries. Now run by the Smith
family, the mill produces more than
three dozen Falling Waters brand flours
and grains and also ships additional
baking ingredients, nut butters, syrup,
and honey. Every year the mill grinds
several thousand bushels of wheat into
kosher flour that is shipped all over the
world for Passover celebrations. The
country store and museum make this
worth a stop if you are traveling near
this part of New York State.

Free price list and brochure
Mail orders
No credit cards

Traditional Vermont favorites—

The Vermont Country Store
P. O. Box 3000
Manchester Center, VT 05255-3000

802-362-2400

This old-fashioned catalog offers a
potpourri of goods, but tucked near the
end you'll find traditional Vermont food
favorites, including a selection of stone-
ground cereals, flours, and baking
mixes. The flour sampler pack and
cereal sampler pack are great ways to
stock the pantry and to try cooking and
baking with some of these Vermont
products.

Free illustrated brochure
Phone and mail orders
MC, VISA

Organic, whole-grain products—

Walnut Acres
Penns Creek, PA 17862

800-433-3998
Fax: 717-837-1146

Suppliers of whole-grain flours for more than 40 years, Walnut Acres still grinds its flour in small batches every day. In addition to bread and pastry flours, there are seven wheat-free flours and a popular 12-grain flour. Whole grains include varieties of wheat, millet, barley, and oat and buckwheat groats; specialty grains and flours include quinoa, amaranth seed and flour, and Maskal Teff grain and flour. Baking mixes for pancakes, waffles, and muffins, as well as sourdough starters and aluminum-free baking powder, are found in this catalog of organic foods.

Free color catalog
Phone, fax, and mail orders
MC, VISA

Stone-ground organic products—

War Eagle Mill
Route 5, Box 411
Rogers, AR 72756

501-789-5343

War Eagle Mill, an historic water-powered gristmill, produces stone-ground flours and meals from certified organic grains. Products include yellow and white cornmeal, cracked wheat, corn grits, breakfast cereal, wheat bran, and wheat germ; flours include whole wheat, buckwheat, and rye. Whole-grain mixes are available for biscuits, cornbread, pancakes and waffles, muffins, and hush puppies. You can also order gift boxes of products or choose one of the whole-grain cookbooks written by the owner of War Eagle Mill, Zoe Caywood.

Free color catalog
Phone and mail orders, gift orders
MC, VISA

Fine flours from the South—

The White Lily Foods Company
Box 871
Knoxville, TN 37901

615-546-5511

White Lily flour has been milled for over 100 years from soft red winter wheat. This flour produces a soft, tender gluten structure favored by Southern cooks for high, light-baked products, including their famed biscuits, cobblers, cakes, and pastries. In addition to plain all-purpose and self-rising flour, White Lily supplies home bakers with bread flour, unbleached self-rising flour, self-rising cornmeal mix, and self-rising buttermilk cornmeal mix. A collection of Southern cake, cookie, and biscuit recipes can be requested at no extra charge.

Free price list
Mail orders
No credit cards

If you're looking for flours milled from nuts, such as chestnut flour, find sources in Chapter 17, "Nuts, Seeds, and Nut Butters."

Find all the pans and other supplies you'll need for baking in Chapter 27, "Equipment and Tools."

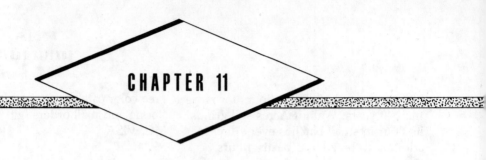

CHAPTER 11

FRUIT, FRESH AND DRIED

Ordering from the orchards in this chapter will ensure that you receive fresh fruit at the peak of ripeness. What could be better than a box of sunny-sweet pink seedless grapefruit or luscious, juicy navel oranges arriving at your door on a dreary winter day? Or opening up a box of exotic California bananas, rare tropical fruits, or freshly picked dates that are never seen in local markets? (Please note that some fruit is available seasonally and there are some shipping restrictions to certain states. Call or write to check.)

The selection of dried fruit, much prepared from organically grown produce without any preservatives, is much wider than you'll find locally. Try your next batch of muffins with dried cherries or dried wild blueberries instead of raisins. Experiment with dried persimmon, starfruit, or mango as a new ingredient for cakes and puddings. Many suppliers offer dried fruit in economical bulk quantities so you can keep a generous supply on hand for healthy snacks and for baking, or you can share orders with friends.

The chapter begins with companies shipping assorted fresh fruit and concludes with sources for dried fruit.

Fresh Fruit

Half a century of growing Florida fruit—

Barfield Groves
P. O. Box 68
Polk City, FL 33868-0068

813-984-1316

The Barfield family celebrated their fiftieth year in business in 1989. They harvest grapefruit (pink or white seedless, ruby red), oranges (navel, Valencia) and tangelos. Order bushels to split with friends or arrange for one of their plans that sends you Florida citrus at its peak through the growing season. Gift baskets available.

Free color brochure
Mail orders, gift orders
MC, VISA

Sending Florida citrus since 1921—

Bilgore Groves
P. O. Box 1958
Clearwater, FL 34617-1958

813-442-2171

You can order seasonally available pink or white seedless grapefruit, Mineola tangelos, navel, Temple, and Valencia oranges (or combinations of these fruits) in five different quantities, ranging from a fifth of a bushel through a whole bushel. Bilgore also combines pineapples, coconuts, avocados, limes, oranges, and grapefruit in a package that suggests some interesting culinary possibilities. Gift selections and club plans available.

Free color brochure
Phone and mail orders, gift orders
MC, VISA

Citrus and tropical fruits—

Blue Heron Fruit Shippers
3221 Bay Shore Road
Sarasota, FL 34234-5725

800-237-3920
813-355-6946 (in FL)

In addition to Florida treats such as tangelos, oranges (navel, Temple and Valencia), and pink, white, and red grapefruit, Blue Heron Fruit Shippers sends pineapples, mangoes, and avocados. Mangoes are available June through mid-August; avocados from mid-July through December. Gift packs mix fruit with nuts, preserves, and honey. There are other Florida specialties available, including a key lime cheesecake.

Free color brochure
Phone and mail orders, gift orders
MC, VISA

Northwest apples and pears—

**Children's Home Society
of Washington**
P. O. Box 15190
Seattle, WA 98115-0190

800-456-3338
206-523-5727
Fax: 206-527-1667

Here's your opportunity to order crisp Washington apples and benefit the state's Children's Home Society as well. Choose Red Delicious or Granny Smith varieties. Walla Walla onions are offered in the summer and Bosc pears are shipped September to May. (A portion of the cost of these products is tax-deductible.) A club plan keeps you or friends supplied with fresh produce throughout the year.

Free color catalog
Phone, fax, and mail orders, gift orders
MC, VISA

Wild berries from the Pacific North-west—

Fresh & Wild, Inc.
P. O. Box 2981
Vancouver, WA 98668

800-222-5578 (orders only)
206-254-8130
Fax: 206-896-8718

Fresh & Wild ships seasonally available red and black currants, gooseberries, black huckleberries, and juniper berries. Figs, French Palladin melons, and dried blueberries are also offered, and the company has plans to introduce a selection of wild Alaskan berries. Fresh & Wild is also a source for a wonderful selection of dried and fresh wild mushrooms, cultivated mushrooms, and truffles (see details in Chapter 16, "Mushrooms and Truffles"), as well as wild salad greens, edible flowers, and unusual produce.

Free color brochure
Phone, fax, and mail orders
MC, VISA

Exotic fruit and a great newsletter—

Frieda's Finest Produce Specialties, Inc.
P. O. Box 58488
Los Angeles, CA 90058

800-421-9477
213-627-2981

Founded in 1962, Frieda's Finest Produce Specialties is a leading marketer and distributor of hundreds of unusual fruits and vegetables. For individual customers the company will ship a basket of exotic fruit from all over the world, including Asian pears, baby pineapples, cherimoyas, feijoas, horned melons, kiwifruit, passion fruit, pepinos, persimmons, prickly pears, and red bananas. Each fruit is identified with a label and recipes are included. The *Club Frieda* bimonthly newsletter supplies recipes and keeps you up to date on what's happening in new and unusual produce. A recent issue described uncommon root vegetables (malanga, yucca root, taro root, boniato and sunchokes) and introduced new varieties of potato (potatoes with beautiful pink or blue marbling throughout the flesh are on the horizon). The newsletter is $6.00 for a year.

Free color brochure
Phone and mail orders, gift orders
AMEX, MC, VISA

Several kinds of crisp Vermont apples—

Grafton Village Apple Company, Inc.
RR 3
Box 236D
Grafton, VT 05146

800-843-4822
802-843-2406
Fax: 802-843-2407

The McIntosh is Vermont's most plentiful apple and accounts for 80 percent of the state's harvest. You can order this popular variety as well as Empire (a cross between McIntosh and Red Delicious that looks like a McIntosh but has a sweeter flavor), or the Crispin (Mutsu), a new variety to Vermont. A descendant from Japan of the Golden Delicious, the Crispin is a large yellow apple that's a bit juicier than Golden Delicious. You can also order other Vermont treats like maple syrup, cheese, preserves, and smoked meats; gift packs combine apples with these items. *The Grafton Country Cookbook*, sent with all orders, contains recipes like Cran-Apple Cheese Cake and Cheddar Apple Cobbler.

Free color catalog
Phone, fax, and mail orders, gift orders
AMEX, MC, VISA

Citrus plus pears and avocados—

Hale Indian River Groves
Indian River Plaza
Wabasso, FL 32970

800-289-4253
407-589-4334
Fax: 407-388-5782

Lots of gift items are offered by this family company that's been around since 1947, and there are some frill-free selections to interest citrus enthusiasts who want to order for their own use. You can choose oranges, grapefruit, or combinations in quantities from a quarter bushel up to a full bushel. A new tangerinelike hybrid called Nova is also grown by Hale. Pears and avocados can be combined with citrus selections. Club plan available.

Free color catalog
Phone, fax, and mail orders, gift orders
AMEX, DC, DISC, MC, VISA

Seasonal California fruit—

Mission Orchards
2296 Senter Road
P. O. Box 6947
San Jose, CA 95150-6947

800-526-0900
408-297-5056

Mission Orchards is a gift-oriented business and it ships California fruit at its seasonal best. Bing cherries are shipped in June, for example, and Rainiers, a rare blushing yellow cherry, are shipped in July. California plums, nectarines, red grapes, kiwi, and pears are also featured. A club plan ships fruit throughout the year.

Free color catalog
Phone and mail orders, gift orders
AMEX, DISC, MC, VISA

Spicy Pear Squares

from Mission Orchards

½ cup butter or margarine
¾ cup sugar
 2 eggs
¾ cup sifted flour
 1 teaspoon baking powder
½ teaspoon baking soda
½ teaspoon salt
 1 teaspoon cinnamon
½ teaspoon nutmeg
¼ teaspoon cloves
¾ cup rolled oats
1½ cups fresh pears, cored and chopped, but not peeled
½ cup raisins
½ cup chopped walnuts
Powdered sugar

In mixing bowl, cream butter or margarine and sugar. Beat in eggs one at a time, mixing thoroughly after each. Sift together flour, baking powder, soda, salt, and spices. Add to creamed mixture. Stir in oats, chopped pears, raisins, and nuts. Spread into a greased 9-inch by 13-inch baking pan. Bake at 375 degrees for 20 to 25 minutes. While still warm, sprinkle lightly with powdered sugar and cut into squares. Makes about 4 dozen 1½-inch squares.

Pears are the pride of this orchard—

Pinnacle Orchards
441 South Fir Street
Medford, OR 97501-0077

800-547-0227

The Comice pear (sometimes called the Christmas pear) is Pinnacle Orchards' most popular product. It has been grown almost exclusively in the Rogue River Valley of Oregon since being introduced from France at the turn of the century. Pinnacle ships boxes of red and green Comice pears, as well as Bosc pears, Red Bartlett pears, and Red Delicious apples plus citrus fruit. Many gift items and gift plans are available. Other Pacific Northwest specialties such as cheese and smoked seafood can also be ordered from Pinnacle.

Free color catalog
Phone and mail orders, gift orders
AMEX, MC, VISA

Citrus fruit, pears, and grapes—

Pittman & Davis
P. O. Box 2227
Harlingen, TX 78551

512-423-2154

Pittman & Davis has been growing and shipping fruit across the country for over 65 years. They'll ship ruby red grapefruit and navel oranges (mid-November to mid-April), Comice pears (November and December), and red grapes (October to December). You can choose from various quantities and combinations of fruit. Gift items and club plans are available, and this is one of the few companies that will still send you a bill. Try the refreshing Starburst Spinach Salad with Ruby Poppyseed Dressing from Pittman & Davis.

Free color catalog
Mail orders
AMEX, MC, VISA

Mix-and-match citrus—

Poinsettia Groves
1481 U.S. Highway 1
P. O. Box 1388
Vero Beach, FL 32961-1388

800-327-8624
407-562-3356

Fruit boxes come in five sizes from a quarter bushel through a full bushel and in three choices: all navel oranges, all grapefruit, or half of each. Also California Comice pears. Gift packs include pecans, coconut patties, honey, and preserves.

Free color catalog
Phone and mail orders, gift orders
AMEX, DISC, MC, VISA

Not your ordinary bananas—

Seaside Banana Garden
6823 Santa Barbara Avenue
La Conchita, CA 93001

805-643-4061

If you have tasted only the yellow bananas carried at your local market, the varieties offered by Seaside Banana Groves will surprise and delight you. This organic farm, the first commercial banana plantation in California, grows over 50 kinds of bananas, all more flavorful than the bland grocery store banana, both because of the variety and because they are allowed to tree-ripen longer than imported shipments that must make a long trip to market. The Garden's catalog describes characteristics of the bananas currently

Starburst Spinach Salad with Ruby Poppyseed Dressing

from Pittman & Davis

Salad:
2 Ruby Red grapefruit
½ pound fresh spinach, rinsed, dried and torn into bite-size pieces
1 pint fresh strawberries, hulled and wiped clean

Peel and section grapefruit. Finely grate 1½ teaspoons peel from grapefruit; set aside for salad dressing. In a bowl combine grapefruit sections, spinach, and strawberries; toss gently. Serve immediately with Ruby Poppyseed Dressing. Makes 4 to 6 servings.

Ruby Poppyseed Dressing:
1 8-ounce bottle excellent-quality red wine vinegar and oil dressing
(or make your own combination of oil and vinegar)
½ cup sugar
½ teaspoon dry mustard
1½ teaspoons finely grated grapefruit peel
¼ cup grapefruit juice
2 tablespoons poppy seeds

Combine all ingredients in the container of an electric blender; cover and blend well. Refrigerate several hours before serving. Makes 1½ cups.

---

available for shipment, and sampler packs are available. Banana trees, which make attractive, fast-growing houseplants, are also sold.

Free catalog
Mail and phone orders
No credit cards

Medjool dates—

Sphinx Date Ranch, Inc.
4041 East Thomas Road
Phoenix, Arizona 85018

800-482-3283
602-224-0195

At the Sphinx Date Ranch, located on the Colorado River near Yuma, Arizona, the growing conditions are ideal for Medjool dates, which are harvested fresh from the palm tree during September and October. Cooks will be interested in the 5-pound boxes of cooking dates or the economical ranch packs of different grades in 15-, 5-, and 3-pound boxes. (You can freeze dates or store them in an airtight container in the refrigerator.) The ranch has prepared a cookbook, which is available for $5.95. Gift packs of stuffed and dipped dates are also available.

Free illustrated catalog
Phone and mail orders, gift orders
MC, VISA

Dried Fruit

Dried cranberries, cherries, wild blueberries—

American Spoon Foods, Inc.
P. O. Box 566
1668 Clarion Avenue
Petoskey, MI 49770-0566

800-222-5886
616-347-9030
Fax: 616-347-2512

Dried Michigan cranberries, cherries, and blueberries from American Spoon Foods will give your favorite baked goods a delicious new flavor—use them instead of raisins in breads, muffins, and cookies. American Spoon Foods has put together sampler selections as well as a Cherry-Berry Nut Mix. Dried cherries can be ordered in a pretty box that illustrates cherry pickers harvesting Michigan's ruby treats.

Free color seasonal catalogs
Phone, fax, and mail orders, gift orders
DISC, MC, VISA

Apricots and more in quantity packs—

The Apricot Farm
2620 Buena Vista Road
Hollister, CA 95023

800-233-4413
408-637-3949

The Apricot Farm has a special grade of apricot pieces for cooks available in economical 4½- or 9-pound packs. Their apricot "mash" is chunky-ground, recipe-ready apricots in 4½-pound packs. In addition to apricots, they ship prunes, dried pears, peaches, nectarines (all in 2¼-, 4½-, or 9-pound packs), dates, figs, mixed fruits, and nuts. You also have an opportunity in the "Merchant's Corner" to order 25-pound quantities—convenient and money-saving for holiday baking. Gift selections are available too.

Free color catalog
Phone and mail orders, gift orders
MC, VISA

A bounty of dried fruit from the West Coast—

Bates Brothers Nut Farm, Inc.
15954 Woods Valley Road
Valley Center, CA 92082

619-749-3333

The Bates family operates two California stores and ships dried fruit, nuts, and snack items all over the country. Dried fruit includes apples, apricots, banana chips, currants, figs, papaya, peaches, pears, pineapples, prunes, raisins, dates, and mixed packages. Many kinds of dried fruit are incorporated in their trail mixes. Glacéd fruit includes mixes, cherries, pineapple, orange and lemon peel, and citron. Dried coconut is available flaked and sliced.

Free price list
Mail orders, gift orders
MC, VISA

Golden and natural raisins—

Grapes-N-More
P. O. Box 16338
Fresno, CA 93755

800-543-2171
209-435-6666

Although Grapes-N-More specializes in gift packs, they will also ship 5 pounds or more of natural or golden raisins. Gift items include selections of chocolate raisins, yogurt-covered raisins, almonds, pistachios, dried apricots, and other items. Raisins come from the company's own vineyards. Request information about bulk quantities when you write or call.

Free price list
Phone and mail orders, gift orders
MC, VISA

California-grown dried fruits—

Hadley Fruit Orchards
P. O. Box 495
Cabazon, CA 92230

800-854-5655
800-472-5672 (in CA)

In addition to a large variety of California dates, Hadley offers dried apples, apricots, figs, papaya, peaches, pears, pineapple, prunes, and raisins. Cooks will be especially interested in Hadley's date brick, date nuggets, and date sugar. For those on restricted diets, this company has thoughtfully provided (and indexed in their catalog) unsalted, unsweetened, and unsulfured products. Many gift items also in this catalog.

Free color catalog
Phone and mail orders, gift orders
MC, VISA

Organic dried fruit—

Jaffe Bros. Inc
P. O. Box 636
Valley Center, CA 92082

619-749-1133
Fax: 619-749-1282

This 40-year-old family business operated on the Jaffe Ranch supplies organically grown, unsulfured and unfumigated dried fruit. Choose from apples, apricots, cherries, figs, nectarines, peaches, pears, prunes, raisins, currants, and persimmons. Dried tropical fruit also available: mangoes, pineapples, papayas, bananas, and unsweetened dried coconut. Order either in 5-pound or 20-pound sizes (ideal to share with fellow cooks); sampler packages are available with 1-pound quantities. Eight varieties of dates are available in 5-pound or 15-pound cases. Organic prune, apple, and apricot juices are also available.

Free catalog
Phone, fax, and mail orders, gift orders
MC, VISA

Dried apples and cherries—

L'Esprit de Campagne
P. O. Box 3130
Winchester, VA 22601

703-722-4224

This company is best known for its sun-dried tomato products, but Carey and Joy Lokey also produce dried apples from local York apples and dried sweet cherries. They plan to introduce more new products soon, including dried peaches, plums, and other fruit.

Free price list
Mail orders
No credit cards

Ruby Raisins from Oregon—

Putney's Specialty Foods
2415 S.E. 10th Street
Portland, OR 97214

800-627-0657
503-236-1169

Ruby Raisins are fresh Oregon cranberries that have been soaked in sweetened cranberry juice before drying, producing moist, plump berries for baking and cooking and snacking. Putney's proprietor, Cathy Farley, also supplies other cranberry specialties: Cranberry-Nut Conserve and Cranberry-Tangerine Chutney.

Free illustrated catalog
Phone and mail orders, gift orders
MC, VISA

From sunny Georgia—

Sunnyland Farms
P. O. Box 8200
Albany, GA 31706-8200

912-883-3085
Fax: 912-888-8332

Jane and Harry Willson pack dried fruit both in gift boxes and what they call the "home box," a plain package that offers you an economical way to enjoy dried fruit for snacking and baking. Select apricots, fruit mix, dates, raisins, or prunes. They sell nuts and candies in home boxes, too.

Free illustrated brochure
Phone, fax, and mail orders, gift orders
MC, VISA

All-natural fruits and nuts—

Timber Crest Farms
4791 Dry Creek Road
Healdsburg, CA 95448

707-433-8251
Fax: 707-433-8255

Timber Crest's dried fruits, all free of any added chemicals, preservatives, or sugar, can be ordered in small or large quantities. For example, order 8 ounces or 5 pounds—a good way to sample an unfamiliar ingredient or stock up on a sizable quantity of your favorites. In addition to unusual dried starfruit, Timber Crest Farms ships dried apples,* apricots,* cherries, dates, white figs, mission figs, mangoes, papayas, peaches,* pears,* pineapples, prunes,* and raisins* (* indicates that these items are organically grown). Also carried are nuts and dried tomato products, fruit butters, and gift baskets.

Free color catalog
Phone, fax, and mail orders, gift orders
AMEX, MC, VISA

Naturally dried fruit—

Walnut Acres
Penns Creek, PA 17862

800-433-3998
Fax: 717-837-1146

Walnut Acres' dried fruits are prepared without sulfur (a bleach) or potassium sorbate (an additive that prevents fermenting and sugaring), which means that the fruit may be a little darker than you are accustomed to and, after a time, some of the fruit's natural sugar may rise harmlessly to the surface. From this organic supplier you can order dried apricots, apples, pears, pineapples, prunes, raisins, dates, and figs. Unsweetened shredded coconut, coarse or medium, is also available.

Free color catalog
Phone, fax, and mail orders
MC, VISA

Dried tomato products can be found in Chapter 6, "Condiments and Savory Sauces."
Look for preserved fruits, conserves, and jellies in Chapter 20.

CHAPTER 12

HERBS AND SPICES

Many of these companies are run by people who established their businesses because they love herbs and spices. You can tell from chatting with them (and from reading their catalogs) how they enjoy sharing their lore and little-known facts about certain flavorings. You'll also get some interesting tips on new ways to use herbs and spices and perhaps learn a little about unfamiliar items like cassia buds (you'll be introduced to them in this chapter). Best of all, you'll get carefully chosen, freshly ground products that are far superior to their supermarket counterparts. To see how they'll enliven your cooking and delight your senses, just try grating your own fresh nutmeg for your next cake or pie!

Fresh onions and garlic are grouped with vegetables in Chapter 23.

Herbs and herb products—

Caprilands Herb Farm
534 Silver Street
Coventry, CT 06238

203-742-7244

All the popular herbs and spices, herb blends, herbal jellies, vinegars, and teas are offered in the Caprilands catalog, which also has a wide selection of seeds and plants, gardening accessories, and books that will appeal to cooks and gardeners. The farm has a shop and also hosts luncheon programs, teas, and special dinners with herbal themes.

Free illustrated catalog
Mail orders
No credit cards

Imported seasoning blends and other specialties—

The Chef's Pantry
P. O. Box 3
Post Mills, VT 05058

800-666-9940
802-333-4141

The Chef's Pantry imports over half a dozen seasoning blends from Bovida of France; they're available to flavor charcuterie, sauces, ragouts, soups, and more. Other imported specialties include tarragon leaves in vinegar from France, dried juniper berries from Yugoslavia, Spanish green peppercorns packed in water and vinegar, and dried peppercorns (green, mixed, or pink) from Madagascar.

Free illustrated catalog
Phone and mail orders, gift orders
MC, VISA

Herbs: blends and "on the branch"—

Dean & DeLuca, Inc.
Mail Order Department
560 Broadway
New York, NY 10012

800-221-7714
212-431-1691

Dean & DeLuca gather herbs and spices from around the world to make their own nine custom blends that include Herbes de Provence, Fines Herbes, Salads Mélange, and Gumbo Filé. Among their individual herbs and spices you'll find your favorites, as well as Spanish saffron and some unusual items (annato seed, African bird pepper, black mustard seed, and pink peppercorns). Seven popular herbs are offered "on the branch."

Color catalog, $2.00
Phone and mail orders, gift orders, and gift certificates
AMEX, MC, VISA

Fresh herbs year round—

Fox Hill Farm
440 West Michigan Avenue
Box 9
Parma, MI 49269-0009

517-531-3179

Fox Hill Farm will deliver garden-fresh herbs to your door by the bunch or the pound all year round. They also offer a variety of dried herbs on the stem, herb-seasoned foods (herbed Brie, fruited herb gels), and books. Gift items such as their pesto 'n' pasta wreath will

be appreciated by friends who enjoy cooking. You can also tour this family-owned farm in Michigan's gently rolling countryside from mid-April to mid-October.

Free illustrated price list
Mail and phone orders, gift orders, and gift certificates
MC, VISA

Seasonally available fresh herbs—

Herb Gathering, Inc.
5742 Kenwood Avenue
Kansas City, MO 64110

816-523-2653

Paula Winchester's company supplies seeds for French vegetables, edible flowers, and *herbes de cuisine* (read all about these in Chapter 28, "Growing Your Own Ingredients"); it also ships fresh herbs to chefs and home cooks across the country. Imported French shallots are available from November to May, weather permitting. Since availability and prices for fresh items change frequently, they are not found in her catalog and it's advisable to call Paula to discuss what you need.

Illustrated catalog (seeds, books, and gift items), $2.00
Mail and phone orders, gift orders, and gift certificates
MC, VISA

Hard-to-find herbs and spices—

The Kobos Company
5620 S.W. Kelly Avenue
Portland, OR 97201

503-222-5226

David Kobos takes special pride in his company's collection of culinary herbs

Balsamic Mustard Relish

from David Kobos, The Kobos Company

½ cup Kobos mustard seed
½ cup dry red wine
⅔ cup balsamic vinegar
½ cup water
1 teaspoon ground allspice
1 teaspoon ground black pepper
2 teaspoons minced garlic
½ cup chopped onion
2 crumbled bay leaves
1 teaspoon dried tarragon leaves
1½ teaspoons salt
1 teaspoon honey

Combine mustard seed, wine, and vinegar in bowl; let stand overnight or at least 3 hours. In bowl of food processor, combine mustard mixture and all remaining ingredients. Whir just until well blended; mixture should still be fairly coarse. Transfer to the top of a double boiler over simmering water. Cook, stirring often, until mixture is slightly thinner than finished mustard, about 10 to 20 minutes. Mustard will thicken as it cools. Scrape into jars and refrigerate. Makes 2 cups.

and spices, and his extensive list includes such hard-to-find items as Italian juniper berries, Tellicherry peppercorns, Persian sumac, and whole-root Indian turmeric. Try the recipe for Balsamic Mustard Relish, a delicious condiment David created using whole mustard seed. The Kobos product line also includes coffees and teas.

Free price list
Phone and mail orders
AMEX, MC, VISA

Mr. Spiceman—

Charles Loeb
615 Palmer Road
Yonkers, NY 10701

914-961-7776

Proprietor Charles Loeb has aptly named himself "Mr. Spiceman." The extensive list of herbs and spices are available in jars and canisters or in 1- and 5-pound bags. He also offers flavoring extracts, essential oils, and teas.

Illustrated catalog, $1.00 (deductible from order)
Phone and mail orders
MC, VISA

Herbs, spices, and seasoning mixes—

Northwestern Coffee Mills
217 North Broadway
Milwaukee, WI 53202

414-276-1031

In addition to a wide selection of coffees and teas, this Milwaukee coffee mill offers spices and herbs, dried vegetables, salt-free seasonings, vanilla, and other flavors and extracts. All products are packaged in four sizes (herbs and spices, for example, are available in 1-ounce, 4-ounce, 1-pound, or 3-pound packages). Most of the seasoning mixes are the company's own, and they include Dixie Chicken Spice, Hot Cider Spice, Lemon Pepper, and Gumbo Filé Powder. This may be one of the few places you can order Door County Fish Boil, an authentic Wisconsin specialty.

Free illustrated catalog (they'll appreciate it if you send 50¢)
Phone and mail orders, gift orders, and gift certificates
MC, VISA

Seasoning mixes their specialty—

Olde Westport Spice & Trading Company
Box 12525
Overland Park, KS 66212

800-537-6470 (orders)
816-361-3452 (information)

Olde Westport Spice & Trading Company sells bulk herbs and spices in small and large quantities and is best known for its many blended seasoning mixes. These include seasonings for sausage, Cajun rice, spaghetti sauce, pizza sauce, chili, and many other Southwestern dishes. Bill Peterson, who runs the company with wife Judy, is an award-winning chili cook and is continually working on new seasoning mixes. The company's catalog shares quite a few of his recipes. Sampler packs and custom gift baskets are available.

Free illustrated catalog
Phone and mail orders, gift orders, and gift certificates
MC, VISA

Paprika is king, but there's much more—

Paprikas Weiss
1546 Second Avenue
New York, NY 10028

212-288-6117

Paprika is the spice that built this business almost a hundred years ago, and Paprikas Weiss claim they import the world's finest from Hungary. This paprika comes in hot, half-sweet, and sweet, and you can also order paprika paste. Dozens of other herbs and spices are available, including saffron, ground or whole poppy seed, pomegranate seed, and St. John's bread (a dried fruit from Cyprus said to have sustained St. John the Baptist in the wilderness).

Seasonal catalogs, $3.00 annual subscription
Phone and mail orders, gift orders and certificates
AMEX, MC, VISA

Southwestern seasonings and more—

Pendery's, Inc.
304 East Belknap Street
Fort Worth, TX 76102

800-533-1870

Although the accent is on Southwestern flavors at this Fort Worth herb and spice company, they also carry a full range of culinary herbs and spices for all cuisines, numerous herbal blends, dried vegetables, and herbal teas; also potpourri and gift items. Pendery's catalog is helpfully indexed, and the characteristics and uses of each herb, spice, and blend are well described.

Free color catalog
Phone and mail orders, gift orders, and gift certificates
AMEX, MC, VISA

Herbs from New Hampshire—

Pickety Place
P. O. Box E
Mason, NH 03048

603-878-1151

Pickety Place is a two-hundred-year-old cottage where the company sells dried culinary herbs and herb blends as well as many charming country-style gifts and potpourri items. You can visit the shop and stay for lunch—menus change throughout the year and feature herb-seasoned specialties. Pickety Place also publishes its own newsletter and has compiled a cookbook.

Color catalog, 50¢
Mail orders, gift orders, and gift certificates
MC, VISA

Salt-free herbal seasonings—

Potluck & Thyme
9 Crescent Street
P. O. Box 1546
Salem, NH 03079-1546

603-893-9965

Ursula St. Louis developed her all-natural, salt-free herbal seasonings in 1983 to help her family lower its sodium intake. Now Potluck & Thyme products are used on the dining-room tables of the famous LaCosta Health Spa in California and in hospitals around the country. You'll find Potluck & Thyme Gourmet Sprinkle, Herbal Sprinkle, and Seafood Sprinkle in some specialty shops (mostly in New England), and Ursula will also mail order. She's currently working on salt-free entrée mixes.

Free price list
Mail orders, gift orders
No credit cards

Everything for the herb enthusiast—

Rathdowney Herbs & Herb Crafts
3 River Street
Bethel, VT 05032

800-543-8885
802-234-9928

Rathdowney has a long list of herbs, herb blends, and recipe kits for items such as Dutch apple cake, Boursin-style cheese, herbed butter with shallots, and down-home barbecue sauce. There are also herbal craft ideas and products for pet owners. The "New Thymes," a newspaper-format newsletter from Rathdowney, is a pleasant potpourri of herbal tips, lore, recipes, and gardening advice

Free newsletter/product list
Mail orders, gift orders
AMEX, MC, VISA

Herbs and spices from A to Z—

G. B. Ratto & Company
821 Washington Street
Oakland, CA 94607

800-325-3483
800-228-3515 (in CA)
Fax: 415-836-2250

G. B. Ratto, the "International Grocers," has put together a wonderful herb and spice list that begins with ancho chili powder and ends with zahter (a mixture of ground sumac and ground thyme used in Middle Eastern cooking). In between you'll discover familiar herbs and possibly a few new ones—berbere (gives Ethiopian dishes spiciness) and mahleb (seed of the wild cherry used to flavor Armenian, Greek, and Arabic breads). Other unusual items include spinach powder to mix with your pasta dough.

Free catalog
Phone, fax, and mail orders, gift orders and certificates
MC, VISA

They'll search for what you want—

Rosemary House
120 South Market Street
Mechanicsburg, PA 17055

717-697-5111 and
717-766-6581

Rosemary House is a charming, crowded herb shop in eastern Pennsylvania, complete with a thriving herb garden. The equally crowded catalog seems to offer anything a cook could want from allspice to zebrovka, but owner Mrs. Reppert tells readers: "If there is something you are seeking and it is not included in this listing, include an extra dollar or two along with your request. We will attempt to locate it for you and refund any excess money you send. We are constantly adding to our collection." She also offers a wide selection of seasoning mixes, imported bouquets garnis, teas, gift items, kitchen accessories, and cookbooks, as well as seeds and plants for your own herb garden.

Illustrated catalog, $2.00
Mail orders, gift orders
No credit cards

Bulk herbs and spices and specialty seasonings—

S. E. Rykoff & Company
P. O. Box 21467
Market Street Station
Los Angeles, CA 90021

800-421-9873 (orders)
213-624-6094 (product inquiries)

Rykoff stocks a large selection of whole and ground herbs and spices by the pound as well as a list of Louisiana Cajun Magic products, Sexton specialty spice blends, and freeze-dried items. Both firm cinnamon stick (recommended for bar use) and soft cinnamon stick (for baking) are offered.

Color catalog, $1.00
Phone and mail orders, gift orders
AMEX, MC, VISA

Herbs and spices from California—

San Francisco Herb Company
250 14th Street
San Francisco, CA 94103

800-227-4530
800-622-0768 (in CA)
415-861-7174 (San Francisco area)

The San Francisco Herb Company, which has been in business since 1973, offers a complete list of culinary herbs and spices. Most products are available in 4-ounce, 1- or 5-pound quantities. Also offered are popular spice blends,

Lemon Herb No-Salt Herbal Blend

from San Francisco Herb Company

Mix together:
- 1 tablespoon dill weed
- 1 tablespoon garlic granules
- 1 tablespoon parsley flakes
- 2 teaspoons basil (California), cut
- 2 teaspoons lemon juice powder
- 2 teaspoons black pepper, ground
- ½ teaspoon cayenne (optional)
- 1 teaspoon celery seed, whole
- 1 teaspoon yellow mustard powder
- 1 teaspoon onion granules
- ½ teaspoon marjoram leaves
- ½ teaspoon rosemary, cut

Zesty No-Salt Herbal Blend

from San Francisco Herb Company

Mix together:
- 1 tablespoon dill weed
- 1 tablespoon garlic granules
- 1 tablespoon onion granules
- 2 teaspoons celery seed, whole
- 2 teaspoons chili (New Mexico), ground
- 2 teaspoons lemon juice powder
- 2 teaspoons black pepper, ground
- 1 teaspoon basil (California), cut
- 1 teaspoon cumin seed, ground
- 1 teaspoon marjoram leaves
- 1 teaspoon yellow mustard powder
- 1 teaspoon parsley flakes
- 1 teaspoon rosemary, cut
- 1 teaspoon sage, rubbed

dehydrated vegetable blends, and herbal teas. Craft items include potpourri blends and individual potpourri ingredients. Try San Francisco Herb Company products to make your own salt-free herbal seasonings: they're much fresher tasting than supermarket blends. (You can also request recipes for vanilla extract, mulling spice mixes, potpourri blends, and sachets.) and sachets.)

Free price list
Phone and mail orders
MC, VISA

Carefully chosen, conveniently packed herb blends—

Select Origins, Inc.
Box N
Southampton, NY 11968

800-822-2092
516-924-5447 (in NY State)
Fax: 516-924-5892

Tom and Kristi Siplon choose their herbs and spices from where they grow best and pack them in airtight wide-mouthed jars. You can order from several selections, including an herb, spice, or baking selection. Individual jars also available, as well as their own cook's blends, salad blends, and bouquet garni kits (you add the fresh parsley). Here's a unique item from Select Origins: freeze-dried California shallots. They have also selected some excellent accessories: cotton seasoning bags, a spice grinder, and a pepper grinder that will give you the exact grind you want.

Free illustrated catalog
Phone, fax, and mail orders, gift orders
AMEX, MC, VISA

Herbs and spices from Milwaukee's historic shopping district—

The Spice House
P. O. Box 1633
Milwaukee, WI 53201

414-768-8799

The Spice House specializes in the finest grades of cinnamons, black peppers, and vanillas (read more about its vanillas in Chapter 1, "Baking Supplies"). The Penzey family grinds all spices on the premises and their spice mixtures are all blended by hand. A source for over 400 items, The Spice House offers many hard-to-find ingredients, including blade mace; jumbo size Penang cloves; pure saffron from Spain; natural tomato, lobster, and shrimp powders; charnuska (also known as black cumin or Russian caraway and as "love-in-a-mist" in Britain); whole and ground cassia buds (used in early American times to scent homes, they're being rediscovered today; also used to flavor preserved fruits and vegetables); and much more. The gift boxes of seasonings are nicely packed with stick cinnamon for fillers, bay leaves to cushion bottles, and whole nutmegs tucked in too. Even the gift cards are "aged" in the pepper sifting room so they have a nice peppery aroma! The Spice House is located in an area of Milwaukee that delights food lovers and counts among its neighbors Usinger's famous sausage store, the Wisconsin Cheese Market, and Mader's, an award-winning German restaurant.

Illustrated catalog, $1.00
Phone and mail orders, gift orders
No credit cards

Special note: The retired owners of The Spice House run a small spice shop in nearby Wauwatosa, Wisconsin. A recent project was grinding and mixing spices for the 1990 Earth Day Mount Everest Peace Climb, an expedition led by climbers from Russia, China, and the United States. For chili enthusiasts, a special chili powder blended for the expedition from peppers from those three countries is available. Call 414-258-7727 for more information.

Herbs from a garden in Maine—

The United Society of Shakers
Herb Department
Sabbathday Lake
Poland Spring, ME 04274

207-926-4597

This Shaker community has been actively involved in the production and sale of herbs since 1799. Members maintain an extensive herb garden to enhance their simple meals and to provide cooks across the country with dried herbs packed in traditional tins.

Herbal vinegars, rose water, herbal teas, fir balsam pillows, and potpourris are also for sale by mail. The Shaker Museum keeps a busy calendar of events for Maine visitors, including herb workshops, basket making, nature walks, and demonstrations of weaving, spinning, and dyeing. Try their recipe for citrus-flecked Rose Water Cookies for tea some afternoon.

Free catalog; send self-addressed stamped envelope
Phone and mail orders
No credit cards

Rose Water Cookies
from The United Society of Shakers

        1 cup butter
        1 cup sugar
        2 eggs, beaten light and fluffy
    2¾ cups flour
        1 teaspoon baking soda
      ½ teaspoon cream of tartar
        2 tablespoons Shaker rose water
      ½ cup chopped orange or lemon peel
Pinch of salt
      ½ cup raisins plus additional raisins for decoration

Cream together butter and sugar. Add beaten eggs. Sift together flour, baking soda, and cream of tartar; add to butter mixture and mix well. Add rose water, fruit peel, salt, and raisins. Blend together. Drop on greased cookie sheet. Dot each with a raisin. Bake at 375 degrees for 20 minutes. Makes 24 to 36 cookies.

Saffron and more—

Vanilla, Saffron Imports
949 Valencia Street
San Francisco, CA 94110

415-648-8990
Fax: 648-2240

This restaurant supplier offers a mail order service to supply home cooks with rare saffron. You can also order dried mushrooms, vanilla extract, and vanilla beans.

Free price list
Mail orders only
No credit cards

Sources for fresh onions and garlic can be found in Chapter 23, "Vegetables."

Also check Chapter 24, "American Regional Foods," and Chapter 25, "The International Pantry," for more sources of unusual herbs and spices.

Refer to Chapter 28, "Growing Your Own Ingredients," for everything you'll need to start your own herb garden.

CHAPTER 13

HONEY, MOLASSES, AND SYRUPS

This is a sweet chapter, filled with delicious honeys that just beg for a fresh-baked scone, molasses for making hearty traditional dishes, and exotic fruit syrups that suggest some equally exotic desserts. For maple syrup, see Chapter 14; this American favorite has found its way into so many products that it merits its own chapter.

Over a dozen flavored honeys—

Abbey of the Holy Trinity
Huntsville, UT 84317

Contact by mail

The monks make their Trappist Creamed Honeys by blending pure honey with fruit, nuts, spices, and other natural flavorings. A sampling of the sixteen flavors includes apricot, date pecan, toasted almond, rum, and maple. These suggestions are from Brother Lawrence: lemon creamed honey is a delightful addition to tea; brandy creamed honey adds a special touch to baked ham; and orange creamed honey makes a delicious sauce for yams. Gift box selections are available.

Free price list
Mail orders, gift orders
No credit cards

Honey from the heartland—

American Spoon Foods, Inc.
P. O. Box 566
1688 Clarion Avenue
Petoskey, MI 49770-0566

800-222-5886
616-347-9030
Fax: 616-347-2512

American Spoon Foods features Michigan varietal honeys—Northern wildflower, raspberry blossom, and blueberry blossom. These varietal honeys are collected at the right time during the season to insure the nectar's source. Then they are warmed just enough to extract them from the comb (no more than 140 degrees) and carefully strained. They are never blended with differing grades. A sampler of three varieties is packed in a folk-art-decorated gift box.

Free seasonal catalogs
Phone, fax, and mail orders, gift orders
DISC, MC, VISA

Liquid and naturally crystallized honey—

Champlain Valley Apiaries
P. O. Box 127
Middlebury, VT 05753

802-388-7724

Charles Mraz started this apiary in 1931, and it's now the largest in New England, with over a thousand hives still tended by Charles with help from his son Bill. You can buy liquid clover honey or natural crystallized honey (a delicious spread) in 1-pound jars, 2½- or 5-pound pails. If you enclose an extra $1.50 with your order, you'll receive *The Vermont Beekeeper's Cookbook*, handsomely illustrated with block-printed woodcuts and containing over 90 recipes made with honey. Try the following one for silky Honey Custard.

Free price list
Mail orders, gift orders
No credit cards

Genuine sorghum molasses—

Clifty Farm
P. O. Box 1146
Paris, TN 38242

800-238-8239
901-642-9740

This purveyor of smoked hams, bacon, and sausage is located close to Benton County, Tennessee, which claims to make the best sorghum molasses in the world. So Clifty Farm offers 2-pound jars of this molasses in their catalog, where you'll also find honey, jellies, and grain mixes.

Free color catalog
Phone and mail orders, gift orders
MC, VISA

Honey Custard

from The Vermont Beekeeper's Cookbook

    3 eggs
    ⅛ teaspoon salt
¼ to ⅓ cup honey
    1 teaspoon vanilla
    2 cups milk, scalded
Nutmeg

Preheat oven to 325 degrees. Add salt to eggs and beat just long enough to combine whites and yolks. Add honey and vanilla to milk and combine with eggs. Pour into 4 custard cups. Top each with a pinch of nutmeg. Set custard cups in a pan of hot water. Bake about 40 minutes or until knife inserted near edge of custard comes out clean. Serves 4.

Rare honeys and Corcellet fruit
syrups—

Dean & DeLuca, Inc.
Mail Order Department
560 Broadway
New York, NY 10012

800-221-7714
212-431-1691

Dean & DeLuca stock honeys from the
Midwest, as well as Hawaiian white
honey (from the nectar of the rare
kiawe tree), and leatherwood honey
from Tasmania. Imported French
Corcellet fruit syrups are available in
cassis or raspberry.

Illustrated catalog, $2.00
Phone and mail orders, gift orders, and
gift certificates
AMEX, MC, VISA

Cane syrup for Southern specialties—

Gazin's
2910 Toulouse Street
P. O. Box 19221
New Orleans, LA 70179

800-262-6410

This New Orleans purveyor carries
some key ingredients for preparing
Southern specialties, including 100
percent pure cane syrup for making
delicious pecan pies and other
traditional dishes.

Color catalog, $1.00 (refundable with
order)
Phone and mail orders, gift orders
AMEX, MC, VISA

Brown rice syrup

Lundberg Family Farms
P. O. Box 369
Richvale, CA 95974-0369

916-882-4551

Brown rice syrup is a golden syrup
made from organically grown brown
rice, water, and natural barley enzyme.
Use it to sweeten beverages or try it on
pancakes, waffles, muffins, or breads as
an alternative to maple syrup or honey.

Free price list
Mail orders
No credit cards

Special California honeys—

Moonshine Trading Company
P. O. Box 896
Winters, CA 95694

916-753-0601

The Gourmet Honey Collection
assembled by this family-run business is
flavored with the flora of California—
eucalyptus, orange blossom, yellow star
thistle, black button sage, and
Christmas berry. Nut butters and
chocolate spreads complete the
collection of products. The beautifully
designed labels make these honeys and
spreads especially nice for gifts.

Free color brochure
Phone and mail orders, gift orders, and
gift certificates
MC, VISA

Imported fruit syrups—

G. B. Ratto & Company
821 Washington Street
Oakland, CA 94607

800-325-3483
800-228-3515 (in CA)
Fax: 415-836-2250

In addition to molasses, honey, and
maple syrup from the United States,

G. B. Ratto is a source for some unusual syrups from around the world. You'll find lingonberry syrup from Sweden, sour cherry syrup from Yugoslavia, and pomegranate concentrate for Persian cuisine (recipes on request). Mix Toroni brand raspberry syrup with seltzer or soda water to make a popular Italian soft drink. French syrups are imported in several fruit flavors, including raspberry, strawberry, blackberry, black currant, and orange.

Free illustrated catalog
Phone, fax, and mail orders, gift orders, and gift certificates
MC, VISA

Imported French honeys—

Schoonmaker/Lynn Enterprises
4619 N.W. Barnes Road
Portland, OR 97210

503-222-5435

Schoonmaker/Lynn Enterprises imports pure flavored honeys from southern France, where beekeepers Peter and Karen Lynn move their hives throughout the season to obtain these special varieties. Among their eight flavors you'll find acacia (gathered from the white flowers of the acacia tree), tournesol (sunflower), orangier (from orange groves), and rare lavender honey.

Free color brochure
Mail orders
No credit cards

Maine honey—

R. B. Swan & Son, Inc.
25 Prospect Street
Brewer, ME 04412

207-989-3622

The Swans have been packing honey for almost fifty years and offer pure Maine raspberry, blueberry, and wildflower honeys. In their leaflet of family-tested honey recipes and information they advise that "a noted advantage of cooking with honey is that . . . foods made with it, especially baked goods, retain their freshness longer." Gift packs and beeswax candles are also available.

Free price list
Mail orders
MC, VISA

Muscadine syrup—

Southern Specialty Foods Corporation
P. O. Box 2853
Meridian, MS 39302

800-233-1736
Fax: 601-483-1864

Southern Specialty Foods' 770-acre vineyard of native muscadine grapes is the largest in the country. This company is also one of the few producers of muscadine syrup, an all-natural pancake and waffle topping. Other products include jellies, jams, preserves, juice, and barbecue sauce flavored with muscadine, as well as other Southern specialties.

Free color catalog
Phone, fax, and mail orders, gift orders
AMEX, DISC, MC, VISA

Honey, molasses, and other natural sweeteners—

Walnut Acres
Penns Creek, PA 17862

800-433-3998
Fax: 717-837-1146

Walnut Acres' honeys are prepared with low heat to preserve nutrients, and this company tells you the highest temperature used during the preparation of each variety of honey it sells. Flavors include clover, wildflower, orange blossom, alfalfa, and tupelo. Table-grade and cooking-grade maple syrups are offered, as well as maple granules. Other sweeteners include Barbados and blackstrap molasses, barley malt syrup, and brown rice syrup. New products are an organic fruit sweetener (made from the concentrated juice of organically grown grapes) and Sucanat® (a granulated product from the juice of organically grown sugar cane that has more nutrients than regular table sugar or brown sugar).

Free color catalog
Phone, fax, and mail orders
MC, VISA

Fruit Sweet syrup—

Wax Orchards
22744 Wax Orchards Road S.W.
Vashon Island, WA 98070

800-634-6132
206-682-8251

Fruit Sweet syrup is a natural sweetener made from a concentrated blend of natural fruit juices. It has only 13 calories per teaspoon and its sweetness is equal to that of honey and surpasses the sweetness of sugar. To use Fruit Sweet in recipes, substitute it for sugar on a one-to-one basis and reduce other liquids by one third the amount of sweetener called for in the original recipe. Wax Orchards also makes an all-fruit mincemeat, dessert toppings, preserves, fruit butters, and

condiments. All are low-calorie and contain very little salt.

Free price list and nutritional information (please send two 25¢ stamps)
Phone and mail orders, gift orders
MC, VISA

Wild huckleberry syrup—

Wilds of Idaho
1308 West Boone
Spokane, WA 99201

509-326-0197

Wilds of Idaho suggests that you "celebrate a stack of pancakes with huckleberry syrup." It's made from wild huckleberries gathered in the mountains of northern Idaho each fall. This company also produces wild huckleberry jam, topping, and dessert filling. All are made without preservatives.

Free price list
Mail orders, gift orders
MC, VISA

Cider syrup—

Wood's Cider Mill
RFD 2, Box 477
Springfield, VT 05156

802-263-5547

Since 1882 the Wood family has been making boiled cider by concentrating the juice of apples pressed on an old-time screw press. They combine it with maple syrup to make their own cider syrup, and Willis and Tina Wood suggest you try it on French toast, pancakes and waffles, as a topping for ice cream, or mixed with plain yogurt. You can also order cider jelly, boiled cider, maple syrup, or a sampler pack of cider products.

Free price list
Mail orders, gift orders
No credit cards

For more fruit syrups, see Chapter 20, "Preserves," and Chapter 22, "Sweet Sauces."

CHAPTER 14

MAPLE SYRUP AND MAPLE PRODUCTS

Maple syrup is a quintessential American product. The first settlers learned how to make it from the Indians, and it is still produced exclusively in North America. Syrup making is a labor-and fuel-intensive process, with 35 to 40 gallons of maple sap needed to make 1 gallon of syrup. Whether it's boiled down the old-fashioned way over a roaring wood fire or in modern plants fueled by oil, the process takes a lot of energy: a full cord of wood to make 20 gallons of syrup the old way, and about 4 gallons of oil for each gallon the new way.

Syrup is probably the first product that comes to mind when we think of maple, but it's been joined by so many other maple products that it merits a chapter of its own. Here you'll discover granulated maple sugar (another age-old product once called "Indian sugar" for its native American inventors) that's produced by boiling off all the water from the syrup and mixing it into a granulated state. Try it in baked goods, candies, and frosting to impart a wonderful maple flavor. It's also a natural and delicious alternative for the sugar bowl. And enjoy discovering the new products, such as maple baking mixes and condiments, that innovative New Englanders have created to showcase one of their most famous regional specialties.

Vermont's sweetness to your home—

American Maple Products
Newport, VT 05855

800-343-0837
800-548-1221 (in VT)

American Maple Products president Roger Ames grew up on a farm in maple country and as a small boy loved to open the mailbox every day to see what exciting glimpse of the outside world had arrived. That experience gives him a special satisfaction in presiding over a company that sends packages from maple country to mailboxes all over the country. You can order syrup in glass bottles, tins, plastic and ceramic jugs. Other products include maple spread, butter, candy, fudge, and a selection of additional Vermont regional foods. Roger invites you to tour his company when you're in the neighborhood.

Free color brochure
Phone and mail orders
MC, VISA

New York State syrup—

Branon Enterprises
Route 2, Box 27A
LaPlante Road
West Chazy, NY 12992

518-493-7090

Barry Branon sells U. S. Grade A light, medium, and dark amber syrup. His products proudly bear the New York State Seal of Quality, for which the standards are more rigid than the U. S. Grade A designation.

Free price list
Mail orders
No credit cards

Suggestions for cooking syrup—

Brookside Farm
Tunbridge, VT 05077

800-832-9482
802-889-3738
Fax: 802-889-3739

Henry and Cornelia Swayze of Brookside Farm offer pints of Vermont grade A syrup in medium or dark amber. They recommend their cooking syrup, which is packed in half gallons, for baking and cooking, and suggest you also try it at the table when the syrup must compete with a strong flavor, such as buckwheat pancakes.

Free brochure
Phone and mail orders, gift orders
No credit cards

A variety of maple products—

Butternut Mountain Farm
Johnson, VT 05656

802-635-7483

Maple Syrup Facts
courtesy of the New York State Department
of Agriculture and Markets

Light Amber is lightest in color with a mild and delicate flavor.
Medium Amber is darker in color and has more flavor.
Dark Amber is still darker and has a strong maple flavor.

While it has virtually the same calorie content as white cane sugar, maple syrup contains significant amounts of calcium and potassium, small amounts of iron and phosphorus, and trace amounts of B vitamins. Its sodium content is low.

Unopened containers of maple syrup should be stored in a cool, dry place. Opened containers should be kept refrigerated. If, after extended storage, mold should form on the surface of the syrup, the original quality can be restored by heating the syrup to the boiling point and skimming, sterilizing the container, and refilling.

The Marvins run a maple farm and country store in the northern Vermont town of Johnson and also ship maple products from their sugarbush across the country. In addition to syrup (four sizes, from a pint to a gallon), they produce their own brand of granulated maple sugar, maple butter, maple candy, and maple mustard. Try the following recipe for Maple Walnut Pie. It will convince you that New England produces a pie every bit as good as the South's famed pecan pie.

Free illustrated brochure
Mail orders, gift orders
MC, VISA

Three grades of syrup from Vermont—

Cherry Hill Cooperative Cannery, Inc.
MR 1, Barre-Montpelier Road
Barre, VT 05641

800-468-3020
802-479-2558

You can order three grades of Vermont maple syrup from Cherry Hill Cooperative Cannery, as well as maple cream and maple granules. For cooking, the economical Grade C with a strong maple flavor is a good choice; it comes in pints, quarts, gallons, and 5-gallon pails.

Free price list
Phone and mail orders
No credit cards

Maple Walnut Pie
from Butternut Mountain Farm and
the Vermont Department of Agriculture

½ cup maple sugar, packed
⅓ cup soft butter
¾ cup white sugar
 3 eggs, slightly beaten
¼ teaspoon salt
¼ cup maple syrup
½ cup milk
½ teaspoon vanilla
 1 cup broken walnut pieces
Unbaked 9-inch pie shell

In the top of a double boiler, beat maple sugar and butter until well blended. Add white sugar and mix well. Add eggs, beating constantly. Stir in salt, maple syrup, and milk. Cook over boiling water for 5 minutes, stirring constantly. Remove from heat; stir in vanilla and walnuts. Pour into unbaked pie shell. Bake at 350 degrees for 1 hour. Makes one 9-inch pie.

Maple syrup, plus maple-sweetened nuts and condiments—

Clearview Farms
RD 1, Box 5070
Enosburg Falls, VT 05450

802-933-2537

Maple syrup from Clearview Farms comes in four sizes from a pint to a gallon; also maple sugar, maple sugared walnuts, pecans, and almonds. Maple syrup is used as an ingredient in a number of Caroline Longe's products, including Maple Glaze Barbecue Sauce and Maple Cran-Orange Relish. Recipes and tips are included in the catalog.

Free illustrated catalog
Phone and mail orders, gift orders
MC, VISA

Maple products, including maple applesauce and mustard—

Cold Hollow Cider Mill
RFD 1
Route 100
Box 430
Waterbury Center, VT 05677-9704

800-3-APPLES
800-U-C-CIDER (in VT)

Although famous for its apple cider products, Cold Hollow Cider Mill also supplies maple syrup, maple butter, and maple granules. Maple is also incorporated into a number of the mill's other products—applesauce with maple syrup, Zesty Maple Mustard, Horseradish Maple Mustard, and Maple Granola. The Cider Mill also has a shop that is open year round.

Free color brochure
Phone and mail orders, gift orders
AMEX, MC, VISA

Maple syrup, sugar, and new maple products—

Dodd Enterprises, Inc.
East Fairfield, VT 05448

802-827-3739

Members of the Dodd family are third-generation maple sugar makers, who still work the old-fashioned way, using horse-drawn sleds to transport the sap and roaring wood fires to boil it down. In addition to maple syrup and sugar, you can order maple glazes and baking mixes developed by Linda Dodd, a home economist and accomplished cook. Gift packs of assorted products are offered too.

Free illustrated brochure
Phone and mail orders, gift orders
MC, VISA

A good source for cooking syrup—

Green Mountain Sugar House
RFD 1
Box 341
Ludlow, VT 05149

802-228-7151

Green Mountain produces light, medium, and dark amber syrup, plus Grade C, the darkest and strongest-flavored pure grade, excellent for cooking—and it's less expensive. For gift selections, Green Mountain packs other Vermont specialties, such as cheese and smoked bacon, with their maple products.

Free illustrated brochure
Phone and mail orders, gift orders
AMEX, MC, VISA

New Hampshire syrup and other native foods—

Harman's Cheese & Country Store
Sugar Hill, NH 03585

603-828-8000

Maxine Aldrich takes great pride in New Hampshire's native food specialties, and she stocks a full range of her state's maple products—syrup, butter, sugar, and confections such as candy and nut brittles. She also sells Cheddar cheese, dressings and condiments, preserves, crackers, and honey. Gift selections available.

Free brochure
Mail orders, gift orders
No credit cards

New Hampshire syrup and an invitation, too—

Dan Johnson's Sugar House
70 Ingalls Road
Jaffrey, NH 03452

603-532-7379

Dan's friendly brochure includes an invitation to come and help tap the trees—"Be here at six in the morning and don't forget your snowshoes!" Wonder how many customers take him up on this? With or without his customers' help, Dan ships his syrup in four sizes—½ pint, pint, quart, and ½ gallon—and you can specify dark, medium, or light amber. Discounts for orders of 6 or 12 containers.

Free brochure
Mail orders, gift orders
No credit cards

Maple syrup from Michigan—

Livingston Farms
2224 Livingston Road
Route 3
St. Johns, MI 48879

517-224-3616

The Livingston family ship their syrup in tin cans or plastic containers; the price is the same for either. They sell one grade in five sizes.

Free price list
Mail orders, gift orders
No credit cards

Cooking syrup with a cookbook—

Maple Grove Farms of Vermont
167 Portland Street
St. Johnsbury, VT 05819

802-748-3136

Maple Grove Farms ships maple syrup in tins, plastic jugs, and stoneware jugs; also maple spread, cream, granulated sugar, candy, and fudge. Especially for cooks there's Grade C maple syrup packed with the *Official Vermont Maple Cookbook*. This company ships a full line of Vermont specialties, including cheese, meats, baking mixes, and baked goods.

Free color catalog
Phone and mail orders, gift orders
AMEX, MC, VISA

A Vermont tradition continues—

Palmer's Maple Syrup
Waitsfield, VT 05673

802-496-3696

Everett and Kathryn Palmer continue to tap trees that were once tapped by

Everett's father and grandfather, and together they produce between 800 and 900 gallons of pure Vermont maple syrup every year. They have put together a pamphlet with photographs that tells the yearly story of the sugaring operation at their farm, where visitors are welcome. Choose light, medium, or dark amber syrup in five sizes, from ½ pint to 1 gallon.

Free price list and brochure
Mail orders
No credit cards

Still doing it the old-fashioned way—

Sugarbush Farm
RFD 1, Box 568C
Woodstock, VT 05091

802-457-1757

Sugarbush Farm still makes its syrup the old-fashioned way. Larry Luce collects the sap with a team of horses and boils it down in the sugar house over a roaring wood fire. You can order a pint, quart, or half gallon of syrup, as well as maple cream and maple candy. Customers can keep up to date on the sugar-making activities through the Luces' newsletter, and you're always welcome to visit the farm. Sugarbush Farm produces cheeses, too. Try the recipe Betsy Luce supplied for Maple Oatmeal Bread—you'll savor the maple fragrance as you knead the dough for this delicious bread.

Free color brochure
Phone and mail orders, gift orders
AMEX, DC, MC, VISA

Maple Oatmeal Bread

from Betsy Luce, Sugarbush Farm

        2 cups milk, scalded
     ½ cup warm water
        2 tablespoons butter
        1 cup old-fashioned oatmeal
     ½ cup pure Vermont maple syrup
     1½ teaspoons salt
        2 packages yeast
6 to 7 cups flour

Combine the scalded milk and warm water and dissolve the butter in the mixture. Pour over oatmeal and let stand 15 minutes. Stir in maple syrup. Mix yeast and salt with half the flour. Add to oatmeal mixture. Stir and knead in the rest of the flour until dough is smooth and elastic. Cover and let rise until double in bulk (about 1 to 1¼ hours). Punch down and form three round loaves. Let rise again (about 45 minutes). If you wish, brush the loaves with oil and sprinkle with oatmeal. Bake at 350 degrees for approximately 30 minutes, or until done. Makes 3 loaves.

Pure Maine syrup—

Sugar Tree Farms
104 Brown Cove Road
Windham, ME 04062

207-892-5135

David and Linda Wasgatt, who operate Sugar Tree Farms, pack pure Grade A Maine maple syrup in ½-pint, 1-pint, and 1-, 2-, or 3-quart jugs. The brochure supplies some appealing recipes developed by the Wasgatts, including apples baked with maple syrup and maple-candied sweet potatoes.

Free brochure
Mail order, gift orders
MC, VISA

Maple syrup and sugar—

Elbridge C. Thomas & Sons
Route 4, Box 336
Chester, VT 05143

802-263-5680

Mr. Thomas sells tins of maple syrup in five sizes, from a half pint to a gallon, and will package syrup in plastic containers on request. He also makes maple sugar to order, and packs eight 2-ounce cakes in an attractive gift box.

Free price list
Mail orders
No credit cards

Maple Sprinkles Shortbread

from Vermont Country Maple, Inc.

½ pound butter
⅔ cup Maple Sprinkles
 2 cups flour
½ cup toasted almonds, coarsely chopped

Cream together butter and Maple Sprinkles until light and fluffy. Add flour and blend gently by hand. Quickly knead in nuts. Gather the dough into a ball, wrap in waxed paper, and chill thoroughly.

Preheat oven to 300 degrees. Divide the dough in half and, on a lightly floured board, roll both halves into neat 8-inch circles, about one third of an inch thick. Place the circles on a buttered baking sheet and score each one into eight wedges. Prick the edges decoratively with a fork. Bake for 30 to 35 minutes or until lightly browned and cooked through. Remove from oven, let cool, and cut into wedges. Makes 16 servings.

You'll find lots of ways to use Maple Sprinkles—

Vermont Country Maple, Inc.
P. O. Box 53
Jericho Center, VT 05465

802-864-7519

This company concentrates on making Maple Sprinkles, an all-natural, granulated version of maple syrup. Lyman Jenkins, who left his job as a chemist in the early eighties to start the company, suggests you try Maple Sprinkles on cereal, fruit, ice cream, toast, and pancakes, as well as for baking. Maple Sprinkles are packed in canisters, shakers, or individual packets, and you can also order a 5-pound bag or 25-pound box. Try them to make the recipe on page 119 for Maple Sprinkles Shortbread—they give new flavor to a traditional classic.

Free brochure
Phone and mail orders
MC, VISA

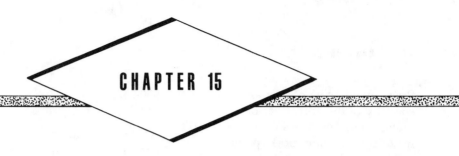

CHAPTER 15

MEATS, POULTRY, CHARCUTERIE, AND SMOKEHOUSE PRODUCTS

Prime steaks and roasts, large game and farm-raised game birds, country hams and bacon, traditional and unusual sausage—all are included in this chapter. To make it a little easier to find what you're looking for, we begin with purveyors who supply a variety of meats, continue with suppliers of just one or two types of product (lamb or veal, for example), then move on to game and game birds, and charcuterie (sausage, pâtés, foie gras). From the selection of smokehouses that concludes the chapter you can order hams, bacon, and other meats cured and smoked just the way you like them—over hickory, applewood, maplewood, or corn cobs.

Purveyors of a Variety of Meats

Meats for easy entertaining—

Balducci's
Mail Order Division
11-02 Queens Plaza South
Long Island City, NY 11101-4908

800-822-1444
800-247-2450 (in NY State)
718-786-9690 (special requests)

Balducci's butchers prepare cuts of beef, veal, and lamb as well as an array of oven-ready items. The holiday roast, for example, is a rack of loin pork chops layered with beef tenderloin, chicken breast, veal tenderloin, provolone, and herbs, all seasoned, rolled, and tied for the oven. Other ready-to-cook selections include stuffed veal roast, chicken galantine, and hams. Balducci's also makes sausages (chicken, lamb, veal, and pork) and offers specialties such as oldani (Italian salami), mortadella, and andouille sausage.

Free seasonal catalogs
Phone and mail orders, gift orders
AMEX, MC, VISA

A wide selection of meat and poultry—

The Bruss Company
3548 Kostner Avenue
Chicago, IL 60641

800-237-3762, ext. 886
312-736-3600

Prime-quality cuts of beef are the specialty of this forty-year-old provisioner. The Bruss Company also features veal, lamb, pork, poultry, smoked, and ready-to-cook items. Combination packs and club plans are available.

Free color catalog
Phone and mail orders, gift orders
AMEX, MC, VISA

A complete mail order butcher—

Cavanaugh Lakeview Farms, Ltd.
P. O. Box 580
Chelsea, MI 48118-0580

800-243-4438
313-475-9391
Fax: 313-475-1133

Browsing through the Cavanaugh catalog is akin to visiting a well-stocked butcher shop. Meats include venison steaks, buffalo burgers, beef steaks, poultry, and game birds (turkey, goose, capon, duckling, pheasant, poussin, squab, quail, and guinea hen). There is also a selection of smoked meats: honey-cured smoked turkey, capon, goose, ham, and bacon; apple-smoked beef, pork, venison, and lamb. Oven-ready entrées include chicken Kiev and chicken cordon bleu, and combination packages offer special values. Cheese and smoked seafood, gift selections, and club plans are available.

Free color catalog
Phone, fax, and mail orders, gift orders
AMEX, MC, VISA

USDA-certified prime beef and lamb—

Certified Prime
4647 South Archer Avenue
Chicago, IL 60632

800-257-2977
312-376-7445

As the name implies, this company supplies only certified prime meats. Choose chateaubriand, filet mignon, sirloin strip, prime rib, top sirloin butt steak, or steak combination packages. Lamb cuts include rib and loin chops.

Free color brochure
Phone and mail orders, gift orders
AMEX

Game and exotic meats—

Czimer Foods
Route 7
Box 285
Lockport, IL 60441

312-460-7152

Czimer Foods supplies the unusual—literally from alligator to zebra. Large game animals include venison, elk, moose, bear, wild boar, buffalo, antelope, and reindeer; also lion, kangaroo, hippopotamus, giraffe, camel, llama, wild goat and mountain sheep, beaver, rabbit, raccoon, and rattlesnake. Oven-ready game birds include pheasant, quail, partridge, guinea hen, duck, goose, squab, wild turkey, and snow grouse. A number of these items are also available smoked.

Free price list
Mail orders
No credit cards

European game, buffalo, boar, game birds, duck, rabbit—

D'Artagnan, Inc.
399-419 St. Paul Avenue
Jersey City, NJ 07306

800-D'ARTAGN
201-792-0748

D'Artagnan supplies unusual and exotic meats. Ducks include Muscovy, mallard, and Pekin. Game birds are poussin, quail, squab, pheasant, wild turkey, guinea hen, partridge, as well as organic turkey and free-range chicken. Various cuts of venison, buffalo, and wild boar are offered, in addition to baby lamb, suckling pig, and kid goat. European game includes grouse, wood pigeon, pheasant, hare, and partridge. Some of these items are available smoked. There is also an extensive variety of foie gras and sausage.

Free price list
Phone orders
AMEX, MC, VISA

Beef, game birds, and smoked meats—

The Forst's Catskill Mountain Foods
CPO Box 1000P
Kingston, NY 12401

800-453-4010
914-331-3500

You can shop at The Forst's from a long list of steaks and game birds (pheasant, partridge, quail, wild turkey, guinea hen, squab, mallard or Muscovy duck). Smoked items include turkey, pheasant, ham, bacon, and sausage. A number of assortments combine these products; some also include cheese. Club plans are available.

Free illustrated brochure
Phone and mail orders, gift orders
AMEX, DC, DISC, MC, VISA

Unusual meats, game birds, rattlesnake, and more—

The Native Game Company
1105 West Oliver
P. O. Box 1046
Spearfish, SD 57783

800-952-6321
605-642-2601

This company, primarily a purveyor to restaurants and hotels, has no minimum order, so home cooks have the opportunity to sample the wide variety of hard-to-find meats. These include buffalo, elk, venison, wild boar, rabbit, goat, and exotic varieties such as kangaroo, zebra, lion, and more. Free-range chicken and domestic duck are offered, as well as a selection of game birds, including pheasant, partridge, squab, quail, and wild turkey. Other items include Texas diamondback rattlesnake meat, alligator fillets, turtle pieces, and smoked eel and salmon. Unusual pâtés and sausage are also offered.

Free catalog
Mail orders
No credit cards

Organic beef, lamb, chicken, and turkey—

Organic Beef, Inc.
P. O. Box 642
Mena, AR 71953

800-634-3058
501-387-7111

Ivan Flanary, Jr., will send you a description of how Organic Beef animals are raised and processed. The company also makes its own fresh beef breakfast sausage without preservatives. First-time customers receive a 10 percent discount on their orders.

Free price list
Mail orders
No credit cards

Fresh frozen and oven-ready meats—

Pfaelzer Brothers
281 West 83rd Street
Burr Ridge, IL 60521

800-621-0226
312-325-9700 (in IL call collect)
Fax: 312-325-0117

Pfaelzer Brothers have a vast selection of beef, pork, veal, plus turkey, goose, duck, and game birds. Highlights from the many oven-ready entrées include whole beef Wellington, stuffed chicken breasts, and marinated fillets. French pâtés and several ready-to-heat hors d'oeuvres make for effortless party giving. Smoked meats and seafood are also available, and holiday and club plans are offered.

Free color catalog
Phone, fax, and mail orders, gift orders
AMEX, DC, MC, VISA

Specialty meats from around the world—

Wild Game, Inc.
2315 West Huron Street
Chicago, IL 60612

312-278-1661
Fax: 312-227-5704

This company ships big game (venison, buffalo, Australian boar) as well as small game (rabbit and hare), and waterfowl (Pekin duck, mallard, and goose). Game birds include pheasant, poussin, quail, partridge, squab, wild turkey, and Scottish grouse and pigeon. (Conveniently, the poussin, quail, and squab may be ordered boned.) Smoked birds include duck, goose, pheasant, turkey, and chicken. Other specialties include sausage (duck, boar, venison),

caviar, smoked fish, pâtés, truffles, and seasonal wild mushrooms.

Free price list
Mail orders
No credit cards

These Suppliers Concentrate on Supplying One or Two Types of Meat

Low-fat beef—

Brae Beef
Stamford Town Center
100 Greyrock Place
Stamford, CT 06901

800-323-4484
203-323-4482

Fred Grant raises Brae beef on a special diet to produce lean, low-fat beef. It is vacuum packed to retain freshness for up to three weeks in the refrigerator. Because of the low fat content, Brae beef cooks up to 20 percent faster than ordinary beef, and stew cooks very quickly.

Color brochure, $2.00 (refundable with order)
Phone orders
No credit cards

A selection of rabbit products—

Classic Country Rabbit Company
P. O. Box 1412
Hillsboro, OR 97123

503-640-1179

Whole rabbits and various cuts, including cutlets and saddle of rabbit, are offered in addition to garlic and hot pizza sausage. You may also order rabbit broth, glace (concentrated rabbit stock), and roux.

Free price list
Mail orders
No credit cards

Spring lamb and suckling lamb—

Jamison Farm
171 Jamison Lane
Latrobe, PA 15650-9419

800-237-LAMB

At their western Pennsylvania farm John and Sukey Jamison raise lamb, breeding their ewes twice a year so that fresh meat is available year round. Order from various suggested cuts and selections (including ready-to-serve lamb stew), or call to arrange for special orders. Young milk-fed lamb is available, and seasonal specials are offered. Try the recipe from Sukey Jamison for succulent Rosemary Lamb Chops.

Free price list
Phone and mail orders, gift orders
MC, VISA

Seasonally available fresh venison—

Lucky Star Ranch
Chaumont, NY 13622

607-VENISON

The von Kerckerinck family raises fallow deer on a 4000-acre ranch in northern New York State. You can order this venison seasonally; cuts include steaks and roasts (with or without bone), saddle of venison, chops, stew meat, liver, heart, and tongue. Fresh meat is shipped by overnight express; delivery of frozen meat is also available. Recipes are sent with each order, and Illiana von Kerckerinck has also prepared a cookbook of recipes for venison and other game.

Free brochure
Phone and mail orders
MC, VISA

Rosemary Lamb Chops
from Sukey Jamison, Jamison Farm

6 lamb chops, cut 1¼ inches thick
2 teaspoons olive oil
1 teaspoon rosemary, crushed
1 teaspoon black pepper, freshly ground

Brush chops with olive oil and rub with rosemary and pepper. Broil under broiler 5 inches from heat or on the grill for 5 to 7 minutes, then turn and finish cooking for 5 to 7 minutes more, or until chops reach desired doneness. Serve with rice pilaf. Serves 4 to 6.

Well-aged, corn-fed beef—

Omaha Steaks International
4400 South 96th Street
P. O. Box 3300
Omaha, Nebraska 68103

800-228-9055

This well-known purveyor of steaks relies on corn-fed beef and a three-week aging process to produce steaks that come with a guarantee of customer satisfaction. The company has introductory offers and regular specials on its products.

Free color brochure
Phone and mail orders, gift orders
AMEX, MC, VISA

Lamb, turkey, capon, and pheasant—

Sugar Hill Farm, Inc.
Smith Hill Road
P. O. Box 50
Colebrook, CT 06021-0050

800-526-2748
800-526-2725 (in CT)

Naturally raised whole and half lambs are available, and you may also select from a choice of cuts. Turkey, capon, and pheasant are also raised on a diet of natural grains, vitamins, and minerals. Recipes accompany orders. Sugar Hill Farm also sells sheepskins, spun yarn, maple syrup, and honey.

Free illustrated brochure
Mail orders
No credit cards

Veal, lamb, and pheasant—

Summerfield Farm
SR 4
Box 195A
Brightwood, VA 22715

703-948-3100

In the foothills of the Blue Ridge Mountains Jamie and Rachel Nicoll produce naturally raised veal, as well as seasonally available lamb, pheasant, squab, and fresh mushrooms. They also make their own glace de veau, a concentrated essence of veal stock, for soups and sauces. You can choose fresh or frozen veal cutlets, roasts, chops, and miscellaneous cuts, or from several assorted veal packages. Customers receive flyers announcing seasonal specials.

Free color brochure
Phone and mail orders, gift orders
MC, VISA

Game Birds

Fresh, frozen, and smoked game birds—

Foggy Ridge Gamebird Farm
P. O. Box 211
Warren, ME 04864

207-273-2357

Ring-necked pheasant, bobwhite quail, and chukar partridge are available from Foggy Ridge Gamebird Farm either fresh, frozen, or smoked. Several samplers are offered, including a Thanksgiving special that combines pheasant and quail. A recipe card is included in every package. Gift baskets of smoked game birds and Maine specialty foods are available for any occasion.

Free illustrated brochure
Phone and mail orders, gift orders
MC, VISA

Fresh and smoked game birds—

Oakwood Game Farm
Box 274
Princeton, MN 55371

800-328-6647
612-389-2077

Jim and Betty Myer started raising game birds for their family in 1967; today their 100-acre central Minnesota facility is one of the largest game bird farms in the country. They ship wild turkey, pheasant, chukar partridge, and mallard duck; turkey and pheasant are available smoked. If you're unsure about how to prepare any of these birds, you may call for recipes and serving ideas. They also sell Minnesota wild rice.

Free color brochure
Phone and mail orders
AMEX, MC, VISA

Vermont game birds—

Wylie Hill Farm
P. O. Box 35
Craftsbury Common, VT 05827

802-586-2887

The fresh game bird selection from Wylie Hill Farm includes pheasant, quail, and partridge. You can also order hickory-smoked pheasant, pheasant pâté, and sampler packages. Tim and Amelia Fritz, owners of Wylie Hill Farm, have included in their brochure two local Vermont products—a maple mustard and an apple chutney—that complement the flavor of their game birds and pâté. You can also order quail eggs, which come with a recipe for pickling them. Try the recipe from Wylie Hill Farm for Quail with Apples.

Free illustrated brochure
Phone and mail orders, gift orders
MC, VISA

Quail with Apples

from Tim and Amelia Fritz, Wylie Hill Farm

4 quail
1 cooking apple, sliced
Paprika
Juice of ½ lemon or lime
1 tablespoon oil

Preheat oven to 350 degrees. Rinse birds and place on a rack in a roasting pan. Stuff birds with apple slices; place any remaining slices on top. Sprinkle with paprika. Combine lemon or lime juice with oil and use this to baste quail every 15 minutes. Bake 50 to 60 minutes. Serves 2.

Variations: Substitute ¼ cup cider for lemon or lime juice (sprinkle with cinnamon); or substitute ¼ cup dry white wine (sprinkle with paprika).

Charcuterie

Sausage, Pâtés, Foie Gras

Unusual fresh and smoked sausage—

Aidells Sausage Company
1575 Minnesota Street
San Francisco, CA 94107

415-285-6660

Before Bruce Aidells founded his company, he was a Berkeley chef making hearty sausages that quickly became his customers' favorites. Now he's supplying chefs and home cooks across the country with unusual sausages. Smoked varieties include andouille, Creole hot sausage, whiskey-fennel sausage, German-style hunter's sausage, and a duck and turkey sausage. Fresh sausages (shipped between October and March) include Italian (hot and mild), Mexican chorizo, duck, pork with fresh herbs, and chicken-apple. The newest varieties are chicken-turkey sausage, flavored with fresh cultured truffles or with red curry and fresh cilantro. If you can't decide, there are several sampler packs. Bruce has published a cookbook and includes booklets of seasonal recipes with all orders. Try the accompanying recipe for Honey-glazed Duck Sausage with Cabbage and Roasted Walnuts from a collection of fall recipes.

Free brochure
Phone and mail orders
MC, VISA

Fresh goose foie gras and international specialties—

Dean & DeLuca, Inc.
Mail Order Department
560 Broadway
New York, NY 10012

800-221-7714
212-431-1691

At Dean & DeLuca you'll find fresh French goose foie gras and authentic Italian specialties: pancetta with bay leaf, soppressatta, toscano salame, and preservative-free prosciutto. Also Hungarian salami, Mexican-style chorizo, and bangers, the traditional English breakfast sausage. Virginia and Vermont hams are also featured.

Color catalog, $2.00
Phone and mail orders, gift orders, and gift certificates
AMEX, MC, VISA

Foie gras from Périgord, France—

François Carrier Foie Gras
5353 West Alabama, Suite 200
Houston, TX 77056

713-963-0787

This company imports luxurious foie gras from Périgord, France. You can order goose or duck foie gras, each with 3 percent truffles. Both are available in gift packs or in individual tins.

Free price list
Mail orders
No credit cards

Portuguese sausage—

Gaspar's Sausage Company, Inc.
P. O. Box 436
North Dartmouth, MA 02747

800-542-2038
508-998-2012

Manuel A. Gaspar brought treasured recipes for making traditional smoked sausage when he immigrated to the United States from Portugal in 1912. Today this company produces over

Honey-glazed Duck Sausage
with Cabbage and Roasted Walnuts

from Bruce Aidells, Aidells Sausage Company
(adapted from American Charcuterie *by V. Wise)*

 8 links Aidells duck sausage with oranges and green peppercorns
½ cup honey
½ teaspoon dried thyme
 1 tablespoon Dijon mustard
½ cup walnuts
 4 tablespoons butter
½ head cabbage, cored and shredded
½ teaspoon salt
½ teaspoon pepper
 3 tablespoons cider vinegar

Preheat the oven to 350 degrees. Place sausage in a shallow baking dish. Combine honey, thyme, and mustard. Coat sausage. Bake for 30 minutes, basting two or three times. Spread walnuts on a cookie sheet and roast in the same oven for about 10 minutes or until they darken and develop a nutty aroma. Set aside and prepare the cabbage. In a large, high-sided frying pan melt butter over medium heat. Add cabbage, salt, and pepper. Toss cabbage so it is well coated with the butter. Cover frying pan and cook 10 to 15 minutes, stirring occasionally, until cabbage is completely wilted. Add vinegar and cook for 2 minutes uncovered. Serve sausage accompanied with the cabbage and garnish with the roasted walnuts. Serves 4.

three million pounds of sausage products each year, including linguiça, chouriço (mild, hot, extra hot), salpicão, kielbasa, and franks. Portuguese sweet bread and coffee syrup are also available.

Free price list
Phone and mail orders, gift orders
MC, VISA

Sausage and additional Portuguese foods—

Lisbon Sausage Company, Inc.
433 South Second Street
New Bedford, MA 02740

508-993-7645

This company offers Portuguese specialties such as linguiça, chouriço, salpicão, and other items. Nonmeat foods include fava and ceci beans, pickled eggs, lupini beans, and hot mixed pickles. The staff at Lisbon Sausage Company will be pleased to try to find items not listed in their pamphlet.

Free price list
Mail orders
MC, VISA

French pâtés and Hungarian salami—

Paprikas Weiss
1546 Second Avenue
New York, NY 10028

212-288-6117

Paprikas Weiss imports from France several kinds of Strasbourg goose liver pâté with truffles; it's available in tins of various sizes, from a modest 2⅝ ounces to a lavish 29 ounces. Hungarian specialties include Paprikas Weiss's own salami and double smoked bacon, as well as Romanian salami.

Seasonal catalogs, $3.00 annual subscription
Phone and mail orders, gift orders, and certificates
AMEX, MC, VISA

Louisiana specialties—

Poche's Meat Market & Restaurant
Route 2, Box 415
Breaux Bridge, LA 70517

318-332-2108

Looking for fresh, marinated sausage or smoked andouille or tasso for making a gumbo? You can order these pork products from Poche's as well as cracklin's, boudin, fresh sausage, stuffed chaudin or tongue, pickled

pork, hog lard, and other items. Poche's will also ship its homemade roux, barbecue sauce, dried shrimp, and peeled crawfish in season.

Free price list
Phone and mail orders
MC, VISA

Pâtés and ready-to-serve meats—

Seyco Fine Foods, Inc.
25574 Rye Canyon Road, #E
Valencia, CA 91355-1109

800-423-2942

Seyco delicacies include several varieties of French goose pâté. Also there is a selection of vegetarian pâtés and ready-to-serve items such as cassoulet, corned beef hash, and chili.

Color catalog, $2.00; 10 percent off first order
Phone and mail orders, gift orders
AMEX, DC, MC, VISA

Wisconsin bratwurst and other specialty sausage—

Fred Usinger, Inc.
1030 North Old World Third Street
Milwaukee, WI 53203-0980

800-558-9998
414-276-9105
Fax: 414-291-5277

Usinger's has been a Milwaukee landmark since 1880 and still makes its sausage from traditional recipes. Frederick Usinger III and his son Fritz represent the third and fourth generations of the family-owned business. The product list of dozens of items includes cervelat or summer sausage, luncheon meats, traditional sausages (bratwurst, knockwurst, frankfurters), liver sausage, and blood sausage. Gift selections are also available.

Free color catalog
Phone, fax, and mail orders, gift orders
MC, VISA

Lamb pâtés, sausage, smoked lamb—

Vermont Country Lamb, Inc.
RFD 1
Route 73
Orwell, VT 05760

800-527-5313
802-948-2294

This company's products are the joint effort of owners Michelle DaVia and Susan Munger. Their unusual pâtés are made primarily from lamb; one variety is flavored with pine nuts and feta cheese, the other with dried apricots, prunes, and walnuts. There's also a mousse of lamb liver pâté, and smoked boneless leg of lamb. Lamb sausage is available with herbs and garlic or with apples and mint.

Free price list
Mail orders
MC, VISA

Traditional German-style sausage—

Wimmer's Meat Products, Inc.
126 West Grant Street
West Point, NE 68788-1856

800-358-0761
800-642-8334 (in NE)

The third generation of the Wimmer family is now involved in running this sausage company founded in 1934. Although the catalog features numerous gift selections, you can also place orders simply for sausage: 2½-pound quantities

of bratwurst, knockwurst, summer sausage, and wieners, or choose from smaller quantities of specialties such as smoked sausage, liverwurst with pistachio nuts, and beef cervelat. Wimmer's fiftieth-anniversary cookbook is also available.

Free color catalog
Phone and mail orders, gift orders
AMEX, MC, VISA

Ham, Bacon, and Other Smoked Products

Traditional German smoking methods continue—

Amana Meat Shop and Smokehouse
One Smokehouse Lane
Amana, IA 52203

800-373-MEAT
319-622-3113

Hickory-smoked ham, bacon, and sausage are produced at the Amana Meat Shop, where the smoking tower has operated since it was built in 1858 by a communal village of German immigrants. German specialties are still available—Kasser Ripchen (smoked pork chops); liverwurst; head cheese; cervelat; Landjager (similar to American beef jerky); and Thuringer, an all-beef sausage.

Free color brochure
Mail orders, gift orders
AMEX, MC, VISA

Smoked meats and Kentucky specialties—

Broadbent's B & B Food Products, Inc.
6321 Hopkinsville Road
Cadiz, KY 42211

800-841-2202
502-235-5294

In addition to cooked and uncooked country hams, Broadbent's supplies ham steaks, ground cooked ham, ham hocks and pieces (ideal for adding to soups and stews). Other smoked products include bacon, pork sausage, turkey, chicken, duck, Cornish hens, and quail. Other foods—baking mixes for spoon bread, corn bread, biscuits, and pancakes, as well as preserves like chowchow and pickled okra—are available separately or can be combined with smoked meats in gift selections.

Free color catalog
Phone and mail orders, gift orders
AMEX, MC, VISA

Hickory-smoked meats from the Ozarks—

Burgers' Smokehouse
Highway 87 South
California, MO 65018

314-796-4111
Fax: 314-796-3137

The Burgers' catalog pictures three generations of Burgers at work in the smokehouse, where they turn out hams (including prosciutto), turkey ham, bacon, smoked pork, turkey, pheasant, and Cornish hens. Other items include barbecued ribs and chicken, and the bargain corner includes country jowl, bacon and ham ends cuts, ham hocks and bacon pieces for seasoning. They also sell steaks, cuts of pork, oven-ready meats, and numerous gift selections. The smokehouse has a museum where visitors can learn about the art of smoking and enjoy a smokehouse sandwich.

Free color catalog
Phone, fax, and mail orders, gift orders
AMEX, MC, VISA

Tennessee country hams, bacon, and sausage—

Clifty Farm
P. O. Box 1146
Paris, TN 38242

800-238-8239
901-642-9740

From Clifty Farm you can order smoked hams in four sizes, slab bacon, and country sausage smoked in cloth bags. Gifts packs include other Tennessee products—jellies, grain mixes, honey, and sorghum molasses.

Free color catalog
Phone and mail orders, gift orders
MC, VISA

Traditional Vermont favorites—

Dakin Farm
Route 7
Ferrisburg, VT 05456

802-425-3971

Dakin Farm cob-smokes ham, bacon, sausage, turkey, pheasant, and pork chops. Two unusual products are Montreal smoked meat, a spicy smoked beef; and very thinly sliced air-dried beef. Dakin also sells cheese and maple syrup and adds these products to its gift packages.

Free color catalog
Phone and mail orders, gift orders
AMEX, MC, VISA

Smoked meats and other Southern treats—

Early's Honey Stand
P. O. Box K
Spring Hill, TN 37174-0911

800-523-2015

Early's started out in the mid-twenties as a roadside honey stand; today the company ships Southern-style foods all over the United States. You'll find hickory-smoked pork sausage, bacon, hams, turkeys, and summer sausage. Also steaks, preserves, baking mixes, and gift baskets.

Free color catalog
Phone and mail orders, gift orders
AMEX, DC, MC, VISA

Virginia hams, bacon, sausage—

S. Wallace Edwards & Sons, Inc.
P. O. Box 25
Surry, VA 23883

800-222-4267
804-294-3121

Three generations of the Edwards family have continued the tradition of smoking Virginia hams, bacon, and sausage over hickory fires. Sampler packs are offered, as well as gift packs that include traditional Virginia favorites such as sparkling cider and smoked peanuts.

Free color catalog
Phone and mail orders, gift orders
AMEX, CHOICE, MC, VISA

From a South Carolina farm store—

Four Oaks Farm
P. O. Box 987
Lexington, SC 29072

803-356-3194

This large farm store on Highway 1 near Lexington specializes in pork products, including hams, bacon, and sausage. Numerous gift selections include preserves, nuts, grits, and dried peas and beans.

Free illustrated catalog
Mail orders, gift orders
MC, VISA

New Hampshire corncob-smoked meats—

Gould's Country Smokehouse
River Road
Piermont, NH 03779

603-272-5856

Gould's has sold cob-smoked meats since 1921. In addition to smoked hams, boneless hams and bacon, you can order smoked cheese (rat trap or mild Cheddar), poultry, pork loins, salmon, and trout. Gift selections and maple syrup are also available.

Free color brochure
Phone and mail orders, gift orders
MC, VISA

Hams and bacon are specialties—

Harrington's
Main Street
Richmond, VT 05477

802-434-4444

This well-known Vermont company has been producing corncob- and maplewood-smoked hams since 1873. Hams and bacon are their specialties, but in Harrington's catalog and New England retail stores you'll also find beef, game birds and poultry, lamb, smoked turkey, beef, seafood, cheese, and other Vermont favorites. Harrington's has introductory offers for new customers and frequent sale flyers. Club plans are also available.

Free color catalog
Phone and mail orders, gift orders
AMEX, DISC, MC, VISA

Hickory-smoked meats from Colorado—

High Valley Farm, Inc.
14 Alsace Way
Colorado Springs, CO 80906

719-634-2944

This Colorado company has been smoking meats for over fifty years. In addition to hickory-smoked ham and bacon, High Valley Farm smokes turkey, chicken, capon, pheasant, Cornish hens, quail, duck, and goose. A selection of pâtés is also available, as are gift selections and club plans.

Free price list
Mail orders, gift orders
No credit cards

Smoked meats, plus steaks and snack items—

Roy L. Hoffman & Sons
Route 6, Box 5
Hagerstown, MD 21740

800-356-3193

Choose Hoffman's country smoked ham, bacon, or a sampler that combines these items with sausage. Hoffman's also ships Delmonico and boneless New York strip steaks. Snackers are remembered with the Snacker's Delight, a combo of smoked beef sticks and beef jerky.

Free illustrated brochure
Phone and mail orders, gift orders
MC, VISA

Old World smoking techniques—

Kohn's Smokehouse
CR 35, Box 160
Thomaston, ME 04861

207-372-8412

Kohn's special technique of smoking over a variety of hardwoods and fruitwoods was brought to Maine from Germany. Kohn's smokes pheasant, chicken, beef, and salami. German specialties include Westphalian beef, bratwurst, and liverwurst. The smoked seafood line includes Maine lobster in the shell.

Free price list
Mail orders
MC, VISA

Mahogany-smoked meats—

Meadow Farms Country Smokehouse
P. O. Box 1387
Bishop, CA 93514

619-873-5311

Roi Ballard has the only company in the country that smokes meats with mahogany wood native to the Sierra Nevada Mountains. At his Bishop store and through mail order he sells smoked ham, pork chops, bacon, chicken, beef jerky, and Cheddar cheese.

Free brochure
Mail orders, gift orders
MC, VISA

Applewood-smoked meats—

Menuchah Farms Smokehouse
Route 22
Salem, NY 12865

800-621-6030
518-854-9423

At Menuchah Farms, meats are marinated in brown sugar, honey, herbs, and spices and slowly smoked over applewood. Choose smoked beef, lamb, pork, turkey, chicken, quail, Cornish hens, pheasant, or duck.

Free color catalog
Phone and mail orders, gift orders
MC, VISA

Hickory-smoked meats from Texas—

New Braunfels Smokehouse
P. O. Box 311159
New Braunfels, TX 78131-1159

800-537-6932
512-625-7316

It seems appropriate that a Texas smokehouse offers all the makings for "smokehouse-style fajitas." Hickory-smoked meats include a variety of cuts of ham, turkey, bacon, pork, chicken, and beef. The smoked sausage selection includes bratwurst, summer sausage, salami, and turkey sausage. Combination boxes, gift selections, and club plans are available.

Free color catalog
Phone and mail orders, gift orders
AMEX, MC, VISA

Kentucky country hams—

Colonel Bill Newsom
127 North Highland Avenue
Princeton, KY 42445

502-365-2482

These hams are cured, hickory smoked, and aged according to a process used for nearly two hundred years in this area of Kentucky. Colonel Newsom's recipe brochure gives you various ways to prepare a Kentucky country ham, provides recipes for red-eye gravy and glazes, and suggests ways to use leftover ham.

Free price list
Mail orders, gift orders
No credit cards

Old-fashioned cob-smoked meats from New Hampshire—

North Country Smokehouse
Box 1415
Claremont, NH 03743

603-542-8323

As well as cob-smoked ham, bacon, sausage, pork chops, and spareribs, North Country Smokehouse prepares smoked turkey, duck, pheasant, chicken, and lamb. You can also order several kinds of specialty sausage—andouille, kielbasa, Montreal smoked meat (Lithuanian pastrami)—and smoked cheese. Special packages combine smoked meats with additional treats: smoked Cornish hens, for example, come with Minnesota wild rice; and bacon comes with maple syrup, griddle-cake mix, and preserves.

Free color brochure
Phone and mail orders
AMEX, MC, VISA

Applewood-smoked meats from Wisconsin—

Nueske Hillcrest Farm Meats
RR 2
Wittenberg, WI 54499

800-382-2266
800-372-2266 (in WI)

This Wisconsin family-run business specializes in pork products— applewood-smoked ham, bacon, sausage, and ribs—and also sells smoked turkey, chicken, duck, quail, pheasant, and Cornish hens. Nueske's, begun in 1933, still slow-smokes meats over chunks of locally grown applewood; bacon is smoked for 18 to 20 hours, hams for 17 to 24 hours.

Free color catalog
Phone and mail orders, gift orders
AMEX, DISC, MC, VISA

Smoked Louisiana meats and sausage—

Oak Grove Smokehouse, Inc.
17618 Old Jefferson Highway
Prairieville, LA 70769

504-673-8657

Turkey, chicken, country-style bacon, ham, and sausage are smoked by this southern Louisiana smokehouse. They also sell tasso and andouille and a list of Creole mixes. Gift selections are available.

Free brochure
Mail orders, gift orders
No credit cards

Smoked turkey and pork products from the Ozarks—

Ozark Mountain Smoke House
P. O. Box 37
Farmington, AR 72730

800-643-3437
800-632-0155 (in AR)

Ozark Mountain Smoke House was founded by Roy Sharp, who started

experimenting with smoking turkeys after retiring to the Ozark Mountains. Now the company has almost a dozen retail outlets in Arkansas and Oklahoma and has a product list that adds smoked hams, slab bacon, pork loin, chicken, and summer sausage to the original product. Gift packs are available.

Free color catalog
Mail orders, gift orders
MC, VISA

Old-fashioned sugar-cured hams and bacon—

Ralph's Packing Company
P. O. Box 249
Perkins, OK 74059

800-522-3979
405-547-2448

Ralph's Packing Company's sugar-cured hams and bacon are popular items. The company also sells a specially trimmed ham (called a "Dieter's Delight" Nugget ham) and extra-lean Arkansas-style bacon. Other products are smoked turkey, Cajun-style sausage, bratwurst, salami, summer sausage, hot links, beef sticks, and smoked cheese. Gift selections are available.

Free color brochure
Phone and mail orders, gift orders
MC, VISA

Maple-cured cob-smoked meats from Vermont—

Roland & Son
Route 14
Box 278
South Barre, VT 05670

802-476-6066

Denis and Debbie Lefebvre are the third generation of their family to run this business, which produces maple-cured cob-smoked hams and bacon as well as smoked turkey, pheasant, beef, trout, cheese, and summer sausage.

Free color brochure
Phone and mail orders, gift orders
MC, VISA

Old World-style meats—

Schaller & Weber
1654 Second Avenue
New York, NY 10028

800-847-4115
212-879-3047

Ferdinand Schaller has run this business since 1937 and is now joined by his four sons in making a variety of sausage and meat products. In addition to roast beef, hams, and bacon, the Schallers make almost a dozen specialty sausages (including fresh and smoked bratwurst), nine liverwursts, ten cold cuts (including a Bavarian-style headcheese), over half a dozen Westphalian-style smoked hams, as well as salami and cervelats.

Free price list
Mail orders
No credit cards

From the ham capital of Virginia—

The Smithfield Collection
P. O. Box 487
Smithfield, VA 23430

800-628-2242
804-357-2121

Various smoked hams, turkey, bacon, and sausage, plus canned specialties

such as peanut soup, beans with ham, Brunswick stew, and barbecued beef and pork are featured. Gift packs are available in wicker hampers.

Free color catalog
Phone and mail orders, gift orders
AMEX, MC, VISA

Smoked pork products and turkey from Smithfield—

Smithfield Packing Company
Smithfield, VA 23430

800-444-9180
804-357-4321

Another company in the Virginia city famed for fine hams, this one offering hams, bacon, ham sausage, smoked turkey, sampler packs, and gift items.

Free color catalog
Phone and mail orders, gift orders
AMEX, MC, VISA

Nitrate-free smoked meats—

Smith's Log Smokehouse
Back Brooks Road
Brooks, ME 04921

207-525-4418

Smith's offers nitrate-free hams, bacon, franks, and smoked chicken and turkey. Blackstrap hams and bacon are processed with molasses rather than sugar, salt instead of nitrates, and smoked over hickory and corncobs. Beef jerky, several varieties of sausage, scrapple, and smoked mozzarella are also available.

Free price list
Phone and mail orders
MC, VISA

From America's oldest meat packer—

E. M. Todd Company, Inc.
1128 Hermitage Road
P. O. Box 5167
Richmond, VA 23220

800-368-5026
804-359-5051

Mallory Todd founded this company in 1779 and cured and smoked hams using a process learned from local Indians. Today's bacon, hams, and jowls are still produced by the same methods—hand curing, smoking over hickory fires, and slow aging. You can order fully cooked or ready-to-cook hams, slab bacon, and sampler packs.

Free illustrated brochure
Phone and mail orders, gift orders
MC, VISA

Smoked meats and Lebanon bologna—

The Daniel Weaver Company
P. O. Box 525
Lebanon, PA 17042

800-WEAVERS
717-274-6100

Lebanon bologna is a ready-to-eat, semi-dry sausage created by the Pennsylvania Dutch who settled Lebanon County in the early 1800s. Weaver's makes its bologna from a closely guarded family recipe that has been handed down from one generation to the next. In addition to this specialty, Weaver's makes smoked hams, bacon, turkey, duck, Cornish hens, and dried beef. Gift items, including Pennsylvania Dutch pretzels, are also available.

Free color brochure
Phone and mail orders, gift orders
AMEX, MC, VISA

If you're looking for a source for rendered goose fat, you can order from these suppliers:

Paprikas Weiss
1546 Second Avenue
New York, NY 10028

212-288-6117

and

G. B. Ratto & Company
821 Washington Street
Oakland, CA 94607

800-325-3483
800-228-3515 (in CA)
Fax: 415-836-2250

MUSHROOMS AND TRUFFLES

Here you will find sources for all kinds of unusual dried and fresh mushrooms. Dried mushrooms are a wonderful ingredient to have on hand, and they will keep in the pantry almost indefinitely. They are intensely flavored, and it takes just a small amount to flavor sauces, pasta dishes, and soups. Don't miss the fresh shiitake mushrooms offered by several suppliers in this chapter—you can't beat their rich, woodsy flavor. Properly stored, fresh shiitake will keep several weeks in the refrigerator.

Sources for several kinds of truffles, those rare subterranean fungi prized by gourmands everywhere, are also included here.

Dried shiitake and cèpe mushrooms—

American Spoon Foods, Inc.
P. O. Box 566
1668 Clarion Avenue
Petoskey, MI 49770-0566

800-222-5886
616-347-9030
Fax: 616-347-2512

American Spoon Foods promotes American regional specialties and highlights two American-grown mushrooms: shiitake, found in the woods of Virginia and West Virginia; and cèpe, found in conifer forests. Both are available dried, and American Spoon Foods sends cooking suggestions with the mushrooms.

Free seasonal catalogs
Phone, fax, and mail orders, gift orders
DISC, MC, VISA

Dried and seasonally available fresh mushrooms—

Caspian Caviars
Highland Mill
P. O. Box 876
Camden, ME 04843

207-236-4436
Fax: 207-236-2740

Fresh morels, chanterelles, and porcini/ cèpes are available seasonally from this caviar importer. Dried varieties include petit morels, black chanterelles, and porcini cèpes. Fresh black winter truffles are offered weekly from January through mid-March and range in size from 8 grams to over 50 grams. Call for prices and to check availability.

Free price list
Phone, fax, and mail orders
AMEX, MC, VISA

Italian tinned truffles, seasonal fresh truffles—

Caviarteria, Inc.
29 East 60th Street
New York, NY 10022

800-4-CAVIAR
212-759-7410
Fax: 718-482-8985

Fresh truffles are available from December to February (call for current prices). Tins and jars of Italian black and white truffles are available year round.

Free price list
Phone, fax, and mail orders
AMEX, MC, VISA

Imported dried and water-packed wild mushrooms—

The Chef's Pantry
P. O. Box 3
Post Mills, VT 05058

800-666-9940
802-333-4141

Dried morels imported from India are available in 4-ounce or 1-pound quantities; dried porcini and porcini powder come from Italy. Mary Spata and Murray Burk of The Chef's Pantry have also selected water-packed mushrooms that include whole and cut cèpes from Germany, medium and extra-tiny chanterelles from France, and mixed wild mushrooms from Germany. Porcini paste and truffle and porcini paste are also available. Revoul brand whole truffles and truffle juice are imported from France. Sliced truffles come from Spain.

Free illustrated catalog
Phone and mail orders, gift orders
MC, VISA

French and Italian dried mushrooms—

Dean & DeLuca, Inc.
Mail Order Department
560 Broadway
New York, NY 10012

800-221-7714
212-431-1691

French dried mushroom varieties include morels, cèpes, chanterelles, and trompettes de la mort (black chanterelles). Dried porcini are imported from the Valtellina region of Italy. Dean & DeLuca suggest using cèpes to add a delicious earthiness to soups and stews, and as an unusual addition the next time you make spoon bread.

Illustrated catalog, $2.00
Phone and mail orders, gift orders and gift certificates
AMEX, MC, VISA

Fresh shiitake—

Delftree Corporation
234 Union Street
North Adams, MA 01247

413-664-4907

In the heart of the Berkshire Mountains, the Delftree Corporation is growing fresh shiitake mushrooms year round. Most of their crop finds its way to restaurants, caterers, and upscale grocers, but Delftree will mail-order 3 or 7 pounds anywhere in the United States. Refrigerated shelf life is up to four weeks. The fabulous recipe for Grilled Shiitake Mushrooms with Garlic, Ginger, and Soy Sauce was supplied by Peter Duble of the Delftree Corporation. It's his favorite shiitake recipe and sure to become one of yours.

Free price list
Phone and mail orders, gift orders
MC, VISA

Dried wild mushrooms and mushroom specialties—

Forest Foods, Inc.
355 North Ashland Avenue
Chicago, IL 60607

312-421-3676

Forest Foods produces the Woodland Pantry brand of dried wild mushrooms: morels, porcini, shiitake, and oyster. Spice rack items include wild mushroom powder and chopped wild mushrooms. You can also order wild mushroom caviars (morel, cèpe, and wild champignon) and four out-of-the-ordinary mushroom soups: a cream of wild mushroom, and mushroom with wild rice, barley, or onion.

Free price list
Mail orders
No credit cards

Fresh and dried exotic mushrooms—

Fresh & Wild, Inc.
P. O. Box 2981
Vancouver, WA 98668

800-222-5578 (orders only)
206-254-8130
Fax: 206-896-8718

Grilled Shiitake Mushrooms with Garlic, Ginger, and Soy Sauce

from Peter W. Duble, Jr., Delftree Corporation

1 pound Delftree shiitakes, stems removed[1]
1 teaspoon minced garlic
1 teaspoon minced ginger
1 teaspoon sugar
3 tablespoons soy sauce
2 tablespoons dry sherry
4 tablespoons peanut oil

Prepare a grill or preheat the broiler to high. In a bowl, combine the mushrooms with the remaining ingredients and toss thoroughly to combine. Set aside to marinate for 15 minutes. Skewer each shiitake through the cap horizontally with a bamboo skewer. Grill the mushrooms for about 2 minutes on each side, until lightly browned and tender. Makes a delicious hors d'oeuvre for 4 to 6.

[1]The reserved stems may be trimmed and added to soups, stews, and other dishes. Or trim and process in a food processor until finely chopped and use as a wonderful addition to sauces and pasta sauce.

Fresh & Wild, a supplier of fresh and dried mushrooms to restaurants across the United States, also offers an enticing selection for the home cook. Among the twenty varieties of fresh, wild mushrooms and seven cultivated mushrooms, you'll find angel trumpet, cauliflower, chanterelles (black, brown, and golden), matsutake, morel, wood ear, portobello, and white chestnut. Seven types of dried mushrooms and a dried mushroom mix of seven varieties are also available. Truffles include premium quality Oregon white and black truffles, fresh and frozen. Many of these items are available seasonally. Fresh & Wild also ships fresh wild berries and unusual produce.

Free color brochure
Phone, fax, and mail orders
MC, VISA

Wild dried mushrooms, powder, and mushroom caviar—

Gourmet Treasure Hunters
10044 Adams Avenue, Suite 305
Huntington Beach, CA 92646

714-964-3355

Gourmet Treasure Hunters have hunted up a collection of dried wild mushrooms from around the world. From Italy: porcini; from France: cèpes, chanterelles, morels; and from the Orient: oyster, shiitake, and Chinese black mushrooms. Try the powder from European wild mushrooms for flavoring soups, sauces, and other dishes, or sample the wild mushroom caviar as a buttery spread for crackers or grilled meat or as an addition to pasta sauces and vinaigrette.

Illustrated catalog (with newsletters for a year), $4.00
Phone and mail orders
AMEX

Baudoin truffles from France—

Paprikas Weiss
1546 Second Avenue
New York, NY 10028

212-288-6117

Paprikas Weiss imports the Baudoin brand of truffles from Périgord, France, in tins and jars of various sizes. They also offer truffle peelings and truffle juice as well as French morels and French mushrooms packed in tins.

Seasonal catalogs, $3.00 annual subscription
Phone and mail orders, gift orders, and gift certificates
AMEX, MC VISA

Fresh shiitake mushrooms—

Michael W. Phillips & Company
P. O. Box 1034
Kennett Square, PA 19348

215-444-3319

Michael W. Phillips & Company ship fresh shiitake mushrooms in 1-, 3-, or 5-pound quantities. The advice from this company about storing and preparing these mushrooms cautions against washing or peeling them, and suggests that, if cleaning is required, simply wiping the mushrooms with a moist towel will do the job.

Free brochure
Mail orders
No credit cards

Italian truffle products and mushrooms from around the world—

G. B. Ratto & Company
821 Washington Street
Oakland, CA 94607

800-325-3483
800-228-3515 (in CA)
Fax: 415-836-2250

On international grocer G. B. Ratto's mushroom shelf you'll find dried chanterelle, porcini, and morel mushrooms from Europe, as well as inexpensive dried Chilean mushrooms. There are also jars of Italian truffled mushrooms and French forest mushrooms. Truffle products include whole truffles, white truffle oil, truffle butter with parmigiano cheese, and both white and black truffle juice. Ratto also stocks truffle puree in a tube—they suggest combining a little with butter for use on poached fish, steak, rice, or pasta.

Free illustrated catalog
Phone, fax, and mail orders, gift orders, and gift certificates
MC, VISA

Imported dried mushrooms—

Select Origins, Inc.
Box N
Southampton, NY 11968

800-822-2092
516-924-5447 (in NY state)
Fax: 516-924-5892

In keeping with their philosophy of supplying foods from where they grow best, Tom and Kristi Siplon stock dried porcini from Italy, morels from France, and shiitakes from Japan. The mushroom sampler includes all three

varieties and comes with tips on how to prepare them.

Free illustrated catalog
Phone, fax, and mail orders, gift orders
AMEX, MC, VISA

Five kinds of dried mushrooms—

Vanilla, Saffron Imports
949 Valencia Street
San Francisco CA 94110

415-648-8990
Fax: 415-648-2240

This restaurant supplier also offers a mail order service for home cooks. Dried mushroom varieties are cèpes/porcini, morels, chanterelles, lobster, and matsutake, available in 1-pound plastic bags or in a smaller "gourmet box." As you'll guess by the name, this company also imports vanilla extract, vanilla beans, and saffron.

Free price list
Mail orders only
No credit cards

White truffles from Oregon—

White Truffle Foods, Inc.
829 Seventh Street
Lake Oswego, OR 97034

503-635-6444

"Damp days, cool nights, and the approaching holiday season mean the Oregon white truffle season has arrived," writes David Lipton in his annual early winter announcement to White Truffle Foods customers. You can order these truffles in quarter, half, or full pounds.

Free information
Mail orders
No credit cards

For more suppliers of dried mushrooms, check the purveyors of Asian ingredients in Chapter 25. "The International Pantry."

If you'd like to try to grow your own mushrooms, you'll find suppliers of spawn and equipment in Chapter 28, "Growing Your Own Ingredients."

CHAPTER 17

NUTS, SEEDS, AND NUT BUTTERS

The next time you want to make a special cake that calls for ground hazelnuts, don't spend hours searching the grocery stores. The sources are here—just call and place your order with one of the many suppliers in this chapter and they'll be at your door within days. You'll also find premium-quality pecans, walnuts, almonds, peanuts, and more, fresh from farms in the South and California. A number of these companies also import specialty nuts such as pignolias and chestnuts. And don't overlook the unusual nut butters—cashew, hazelnut, and almond.

Ordering nuts in bulk is a definite money saver. They'll store well in the freezer for long periods (see the storage tips for pecans, which also apply to other nuts). Get together with fellow cooks and place bulk orders for several kinds of nuts; that way, you'll all have the pleasure of a well-stocked pantry.

Nuts from the United States and around the world—

Ace Specialty Foods
P. O. Box 100
Cordele, GA 31015-0100

800-729-8999

Pecan halves and pieces come in various quantities up to 5-pound cartons; cracked and in-shell pecans come in 5-pound sacks. Red and natural pistachios, peanuts, sunflower seeds, and almonds are also available in large quantities. Ace's selection of international nuts includes marcona almonds from Spain, pignolias from Italy, piñons and pepitas (pumpkin seeds) from Mexico, and Turkish

pistachios. A wide selection of gifts, nut cakes, and candies is offered.

Free color catalog
Phone and mail orders, gift orders
AMEX, DISC, DC, MC, VISA

An array of almond products—

Almond Plaza
P. O. Box 500
Sacramento, CA 95812-0500

800-225-6887

This large Sacramento firm has several stores in California and has been mail-ordering nuts for more than forty years. You'll find every kind of almond here—diced, sliced, slivered, natural and blanched, even green-onion-flavored almonds for salads. You'll also find almond oil, almond butter, and a 7-pound tin of almond paste that should see you through your holiday baking (1½-pound tins also available). Also hazelnuts, pistachios, flavored nuts, nut confections, and gift packs.

Free color catalog
Phone and mail orders, gift orders
AMEX, MC, VISA

Native wild nuts—

American Spoon Foods, Inc.
P. O. Box 566
1668 Clarion Avenue
Petoskey, MI 49770-0566

800-222-5886
616-347-9030
Fax: 616-347-2512

This company, one of the few sources for native wild nuts, supplies black walnuts, hickory nut meats, and wild pecan meats from Missouri. American Spoon Foods is involved in an effort to help the American chestnut tree recover from near extinction. They will send you native American chestnut seedlings and put you in touch with a conservation group, the Great Lakes Chestnut Alliance. And if you don't have room to plant your own trees, you can order Great Lakes-grown chestnuts in 1- and 4-pound boxes.

Free seasonal catalogs
Phone, fax, and mail orders, gift orders
DISC, MC, VISA

Nuts and seeds from California—

Bates Brothers Nut Farm, Inc.
15954 Woods Valley Road
Valley Center, CA 92082

619-749-3333

The Bates family has run this farm since the 1920s, when they started selling walnuts in their garage. Now they have two large stores in California, and they ship nuts, fruits, and snack items all over the country. Raw nuts include almonds (whole, slivered, sliced, and blanched), Brazil nuts, cashews, hazelnuts, peanuts, pecans, pignolias, and walnuts. Pumpkin, sesame, and sunflower seeds are also offered. Most of these items are available roasted, with or without salt, and there are some smoked nuts, too.

Free price list
Mail orders, gift orders
MC, VISA

Roasted Chestnuts

from American Spoon Foods

With a sharp knife, cut an X on the rounded side of the chestnuts. Place the chestnuts in a pan, cut side up. Cover the pan and roast them at 425 degrees for approximately 45 minutes.

California almonds—

Cal-Almond, Inc.
6049 Leedom Road
Hughson, CA 95326

209-883-0478

Order whole natural almonds in 3-, 5-,
and 25-pound packs. Three-pound
boxes of hickory-smoked almonds are
also available.

Free price list
Mail orders
No credit cards

Imported chestnut products and
specialty nuts—

The Chef's Pantry
P. O. Box 3
Post Mills, VT 05058

800-666-9940
802-333-4141

From France, Chef's Pantry owners
Mary Spata and Murray Burk import
Faugier sweetened chestnut spread and
unsweetened chestnut puree; also
Minerve ready-to-use whole roasted
chestnuts and two brands of French
brine-packed whole chestnuts. Italian
chestnut pieces in syrup complete the
selection. You'll also find macadamia
nuts and shelled pistachio nuts by the
pound, and whole, roasted hazelnuts,
grains, and flour.

Free illustrated catalog
Phone and mail orders, gift orders
MC, VISA

Pecan specialties and a cookbook—

Country Estate Pecans
P. O. Box 7
1625 East Helmet Peak Road
Sahuarita, AZ 85629

800-327-3226
602-791-2062

Shelled pecan halves (mammoth and
medium) are shipped in bulk quantities
of 24 and 30 pounds. Smaller quantities
and gift selections are available, as well
as pistachios and almonds. Numerous
tempting pecan confections beckon, and
Country Estate Pecans also stocks a
Pecan Lovers Cookbook.

Free price list
Phone and mail orders
MC, VISA

Peanuts and pecans—

DeSoto Confectionery & Nut Company
P. O. Box 72
DeSoto, GA 31743

800-237-8689
912-874-1200

Order Georgia redskin peanuts in the
shell (raw or roasted in 10-pound
boxes); shelled (in 5-pound bags); and
shelled, roasted, and salted (in 1-pound
bags, 28-ounce pails, or 5-pound boxes).
Pecans are available in the shell (10-
pound boxes); shelled (in 2- or 5-pound
boxes); and roasted and salted (in
1-pound bags, and 2- and 5-pound
boxes). For baking, pecan pieces in
1-, 2-, or 5-pound quantities are a good
choice. Nut confections and gift baskets
are also offered.

Free color catalog
Phone and mail orders, gift orders
AMEX, MC, VISA

Hazelnuts and pure hazelnut butters—
Dundee Orchards
P. O. Box 327
Dundee, OR 97115

503-538-8105

Dundee Orchards ship bags of hazelnuts in the shell and shelled raw hazelnuts. You can also order roasted and skinned jumbo hazelnuts in 2-pound bags. Hazelnut butters, made without salt, sugar, or oil, include crunchy and creamy varieties, chocolate hazelnut butter, and walnut hazelnut butter. Sampler packs are available.

Free illustrated brochure
Mail orders, gift orders
MC, VISA

Vacuum-packed nuts—

Durey-Libby
P. O. Box 345
Carlstadt, NJ 07072

201-939-2775

Durey-Libby packs nuts in vacuum tins: almonds, cashews, and macadamia nuts come in 4-pound tins; walnuts and pecans come in 3-pound tins. California pistachios are packed in 5-pound triple-lined bags. Lightly salted mixed nuts are also available.

Free price list
Mail orders
MC, VISA

Fresh Oregon hazelnuts—

E & S Farms
10902 Old Sheridan Road
McMinnville, OR 97128

503-472-5320

This family-run farm in Oregon's Willamette Valley ships fresh shelled whole hazelnuts in 1-, 2½-, and 5-pound packs. For cooking and baking, their mixture of whole and broken nuts is a good buy. Lelah Selby of E & S Farms provided the recipe for rich and

creamy Willamette Hazelnut Cheesecake. To get the fullest flavor, it's a good idea to follow her instructions for roasting hazelnuts whenever a recipe calls for them.

Free brochure
Mail orders, gift orders
No credit cards

Bulk quantities of many nuts—

Fiesta Nut Corporation
P. O. Box 366
75 Harbor Road
Port Washington, NY 11050

800-645-3296
516-883-1403

In addition to gift items, Fiesta Nut ships almonds, Brazil nuts, cashews, hazelnuts, macadamias, pistachios, pecans, walnuts, and pine nuts; also sunflower and pumpkin seeds. Most are available in 2- or 3-pound quantities, with walnuts, almonds, hazelnuts, and pecans also available in 25-pound quantities. Gifts include mixed nuts, dried fruit, cakes, and confections.

Free color catalog
Phone and mail orders, gift orders
AMEX, CB, DC, MC, VISA

Pecans, some just right for cooks—

Fran's Pecans
110-140 Hicks Street
P. O. Box 188
Harlem, GA 30814

800-476-6887
404-556-9172

Fran's packs its pecans in 1-pound bags of mammoth halves, extra-large pieces, roasted and salted halves, and pralines

Willamette Hazelnut Cheesecake

from Lelah J. Selby, E & S Farms

Crust:
 1 cup coarsely ground roasted hazelnuts (see Hazelnut Hints following)

Filling:
 2 pounds cream cheese at room temperature
¾ cup sugar
 6 eggs
½ cup Frangelico (hazelnut liqueur)

Topping:
 1 cup semi-sweet chocolate chips
 2 tablespoons corn syrup
¾ cup sour cream
 2 tablespoons Kahlúa (optional)
 1 cup hazelnuts, roasted and chopped, for garnish

Generously butter an 8-inch springform pan. Sprinkle ground hazelnuts over bottom of pan. In bowl beat cream cheese and sugar; add eggs one at a time, beating well after each. Stir in liqueur. Pour mixture into nut-lined pan. Bake at 350 degrees for 55 minutes. Remove from oven and let cool. Melt chocolate chips and corn syrup in a double boiler over hot water. Add sour cream gradually, beating by hand until smooth. Stir in Kahlúa, if you wish. Pour over cooled cake. Garnish with 1 cup chopped roasted hazelnuts. Chill overnight. Serves 10 to 12.

Hazelnut Hints

Roasting: Always roast hazelnuts for full flavor. Spread nuts on a cookie sheet in one layer. Roast at 350 degrees for 10 to 15 minutes. To remove skins, rub nuts vigorously between two coarse towels. Any skin remaining will not affect texture or taste of nuts.

Storage: Shelled nuts may be stored for 2 to 3 months at room temperature. For longer periods, they should be refrigerated. Nuts may be frozen for up to 2 years.

and lets you mix and match selections. Cooks will be interested in 5-pound quantities of seedling halves and economical cooking pecans. You can also request salt-free roasted pecans for snacking and gifts.

Free color brochure
Phone and mail orders, gift orders
MC, VISA

Plain and flavored nuts in various quantities—

Golden Valley Nut Company
170 Rucker Avenue
Gilroy, CA 95020

408-842-4893

Golden Valley Nut Company ships pistachios (natural or with garlic or jalapeño flavor), almonds (plain or flavored with hickory or salsa ranchera), cashews, macadamias, walnuts, and pecans. There is also a bulk price for these products packed in 25-pound boxes. In addition, the company sells dried apricots, prunes, and mixed fruit.

Free price list
Mail orders
No credit cards

Almond products and pistachios—

Gourmet Nut Center
1430 Railroad Avenue
Orland, CA 95963

916-865-5511

Whole and sliced natural, or blanched whole, slivered, and sliced almonds come packed in 3- or 4-pound tins. Almond oil and butter are available, and a kitchen pack gives you a selection of almonds, including almond meal for

garnishing. Pistachios and combination or gift packs are also offered.

Free color catalog
Mail orders, gift orders
MC, VISA

Hazelnuts and walnuts—

Hazy Grove Nuts
P. O. Box 25753
Portland, OR 97225

503-244-0593

In-shell hazelnuts and raw or toasted hazelnut kernels are shipped from this Oregon nut farm. Walnuts are also available. The nuts come in 2-pound quantities with discounts for orders of 2 or 3 bags. Gift boxes are also available, and recipes are included.

Free price list
Mail orders, gift orders
MC, VISA

From Oregon's Willamette Valley—

Henry's Farm
1216 East Henry Road
Newburg, OR 97132-9134

503-538-5244

This farm is run by the grandchildren of Henry Wilhoit, who first began planting the hazelnut orchards in 1939. In addition to ready-to-roast hazelnut kernels for your favorite recipes or for snacking, Henry's Farm sells hazelnut butter, vacuum-packed roasted hazelnuts, and honey-roasted hazelnuts. With your order Henry's Farm will send some of the recipes they have developed, including Hazelnut Mushroom Sauce, Chocolate and Filbert Butter Pie, and Oriental Main Dish Salad.

Free price list
Mail orders
No credit cards

Peanuts from Virginia—

Hubbard Peanut Company
P. O. Box 94
Sedley, VA 23878

804-562-4081

You can order Hubbard home-cooked peanuts in 20-, 32-, or 48-ounce cans (specify salted or unsalted). You may also order 5-pound quantities of raw peanuts most of the year, although they are not available from June 1 to October 1. Various club plans are available to ensure that you'll always have a fresh supply of peanuts on hand.

Free price list
Mail orders, gift orders
No credit cards

Organic nuts and seeds—

Jaffe Bros. Inc
P. O. Box 636
Valley Center, CA 92082

619-749-1133
Fax: 619-749-1282

You can order raw, unbleached, shelled, or in-shell nuts from Jaffe in 5- or 25-pound quantities, ideal for splitting with fellow cooks for holiday baking. Choose almonds, Brazil nuts, peanuts, cashews, pecan halves, walnuts, macadamias, hazelnuts, pine nuts, or a nut sampler featuring 1 pound of almonds, hazelnuts, cashews, and pecans. Seeds, also available in 5- and 25-pound quantities, include sunflower (hulled or in shell), sesame (hulled or unhulled), flax, pumpkin, fenugreek, and chia. Sprouting seeds include alfalfa, red radish, and red clover. Nut butters, made without

Interesting Facts About Hazelnuts
from Henry's Farm

The European filbert (a French name; the English use the word hazelnut) was first introduced to the Willamette Valley in the late nineteenth century and commercial production began in earnest in the 1920s.

Today, over 98 percent of the hazelnuts grown commercially in the United States come from Oregon's Willamette Valley, where close proximity to warm Pacific air provides a mild winter and summer that closely resemble climatic conditions in the main hazelnut-producing regions of the world: Spain, Italy, and the world's largest producer, Turkey.

Hazelnuts are a tasty and nutritious food, providing an excellent and cholesterol-free source of protein, calcium, and potassium. Raw, dry kernels are great to eat as a snack and when roasted become a wonderful addition to many recipes. When ground into butter, hazelnuts can be spread on many foods for a quick nutritious meal or be added to your favorite recipes.

additives or preservatives, include peanut, almond, sesame tahini, cashew, and macadamia.

Free catalog
Phone, fax, and mail orders, gift orders
MC, VISA

Seasonally available Georgia pecans—

Koinonia Partners, Inc.
Route 2
Americus, GA 31709-9986

Contact by mail

Koinonia Partners pack pecans in the shell, shelled pecan halves and pieces, and raw peanuts. They also ship pecan and peanut confections, granola, and cakes. Foods are shipped from mid-September to May 1. The mail order business supports the efforts of the Koinonia Partners in various ministries that include building low-cost homes for area residents.

Free color catalog
Mail order, gift orders
No credit cards

Shelled and in-shell almonds and walnuts—

Mariani Nut Company
P. O. Box 808
709 Dutton Street
Winters, CA 95694

916-795-3311

Choose either in-shell or freshly shelled walnuts and almonds in 5- and 25-pound quantities.

Free price list
Mail orders
No credit cards

Pecans year round, and seasonal Vidalia sweet onions—

Mascot Pecan Company
P. O. Box 765
Glennville, GA 30427

800-841-3985
912-654-2195

You can order cellophane bags of fancy pecans in halves and pieces, extra-large halves, mammoth halves, extra-large pieces, and roasted and salted mammoth halves. Choose 1-pound or 13-ounce bags, which come with a collection of recipes that includes no-crust pecan pie, pralines, and tropical banana-pecan salad. Vidalia sweet onions are also available in May and June.

Free price list
Mail orders
No credit cards

A variety of nuts—

Missouri Dandy Pantry
212 Hammons Drive East
Stockton, MO 65785

800-872-6879
800-872-6880 (in MO)

Black walnuts, pecans, cashews, almonds, pistachios, macadamia nuts, and sunflower kernels—this company sells them all. They have put together two selections especially for cooking, and offer 5-pound home boxes of all varieties. Also numerous nut candy confections and gifts.

Free color catalog
Phone and mail orders, gift orders
AMEX, MC, VISA

Peanuts, peanut butter, and oil—

Nuts D'Vine
185 Peanut Drive
P. O. Box 589
Edenton, NC 27932

800-334-0492
919-482-2222

Nuts D'Vine has the cook in mind with a sampler that includes cold-pressed peanut oil, water-blanched peanuts, and a recipe booklet. You can buy these items separately (the blanched peanuts come in 12-ounce bags and 25-pound boxes), as well as recipe-ready peanut pieces, peanut butter, raw and roasted peanuts, hot Thai peanut sauce, peanut butter fudge sauce, and numerous other products for peanut enthusiasts.

Free color catalog
Phone and mail orders, gift orders
AMEX, MC, VISA

Seven ways to enjoy chestnuts—

Paprikas Weiss
1546 Second Avenue
New York, NY 10028

212-288-6117

Paprikas Weiss imports dried chestnuts, tins of whole chestnuts, a chestnut puree, and chestnut flour. Sweet treats include chestnuts in vanilla syrup, a crème de marrons (chestnuts with vanilla and sugar), and marrons glacés (candied chestnuts). Their list of other nuts includes almonds, Brazil nuts, hazelnuts, macadamia nuts, pecans, pignolias, pistachios, and walnuts.

Seasonal catalogs, $3.00 annual subscription

Phone and mail orders, gift orders, and gift certificates
AMEX, MC, VISA

Pecans and pecan specialties—

Priester's Pecans
Fort Deposit, AL 36032

800-633-5725
800-231-1084 (in AL)

This company produces numerous pecan specialties and baked goods but also remembers cooks with their tubs of natural pecans in plain packaging. Order 1¼-, 2¼- or 4¼-pound tubs; cases of these tubs are also available for additional savings.

Free color catalog
Phone and mail orders, gift orders
AMEX, CB, DC, MC, VISA

Chestnut products—

G. B. Ratto & Company
821 Washington Street
Oakland, CA 94607

800-325-3483
800-228-3515 (in CA)
Fax: 415-836-2250

G. B. Ratto stocks dried chestnuts from Italy that can be reconstituted overnight; Ratto recommends them for stuffing fowl. There's also chestnut spread and puree. Pine nuts are available in 4-ounce or 1-pound bags; also, pistachios and hazelnuts. Almond paste from Denmark is also available.

Free catalog
Phone, fax, and mail orders, gift orders, and gift certificates
MC, VISA

Fresh pecans and a cook's combo—

Road Runner Pecans
1985 Salopek Road
Las Cruces, NM 88005

505-526-5949

Fancy pecan halves and large pieces are available from this New Mexico farm in 1-, 2½-, and 5-pound quantities. The cook's combo combines 2½ pounds of halves with 2½ pounds of large pieces.

Free color brochure
Phone and mail orders, gift orders
MC, VISA

Seasonally available fresh pecans—

Sternberg Pecan Company
P. O. Box 193
Jackson, MS 39205

601-366-6310

The Sternberg Pecan Company has sold just one product—mammoth shelled pecan halves—since it was established in 1938. Since Sternberg's owner, James Hand, is committed to selling fresh-shelled pecans, you can order only between November 1, when the new crop comes in, and March. Four quantities are available from 1 pound, 10 ounces through 10 pounds.

Free price list
Mail orders, gift orders
No credit cards

Pecans and more—

Sunnyland Farms
Willson Road at Pecan City
P. O. Box 8200
Albany, GA 31706-8200

912-883-3085
Fax: 912-888-8332

Pecans are the main crop of this Georgia company, which has been shipping nuts for more than forty years. Home boxes of pecans come in 3-, 5-, 10-, and 25-pound sizes and there are several pages in the Sunnyland catalog devoted to other nuts for cooking—almonds, walnuts, pecans, Brazil nuts, cashews, peanuts, macadamia nuts, and hazelnuts. Also pecan meal, dried fruit, gift items, and regional specialties such as mayhaw jelly. (A mayhaw is a small crabapple-like fruit that grows wild in the Georgia wetlands.)

Free color catalog
Phone, fax, and mail orders, gift orders
MC, VISA

Almonds, almond butter, and gifts—

Theodore's California Almonds
23073 Frederick Road
Ripon, CA 95366

800-525-6663
800-237-8688 (in CA)

The sixth generation of the Nocolaysen family runs this business, which was begun during the San Francisco gold rush. Cooks will be interested in the 10-pound boxes of whole natural almonds. Hickory-roasted and salted or salt-free roasted almonds are also available in quantity. Almond butter comes in both creamy and crunchy. There are also numerous gift boxes.

Free color catalog
Phone and mail orders, gift orders
AMEX, MC, VISA

Natural and blanched almonds—

Treehouse Farms, Inc.
P. O. Box 168
Earlimart, CA 93219

805-849-2606

Order whole natural almonds in quantities of 2½ to 5½ pounds, or choose sliced, diced, or slivered blanched almonds in 2½-pound bags.

Free price list
Mail and phone orders, gift orders
MC, VISA

Organic nuts and seeds—

Walnut Acres
Penns Creek, PA 17862

800-433-3998
Fax: 717-837-1146

Choose from Walnut Acres' selection of walnuts, pecans, Brazil nuts, almonds, cashews, peanuts, hazelnuts, and pignolias. Seed varieties include sunflower, pumpkin, sesame, flax, and psyllium. Walnut Acres' nut butters include peanut butter, almond butter, and sesame tahini, as well as some unusual peanut spreads—banana

peanut, date peanut, peanut honey, and peanut honey sesame. You will also find sprouting seeds and trail mixes in this complete catalog of organic foods.

Free color catalog
Phone, fax, and mail orders
MC, VISA

Oregon hazelnuts—

Westnut
P. O. Box 125
Dundee, OR 97115

503-538-8211

Natural Oregon shelled hazelnuts are shipped in 1-, 2½-, and 5-pound boxes. Chocolate-covered hazelnuts are available in gift boxes. For $2.00 you can order "An Oregon Hazelnut Primer" with 32 recipes for cookies, candies, desserts, breads, and more.

Tips on Storing Shelled Pecans

from Young Pecan Sales Corp.

Shelled pecans need to be properly stored to assure maximum freshness and flavor for cooking and snacking. Generally, pecans may be stored at room temperature for weeks, in the refrigerator for months, and in the freezer for years.

Refrigerator storage: Shelled pecans tend to absorb foreign flavors, so pack them in tightly closed glass, metal, or plastic containers when storing them in the refrigerator for long periods.

Freezer storage: Your home freezer is ideal for storing pecans. Just place closed cellophane bags of pecans in the freezer until ready for use. You will find that the pecans do not stick together when frozen and are ready for instant use. Pecans may be refrozen repeatedly without harm.

Free illustrated brochure
Phone and mail orders, gift orders
MC, VISA

Fresh pecans shipped in tubs—

Joe C. Williams
P. O. Box 640
Camden, AL 36726

205-682-4559

These Alabama pecans are available from November 1 through August 31 and are delivered in 2-pound, 13-ounce plastic tubs. Choose pecan halves or large pieces. Discounts on orders for more than four tubs.

Free illustrated brochure
Mail orders, gift orders
No credit cards

Pecans from South Carolina—

Young Pecan Sales Corporation
P. O. Drawer 5779
Florence, SC 29502

800-845-4366
803-662-2452

Fresh mammoth pecan halves and pieces in 1-pound bags or 34-ounce tubs, with discounts for orders of more than 8 pounds. Roasted, salted, and chocolate-dipped pecans and cashews are also available.

Free color brochure
Phone and mail orders, gift orders
AMEX, MC, VISA

CHAPTER 18

OILS AND VINEGARS

Here are the essentials (and a recipe) for a fine vinaigrette. But don't stop with the classic red wine vinegar-olive oil combination. Try some of the fragrant fruit and herb vinegars in this chapter and experiment with some unusual oils—pure nut oils such as walnut and pecan, as well as olive oils flavored with garlic or hot red chilies.

Also, enjoy an expert's explanation of just exactly what "extra-virgin" means and how balsamic vinegar acquires its very special and robust flavor.

Fruit vinegars—

American Spoon Foods, Inc.
P. O. Box 566
1668 Clarion Avenue
Petoskey, MI 49770-0566

800-222-5886
616-347-9030
Fax: 616-347-2512

American Spoon Foods make two popular fruit vinegars—red raspberry and black raspberry—by steeping berries in white wine vinegar and adding a touch of wildflower honey.

Free seasonal catalogs
Phone, fax, and mail orders, gift orders
DISC, MC, VISA

Fruit and herb vinegars—

Bear Meadow Farm
Route 2
Moore Road
Florida, MA 01247

413-663-9241

Hilary and George Garivaltis's product list includes a wonderful variety of herb vinegars, including basil, dill, garlic-herb, and combinations such as savory, marjoram, chives, and thyme. Fruit vinegars include cranberry, blueberry, and raspberry. Some very special herb jellies are also made at Bear Meadow Farm.

Free price list
Mail orders
No credit cards

Imported oils and vinegars—

The Chef's Pantry
P. O. Box 3
Post Mills, VT 05058

800-666-9940
802-333-4141

From the selection of French Vilux vinegars, choose cider and honey, garlic, herbes de Provence, raspberry, red wine, or white vinegar. Or select from other imported vinegars: champagne vinegar from France, balsamic vinegar from Italy, or aged sherry vinegar from Spain. Quite a few of these are available in restaurant-size 5-liter jugs. Several Italian extra-virgin olive oils are offered in sizes ranging from 1 to 5 liters. French walnut, hazelnut, and almond oils are also available.

Free illustrated catalog
Phone and mail orders, gift orders
MC, VISA

Vinegars from a Martha's Vineyard winery—

Chicama Vineyards
Stoney Hill Road
West Tisbury, MA 02575

508-693-0309

Chicama Vineyards, situated on Martha's Vineyard, grow a variety of grapes: Chardonnay, Chenin Blanc, Riesling, and Pinot Noir, among others. From their wines the Vineyards produce oak-aged vinegars that include a red and a white wine vinegar, over a dozen herb wine vinegars (including shallot, opal basil, and ginger and lemon) and four fruit wine vinegars (cranberry, blueberry, raspberry, and spicy orange). Oils include extra-virgin olive oil, Cajun, Moroccan, or Thai. Salad dressings, mustards, jams, and dessert sauces are also available. Sampler packages are offered. You may tour this island winery from May through October.

Free price list
Mail orders
MC, VISA

A variety of imported products—

Dean & DeLuca, Inc.
Mail Order Department
560 Broadway
New York, NY 10012

800-221-7714
212-431-1691

Dean & DeLuca have selected cold-pressed extra-virgin olive oils from Tuscany, Umbria, and Provence. Soleillou herbed grapeseed oils are available for salads and meats; French nut oils include almond and walnut. There are also balsamic, red and white wine vinegars, herb and fruit vinegars, as well as a basic barley malt vinegar from England.

Illustrated catalog, $2.00
Phone and mail orders, gift orders, and gift certificates
AMEX, MC, VISA

Hard-to-find oils—

Gourmet Treasure Hunters
10044 Adams Avenue, Suite 305
Huntington Beach, CA 92646

714-964-3355

The unusual oils stocked by Gourmet Treasure Hunters include pecan, avocado, walnut, garlic, palm, and Greek olive. For ethnic cuisines, try Spanish chili rojo oil (spiced with chili peppers), Cajun oil, Singapore curry oil, and mustard oil (for Indian dry curries). Vinegar varieties include balsamic, raspberry, blueberry, white wine with tarragon and shallots, and Fiesta (with cilantro and red chili pepper).

Notes on Oil and Vinegar

from Dean & DeLuca

About "extra-virgin" olive oil: This phrase refers to oils with a level of acidity below 1 percent. Low acidity—when naturally achieved—makes for a peppery, highly fruity olive oil. High acidity destroys the flavor of the oil. While the first cold pressing of top-quality olives will yield the desired level of acidity, so, too, can chemical refining of inferior oil. Faced with hundreds of adulterated oils, it is best to rely on trusted names and producers whose standards and integrity you can count on.

About balsamic vinegar: Balsamic vinegar is made from the juice of the Trebbiano di Spagna grape, which is slowly reduced in copper cauldrons until concentrated, thick and sweet. After a year-long fermentation, aging in small wooden barrels for a minimum of nine years completes the process and gives vintage balsamic vinegar its distinctive character.

Illustrated catalog (with newsletter for a year), $4.00
Phone and mail orders
AMEX

Unrefined salad oils—

Jaffe Bros., Inc
P. O. Box 636
Valley Center, CA 92082

619-749-1133
Fax: 619-749-1282

Jaffe offers three cold-pressed unprocessed oils: sesame, olive, and safflower. The oils are packed in gallon tins (sesame and olive oil also available in 5-gallon tins), and you can order money-saving cases to split with friends.

Free catalog
Phone, fax, and mail orders, gift orders
MC, VISA

Italian oils and vinegars—

Manganaro Foods
488 Ninth Avenue
New York, NY 10018

800-472-5264
212-563-5331

This Italian grocery has been serving customers from the same spot on New York City's West Side for almost a hundred years, and the mail order side of the business supplies cooks across the country with fine ingredients for Italian cooking. Manganaro imports extra-virgin oils from Italy. The vinegars include red and white wine vinegars; a Chianti wine vinegar; balsamic vinegar; and raspberry vinegar from France (that Manganaro assures you is delightful, "even if it's not Italian!"). They will also try to find other special oils at your request.

Free color catalog
Phone and mail orders, gift orders
AMEX, DC, MC, VISA

Several American oils and California
vinegars—

Market Square Food Company, Inc.
1642 Richfield Avenue
Highland Park, IL 60035

800-232-2299 (orders)
312-831-2228
Fax: 312-831-3533

Market Square Food Company
recommends its peanut oil from
Virginia for stir frying, and suggests
you try its light sunflower oil from
North Dakota for salads and baking.
The California olive oil is extra-virgin
and cold pressed to achieve a light,
fruity flavor that will enhance many
foods. The vinegars, oak-barrel aged,
are made from California wines: red
from Cabernet, white from
Chardonnay. You can also order
Cowboy Marinade barbecue sauce.

Free price list
Phone, fax, and mail orders, gift orders
MC, VISA

Oils and vinegars from around the
world—

G. B. Ratto & Company
821 Washington Street
Oakland, CA 94607

800-325-3483
800-228-3515 (in CA)
Fax: 415-836-2250

G. B. Ratto has searched the world to
bring you top-quality extra-virgin olive
oils from France, Italy, Greece, Spain,
and Portugal. Ratto's own brand is
cold-pressed from freshly picked
California olives. Ratto also stocks some
uncommon oils: avocado, walnut,
grapeseed, hazelnut, sesame, and chili.
The vinegar selection is equally good
and includes Ratto's own brand of red
and white wine vinegars as well as
balsamic vinegar, French and Spanish
wine vinegars, sherry wine vinegar,

Sauce Moutarde du Dauphin
(French Vinaigrette with Mustard)
from G. B. Ratto

1 to 2 heaping tablespoons Maille Dijon mustard
3 tablespoons Sasso olive oil
3 teaspoons Ratto's red wine vinegar
Salt and pepper to taste

Combine ingredients to make the base dressing. To this you can add either
minced garlic, herbes de Provence, tapenade, Italian herbs, San Francisco seasoning, or your own favorite combination. For a stronger olive oil flavor, add 1
teaspoon Ratto's olive oil.

and pear, raspberry, champagne, and rice vinegars.

Free illustrated catalog
Phone, fax, and mail orders, gift orders, and gift certificates
MC, VISA

Hard-to-find oils and vinegars—

S. E. Rykoff & Company
P. O. Box 21467
Market Street Station
Los Angeles, CA 90021

800-421-9873 (orders)
213-624-6094 (product inquiries)

Rykoff has assembled a fine selection of oils and vinegars. Italian and California extra-virgin olive oils are offered, as well as Spanish olive oil. Nut oils include sesame, walnut, hazelnut, and almond. There are hard-to-find oils such as grapeseed, pineseed, and rare and expensive truffle oil. The vinegars offered are red wine and sherry wine vinegar, fruit and herb vinegars, balsamic vinegar, champagne vinegars (one with mango), and seasoned and unseasoned rice vinegar.

Color catalog, $1.00
Phone and mail orders, gift orders
AMEX, MC, VISA

Specialty oils and vinegars—

Santa Barbara Olive Company
1661 Mission Drive
Solvang, CA 93463-2631

800-624-4896
800-521-0475 (in CA)

In addition to extra-virgin olive oil, Santa Barbara Olive Company supplies sesame seed oil, grapeseed oil, and garlic oil. Vinegars include garlic and pepper, green peppercorn, and several herb vinegars. Among the fruit vinegars, there are some unusual flavors—lemon, mango, and black currant. Sampler packs allow you to try different varieties. This company may also have the longest list of olives you've ever seen—find details in Chapter 6, "Condiments and Savory Sauces."

Free price list
Phone and mail orders
AMEX, MC, VISA

California extra-virgin olive oil—

Nick Sciabica & Sons
P. O. Box 1246
1525 Encina Avenue
Modesto, CA 95353

209-577-5067

This California company has been producing olive oil for more than fifty years and each batch is still personally tasted by Gemma Sciabica. The oil is cold pressed from early fall until late winter. Fall-harvested olives produce a green, tangy, fresh-flavored oil (best for cooking); black olives harvested in the late winter and early spring yield a golden sweet, mellow oil (great for baking and salads). You can order sampler packs of the six oils produced by the Sciabica family. Try Gemma Sciabica's delicious and simple recipe for pasta with garlic and oil, which cooks a generous amount of fresh Italian parsley along with the pasta.

Free color catalog
Mail orders
No credit cards

Pasta Aglio e Olio

(Pasta with Garlic and Oil)

from Gemma Sciabica of Nick Sciabica & Sons

8 ounces linguine, thin spaghetti, or twists
1 to 1½ cups fresh chopped Italian parsley
4 tablespoons Sciabica extra-virgin olive oil
5 or 6 cloves of garlic, minced
Pinch of cayenne pepper
Salt and white pepper to taste
½ cup Romano cheese, grated

Cook pasta according to directions on package with parsley in water. In a small skillet, place oil, garlic, and cayenne and cook a few seconds. Do not burn garlic or it will become bitter. Drain pasta/parsley and place in serving plate. Add oil and garlic mixture, salt and pepper, and toss gently. Sprinkle with cheese. Serves 4.
Serving variation: sprinkle with ¼ cup ground walnuts.

Selections of oils and vinegars—

Select Origins, Inc.
Box N
Southampton, NY 11968

800-822-2092
516-924-5447
Fax: 516-924-5892

Tom and Kristi Siplon have put together what they call "The Vinegar Arsenal"—a trio of vinegars to use as flavoring tools. It includes balsamic vinegar, Spanish sherry vinegar, French red wine vinegar, and recipes; you may order these separately, or save when you order the trio. Imported and domestic extra-virgin olive oils are available. Select Origins blends three oils especially for salads, sautéing, and marinating and grilling; order them individually or in sampler packs.

Free illustrated catalog
Phone, fax, and mail orders, gift orders
AMEX, MC, VISA

Try this suggestion for champagne vinegar—

Seyco Fine Foods, Inc.
25574 Rye Canyon Road, #E
Valencia, CA 91355-1109

800-423-2942

Seyco features Italian extra-virgin olive oil, as well as Spanish apricot oil and French walnut oil. Vinegars include balsamic and French champagne. Here's a serving suggestion for the latter: sauté some mushrooms, add heavy cream, and pour a few drops of champagne vinegar over top.

Color catalog, $2.00; 10 percent off first order
Phone and mail orders, gift orders
AMEX, DC, MC, VISA

Fruit vinegars, walnut oil, and dressings—

The Silver Palate
274 Columbus Avenue
New York, NY 10023

212-799-6340

The Silver Palate cookbooks helped popularize fruit vinegars, and their raspberry and blueberry vinegars can be ordered by mail, as can their walnut oil. Their prepared salad dressings include Balsamic Country, Julee's Caesar, Raspberry Sun, Pesto Garden, and Sweet and Rough.

Free price list
Phone and mail orders
AMEX, MC, VISA

Organic oils and vinegars—

Walnut Acres
Penns Creek, PA 17862

800-433-3998
Fax: 717-837-1146

Among the Walnut Acres selection of organic foods you'll find rice vinegar flavored with basil and garlic, French tarragon, or raspberries; also, old-fashioned apple cider vinegar. Vegetable oils include safflower, extra-virgin olive, canola, virgin peanut, corn germ, and sesame. Walnut Acres also supply mayonnaise and a selection of preservative-free salad dressings.

Free color catalog
Phone, fax, and mail orders
MC, VISA

Check Chapter 25, "The International Pantry," for additional oils and vinegars.

Some of the suppliers in Chapter 12, "Herbs and Spices," also make herb vinegars— peruse that chapter, too, to see what they offer.

CHAPTER 19

PASTA AND NOODLES

Even if you think you've seen a pretty good variety of pasta on the shelves of your best-stocked local market, these sources will introduce you to a new world of variety and flavor! You'll find everything from the finest traditional imported Italian pastas to inventive new flavors created by American companies. Try them—lemon pasta or walnut pasta might bring a new dimension to your favorite summertime pasta salad!

Throughout this chapter you'll discover the pastas and noodles that are often difficult to find locally, including spaetzle and Greek orzo; there are also nutritious whole wheat pastas and, for special diets, pastas that are completely free of wheat.

Traditional imported Italian pastas—

Dean & DeLuca, Inc.
Mail Order Department
560 Broadway
New York, NY 10012

800-221-7714
212-431-1691

To introduce its pasta selection, Dean & DeLuca describe the two basic varieties of Italian pasta: the water and flour pasta of Naples and the egg pasta of Emilia Romagna. Both are stocked, the former from the only Italian company still making this pasta the traditional way, extruding it through bronze tubes and hand-hanging it to dry. Also available: spaetzle, orzo (Greek rice-shaped pasta), and pizzocheri (a speckled buckwheat noodle).

Illustrated catalog, $2.00
Phone and mail orders, gift orders, and gift certificates
AMEX, MC, VISA

Organic whole wheat pasta—

Jaffe Bros., Inc
P. O. Box 636
Valley Center, CA 92082

619-749-1133
Fax: 619-749-1282

Jaffe's organic whole wheat pasta is made with hard spring wheat. Choose from nine kinds, including all the popular varieties plus veggie elbows (tomato, spinach, celery), artichoke spaghetti, and spinach noodles. Nonwheat corn elbows are also available. Order them in 5-pound or pantry-stocking 20-pound quantities.

Free catalog
Phone, fax, and mail orders, gift orders
MC, VISA

Pasta exclusively from Italy's Abruzzi region—

Manganaro Foods
488 Ninth Avenue
New York, NY 10018

800-472-5264
212-563-5331

This landmark Italian grocery on New York City's West Side takes special pride in its collection of pastas—all made in Italy's Abruzzi region from 100 percent durum wheat semolina. Manganaro's most requested varieties include spaghetti, linguini, ziti, rigatoni, fusilli, and lasagne, but if you have something more exotic in mind, chances are they have it, and they will be pleased to send it to you.

Free color catalog
Phone and mail orders, gift orders
AMEX, DC, MC, VISA

Over 200 varieties (and counting)—

Morisi's Pasta
647 Fifth Avenue
Brooklyn, NY 11215

718-499-0146

Perusing this list lets you know that the Morisis are an imaginative family—their pasta company makes over 200 varieties of pasta, and they haven't run out of ideas yet! Here are just a few highlights from the various categories: vegetable (asparagus, beet, sweet red pepper); spice (saffron, tarragon, triple hot chili pepper); fruit (black fig, lemon, apricot); nut (hazelnut, pecan, walnut); fish (calamari, lobster); cheese (Cheddar, Roquefort, goat cheese/walnut); special blends (red wine, black olive, Cajun). There are also mixed flavors (equally fascinating), and, if you wish, pasta from egg and original formulas. Their shapes include the traditional favorites and some whose definition will challenge the most devoted pasta lover —bumbola, ricciolini, spacarelli, quadrefiore. (You'll have to order Morisi's brochure to find out!)

Free color brochure
Phone and mail orders
No credit cards

Hungarian-style pasta—

Paprikas Weiss
1546 Second Avenue
New York, NY 10028

212-288-6117

The pasta stocked by Paprikas Weiss is made from semolina flour and egg yolk. Choose egg barley, large and small squares, shell noodles, spaetzle, various-size noodles and bow ties, and angel hair.

Seasonal catalogs, $3.00 annual subscription
Phone and mail orders, gift orders, and gift certificates
AMEX, MC, VISA

Fresh pasta from the highest-quality ingredients—

Providence Cheese and Tavola Calda
407 Atwells Avenue
Providence, RI 02909

401-421-5653

Ginny Wheatley and her son carry on the tradition of making fine pastas, cheeses, and sauces that was begun by her father when he opened this shop more than twenty years ago. Providence Cheese and Tavola Calda uses only organically grown, stone-ground durum wheat flour, and fresh eggs, and milk to make their products. All fats, shortenings, preservatives, salt, sugar, and honey are eliminated. The pastas include linguine, fettucine, shells, and lasagne sheets. Depending on what's fresh that day, vegetables may be added to create pasta flavored with sweet red peppers, spinach, carrots, or tomato. For ravioli, tortellini, and tortelloni, the cheese is made daily from fresh cow and goat milk. Breads, focaccia, pizza, calzone, sauces, and desserts are all made fresh in the shop. There's a product list but since it changes from day to day, it's best to call to discuss what's available.

Free product list
Phone and mail orders
No credit cards

From the "pasta capital of the world"—

G. B. Ratto & Company
821 Washington Street
Oakland, CA 94607

800-325-3483
800-228-3515 (in CA)
Fax: 415-836-2250

G. B. Ratto imports more than 30 kinds of pasta from Delverde in Fara San Martino, which Ratto calls "the pasta capital of the world." The varieties are illustrated on the pasta page of their catalog, which is a great help in identifying the unusual ones. Most are available in 1-pound packages; some of the most popular types come in

5-pound boxes. A great product from Delverde is "instant lasagne"—pasta sheets that don't need to be parboiled. (You can also use them for cannelloni by dipping the sheets in water before rolling them.) Dried tortellini and whole wheat pastas are also available.

Free illustrated catalog
Phone, fax, and mail orders, gift orders, and gift certificates
MC, VISA

Authentic pasta . . . from southeastern Ohio—

Rossi Pasta
P. O. Box 759
Marietta, OH 45750

800-227-6774
Fax: 614-373-5310

Rossi Pasta, which stresses high-quality ingredients, raises its own garlic and uses free-range eggs from neighboring farmers and unbleached, enriched spring wheat to make its pasta. Highlights from the 25 flavors include basil black pepper, leek and onion, wild mushroom, and garlic, as well as 2 egg-free and a cholesterol-free variety. Sauces include House Red, Emilio Red (with enoki mushrooms, ginger, and leeks), and Gaitana Red (with black olives and artichoke hearts). John Rossi, who has written one of the wittiest catalogs around, believes that dinner without music is only food, so his catalog also includes cassette tapes (Frank Sinatra, Tony Bennett, and other legends). You can send a tape along with a pasta gift. Try Rossi linguine in the following recipe for Cold Sesame Noodles.

Free color catalog
Phone, fax, and mail orders, gift orders
AMEX, DISC, MC, VISA

Cold Sesame Noodles

from Ellen Morgenthaler of Rossi Pasta

⅓ cup vegetable oil
¼ cup tamari or soy sauce
2 tablespoons sesame oil
1 tablespoon fresh ginger, chopped
4 to 6 scallions (white and green parts), chopped
¼ to ½ teaspoon hot chili oil, *or* ¼ to ½ teaspoon hot pepper flakes
12 ounces Rossi linguine

Combine all the dressing ingredients in a large bowl while you're waiting for the water to boil. Cook the linguini, drain, and immediately run under cold water until thoroughly cooled—drain well and toss with dressing. Garnish with toasted sesame seeds and/or shredded red cabbage and/or thinly sliced radishes. Serves 4. *Variations*: Add lightly steamed broccoli or snow peas.

Flavored pasta, California style—

S. E. Rykoff & Company
P. O. Box 21467
Market Street Station
Los Angeles, CA 90021

800-421-9873 (orders)
213-624-6094 (product inquiries)

From northern California come these varieties of flavored fettucine—tomato basil, lemon pepper, and garlic basil. A sampler gives you a ½-pound package of each plus recipes. An Italian pasta sampler lets you try six different traditional varieties.

Color catalog, $1.00
Phone and mail orders, gift orders
AMEX, MC, VISA

Semolina and egg pasta from Italy—

Select Origins, Inc.
Box N
Southampton, NY 11968

800-822-2092
516-924-5447
Fax: 516-924-5892

Select Origins imports semolina and egg pastas from Italy. The semolina pasta, available in twin 1-pound packs, includes spaghetti, spirale, penne, and spirale verde (with spinach). Egg pasta, in twin 8.8-ounce packages, comes in capellini (angel's hair), tagliatelle (medium size), and tagliolini (slightly smaller than tagliatelle). Recipes are included.

Free illustrated catalog
Phone, fax, and mail orders, gift orders
AMEX, MC, VISA

Pasta from organically grown wheat and grains—

Walnut Acres
Penns Creek, PA 17862

800-433-3998
Fax: 717-837-1146

Walnut Acres is a good source for whole wheat pasta, available in rigatoni, spaghetti, elbow macaroni, egg noodles, and vegetable spirals. Unusual pastas include wheat-free corn pasta, quinoa pasta (from high-protein quinoa grain), and lupini pasta (from durum whole wheat triticale and sweet lupin flours). All are made from organically grown grain.

Free color catalog
Phone, fax, and mail orders
MC, VISA

CHAPTER 20

PRESERVES: JAMS, JELLIES, MARMALADES, COMPOTES, AND FRUIT BUTTERS

In addition to offering delectable treats for your morning muffin (how about pear conserve or tangerine marmalade for a change?), this chapter may suggest surprising new ingredients for baking and cooking. Some of these delicious conserves are perfect for making dessert crepes or for wrapping in squares of puff pastry for quick, melt-in-your-mouth turnovers. Try the jams to flavor plain yogurt or to top ice cream or your favorite cheesecake. The recipes will give you more ideas—you'll see how fruit butters and jellies can make a quick and elegant soup, add the finishing touch to a succulent braised pork loin, and produce a fast multipurpose glaze.

A taste of Alaska's wild berries—

Alaska Wild Berry Products
528 East Pioneer Avenue
Homer, AK 99603

907-235-8858

Since 1946, Alaska Wild Berry Products has been making use of Alaska's abundant variety of wild berries. Jellies are made from wild rose hips, lingonberries, raspberries, elderberries, and salmonberries. Rhubarb jam, cranberry-apple butter, low-bush cranberry sauce, and sourdough sauce (a sweet and sour apple cranberry blend) are also available. Wooden gift crates can be packed with additional Alaskan specialties, including sourdough starter, salmon, and smoked reindeer sausage. Their shop, with a small museum, is open year-round.

Free color catalog
Mail orders, gift orders
MC, VISA

Handmade preserves from Michigan—

American Spoon Foods, Inc.
P. O. Box 566
1668 Clarion Avenue
Petoskey, MI 49770-0566

800-222-5886
616-347-9030
Fax: 616-347-2512

American Spoon Foods' wild fruit preserves are made from berries picked in the wilds of northern Michigan and include blackberry and thimbleberry preserves and elderberry, grape, and chokecherry-apple jelly. Additional products include traditional favorites as well as blueberry-lime, damson plum, nectarine, and sour cherry preserves. Pumpkin butter, gooseberry marmalade, rhubarb marmalade, and pear conserve complete the list. Order these products individually, select a group of your favorites, or choose gifts packed in folk art boxes or birch-bark baskets.

Free seasonal catalogs
Phone, fax, and mail orders, gift orders
DISC, MC, VISA

Preserves and jellies from a
Massachusetts farm—

Bear Meadow Farm
Route 2
Moore Road
Florida, MA 01247

413-663-9241

Bear Meadow's owners, Hilary and George Garivaltis, make good old-fashioned fruit products including spiced wild blueberries, bramble preserves made with wild blackberries, and Shaker-style, sugar-free apple butter. They offer red and black raspberry jam, wild blueberry preserve, and cranberry-wine, grape, and apple jelly as well as fruit catsups, vinegars, and herbal jellies and vinegars.

Free price list
Mail orders
No credit cards

French preserves—

The Chef's Pantry
P. O. Box 3
Post Mills, VT 05058

800-666-9940
802-333-4141

The Chef's Pantry imports Brunet fruit purees, made without sugar, in several flavors—black currant, pear, strawberry, and passion fruit puree. Mary Spata and Murray Burk of The Chef's Pantry suggest you try them for making sorbets, ice cream, mousses, cakes, sauces, and beverages—or just enjoy them over ice cream. In addition, The Chef's Pantry imports Biassac preserves from France in a range of flavors, of which the apricot, black currant, raspberry, and strawberry can be ordered in 5-kilo tins.

Free illustrated catalog
Phone and mail orders, gift orders
MC, VISA

A selection of Vermont preserves—

Cherry Hill Cooperative Cannery, Inc.
MR 1, Barre-Montpelier Road
Barre, VT 05641

800-468-3020
802-479-2558

The preserves and fruit butters offered by Cherry Hill Cooperative Cannery are the products of small, independently owned companies in Vermont. Conserves include varieties such as apple-rum-walnut, blueberry bourbon, and banana-berry. Applesauces are available mixed with raspberries, peaches, strawberries, and other fruit; fruit-flavored and spiced apple butters are also available. The applesauces and butters are sweetened with maple syrup. The Cannery also sells condiments and maple syrup.

Free price list
Phone and mail orders
No credit cards

Fruit spreads sweetened with fruit concentrate—

Clearbrook Farms
5514 Fair Lane
Fairfax, OH 45227

800-888-3276
513-271-2053

Clearbrook Farms fruit spreads are made from pure fruit sweetened with fruit concentrate, making a highly flavored but low-calorie preserve (only 16 calories a teaspoon). Try Michigan Red Tart Cherry, Maine Wild Blueberry, Oregon Red Raspberry, and Michigan Strawberry. Clearbrook also makes other preserves, marmalades, and dessert sauces. Although they are available in specialty shops, you can order a selection of Clearbrook products directly from the company.

Free price list
Phone and mail orders
MC, VISA

Apple cider jelly and fruit preserves—

Cold Hollow Cider Mill
RFD 1
Route 100
Box 430
Waterbury Center, VT 05677-9704

800-3-APPLES
800-U-C-CIDER (in VT)

Apple cider jelly is the most requested product of Cold Hollow Cider Mill, both at the store and through its mail order business. Other apple products include cider syrup and concentrate, applesauce (plain or with cranberry, raspberry, strawberry, or maple), and apple juices. Also, wild elderberry, beach plum, and rose hip jellies, as well as blackberry, blueberry, gooseberry,

strawberry, and strawberry-rhubarb jams. The Mill also sells condiments, honey, and maple products.

Free color brochure
Phone and mail orders, gift orders
AMEX, MC, VISA

Unusual fruit butters—

Drake's Ducks
RD 2
Box 810
Keene, NH 03431

800-533-8257
603-357-5858

Marie and Chris Drake once raised ducks on their New Hampshire farm, but these days they keep busy making herb products and smooth fruit butters, which are sold in specialty shops. For mail order customers they will ship sampler packs that contain six products —three fruit butters, herb cheese, herb butter, and pesto. The fruit butters included are raspberry, blueberry, and cranberry-orange, ready to use as spreads and toppings or to incorporate into the recipes that Marie has created and includes with all orders. Try the following simple and delicious recipe for Creamed Cranberry-Orange Squash Soup.

Free price list
Mail orders
No credit cards

Old-fashioned and sun-cooked preserves—

Green Briar Jam Kitchen
6 Discovery Hill Road
East Sandwich, MA 02537

508-888-6870

Creamed Cranberry-Orange Squash Soup
from Marie Drake of Drake's Ducks

1 container Drake's Ducks Cranberry-Orange Butter
3 cups squash, mashed (butternut is a good, dry squash for this)
3 cups light cream or milk
2 cups chicken or veal stock
Salt and pepper to taste
Nutmeg as garnish

Whisk together all ingredients in heavy saucepan. Heat until hot, but be careful not to boil. Serves 6.

The Green Briar Jam Kitchen has been on Cape Cod since 1902, and today it is operated by the nonprofit Thornton W. Burgess Society. You can visit the restored kitchen and buy jams in the gift shop or order them by mail. Old-fashioned favorites include plum, raspberry, and strawberry jams; apple, crab apple, mint, quince, and cinnamon jellies. Sun-cooked preserves include plums with rum and blueberries with kirsch. Cape Cod cranberry products range from sauce and conserve to chutney and marmalade with orange and pineapple. Thornton Burgess, the well-known naturalist and author for whom the society is named, had this to say: "It is a wonderful thing to sweeten the world which is in a jam and needs preserving."

Free color catalog
Mail orders, gift orders
MC, VISA

From Pennsylvania Dutch country—

Kitchen Kettle Village
Box 380
Intercourse, PA 17534

800-732-3538
717-768-8261

Kitchen Kettle Village, situated in the heart of Pennsylvania Dutch country, started as a farm kitchen where neighbors stopped to buy the Burnley family's jams and relishes. Today it's a community of shops where you can still see jams being made in copper pots. Order from the dozens of jams, jellies, and preserves that include such old-fashioned specialties as apple elderberry jelly, red beet jelly, tomato jam, pear blueberry spread, peach or pear butter, and spiced peaches. If you're near the Village in May, stop by for the annual Rhubarb Festival.

Free price list
Mail and phone orders, gift orders
MC, VISA

Montana wild fruit jellies and syrup—

Kountry Kitchen
406 South Strevell
Miles City, MT 59301

406-232-3818

Jellies from Kountry Kitchen are made from the wild fruit of Montana's Yellowstone Valley—buffalo berries, grapes, currants, plums, and chokecherries—in small batches without additives. Chokecherry syrup comes in bottles or pretty stoneware jugs. You can also order assorted selections of these wild berry products.

Free illustrated brochure
Mail orders
No credit cards

Preserves from Sonoma County—

Kozlowski Farms
5566 Gravenstein Highway
Forestville, CA 95436

707-887-1587

Kozlowski Farms products have been developed from the Kozlowski family's many years of home canning experience. They now offer more than forty products, including over a dozen old-fashioned jams (among them boysenberry, blackberry, and kiwi); conserves and fruit butters (apple, plum, and pear) without added sugar; orange and pink grapefruit marmalade; wine jellies; and fruit chutneys. Fruit vinegars and a barbecue sauce are also available.

Free color brochure
Mail orders, gift orders
MC, VISA

Preserves from a California restaurant—

La Casa Rosa
107 Third Street
San Juan Bautista, CA 95045

408-623-4563

La Casa Rosa, a California restaurant established in 1935, maintains a mail order business that supplies customers all over the country with favorites from the restaurant kitchen. Fruit specialties include Jubilee Cherries, spiced cranberries, apple butter, pomegranate jelly, marmalades (including lemon and tangerine), as well as preserves such as Kadota fig, peach, plum, wild blackberry, and more. Also chutneys and other condiments.

Free price list
Mail orders, gift orders
MC, VISA

Yankee Citrus Marmalade and fruit preserves—

The Lollipop Tree
Box 518
Rye, NH 03870

800-842-6691
603-436-8196

Laurie and Bob Lynch of The Lollipop Tree make their preserves in small batches, using all natural ingredients. Choose from these preserves: cranberry pineapple walnut, raspberry pecan, strawberry walnut, triple berry (raspberry, strawberry, and blueberry), or wild blueberry. Yankee Citrus Marmalade is a combination of lemon, lime, and orange that Laurie and Bob suggest as a glaze for vegetables, fowl, and pork. Additional products from The Lollipop Tree include baking mixes for beer breads, scones, and muffins; a range of condiments; and gift selections that combine these products.

Free color catalog
Phone and mail orders, gift orders
MC, VISA

From a Puget Sound island—

The Maury Island Farming Company
Rte 3, Box 238
Vashon, WA 98070

800-356-5880
206-463-5617

Maury Island Farm is located on Vashon Island in Puget Sound, west of Seattle. Started in 1976 by Pete and Judith Shepherd, the farm quickly became known for its red currant jelly produced from island-grown berries. Since then the jam, jelly, and marmalade line has expanded to over a dozen products that include traditional favorites as well as some unusual flavors: gooseberry, tayberry, and marionberry jams, and tangerine marmalade. Raspberry, boysenberry, and blackberry fruit toppings are also available.

Free illustrated brochure
Phone and mail orders, gift orders
AMEX, MC, VISA

Wine jellies—

Napa Valley Connection
P. O. Box 509
St. Helena, CA 94574

707-963-1616 (nationwide)
800-422-1111 (in CA only)

Napa Valley Connection makes jellies from Cain Cellars wines, both Cabernet Sauvignon and Sauvignon Blanc. Try spreading them on toast, muffins, or

croissants—or use them as a new ingredient for cooking. Napa Valley Connection will send with your order recipe cards for main dishes and desserts, including Cabernet Wine Jelly Ice Cream with Currants and Sauvignon Blanc Wine Jelly Bavarian Cream. Try the following recipe for Braised Pork Loin in Cabernet Wine Jelly.

Free price list
Phone and mail orders
MC, VISA

Conserves in tempting flavors—

Pan Handler Products
Percy Hill Road
RR 2, Box 399
Stowe, VT 05672

802-253-8683

Vermont Harvest conserves from Pan Handler Products are available in eight tempting flavors, including Strawberry Amaretto, Blueberry Bourbon, Brandied Peach, and Apple Rum Walnut. Jams include BananaBerry (strawberries, raspberries, and bananas) and Blackberry. You can also order pepper jellies and sampler packages of conserves.

Free illustrated brochure
Phone and mail orders, gift orders
MC, VISA

Hungarian specialties—

Paprikas Weiss
1546 Second Avenue
New York, NY 10028

212-288-6117

Paprikas Weiss imports prune levkar (a rich spread made from pitted prunes), apricot butter, and plum jam. You'll

Braised Pork Loin in Cabernet Wine Jelly

from Napa Valley Connection

1¾ pounds pork tenderloin
Salt and pepper to taste
   2 tablespoons vegetable oil
   4 tablespoons butter
   2 garlic cloves, chopped
   1 shallot, chopped
   1 tablespoon chopped fresh thyme
   1 red onion, finely diced
   1 tablespoon orange zest
   ½ cup Cain Cellars Cabernet Sauvignon wine
   1 cup beef broth
10-ounce jar Napa Valley Connection Cabernet Sauvignon Wine Jelly

Season pork tenderloin with salt and pepper and sear in hot oil; brown well. Place on a warm plate. Drain oil and to the pan add butter, garlic, shallot, thyme, onion, and orange zest. Cook for 4 minutes. Add wine and cook down by half. Then add beef broth and Napa Valley Connection Cabernet Sauvignon Wine Jelly. Place tenderloin back in pan. Cook at 425 degrees for 40 minutes, basting twice during cooking. Serves 4 to 5.

also find imported gooseberries (recommended for fruit soup or for a sauce with boiled beef) and pitted morello cherries ready for making a strudel. This company also makes more than two dozen of its own jams, jellies, and preserves, in flavors that include all the traditional favorites as well as Dutch apple, rose hip, and gooseberry jams, blackberry, quince, and mint jellies, and mincemeat.

Seasonal color catalogs, $3.00 annual subscription
Phone and mail orders, gift orders, and gift certificates
AMEX, MC, VISA

Fruit compotes from a Wisconsin restaurant—

The Postilion
615 Old Pioneer Road
Fond du Lac, Wisconsin 54935

414-922-4170

The Postilion School of Culinary Art has been teaching classic cooking techniques since 1951. It is run by Madame Liane Kuony, an energetic woman who also presides over the highly regarded Postilion Restaurant and still finds time to supply shops and individual customers with specialties of the house. These include fruit liqueur compotes—apple kirsch with kirschwasser, apricot prune with rum, cherry pineapple with cognac, pear ginger with Cointreau, and cranberry hickory nut with rum. Other items include chocolate sauce, mincemeat, yule log cakes, plum pudding, and hard sauce.

Free illustrated brochure
Phone and mail orders, gift orders
No credit cards

Preserves from around the world—

G. B. Ratto & Company
821 Washington Street
Oakland, CA 94607

800-325-3483
800-228-3515 (in CA)
Fax: 415-836-2250

At G. B. Ratto you'll find Poiret all-fruit spreads from Belgium in several tempting flavors and French preserves by Les Confituriers de Haute-Provence in your favorite flavors plus some unusual ones like greengage plum, fig, and black currant. Other specialties: quince and guava paste from Brazil, brandied cherries from California, rose petal or sour cherry spoon sweets from Greece, and ginger stems from Hong Kong or Taiwan. If you would like to make your own marmalade, order a can of prepared Seville bitter oranges to make six pounds of marmalade in just 30 minutes.

Free illustrated catalog
Phone, fax, and mail orders, gift orders, and gift certificates
MC, VISA

Fruit products from a Michigan hilltop—

Rocky Top Farms
Route 1, Essex Road
Ellsworth, MI 49729

616-599-2251

This northern Michigan company makes almost twenty varieties of preserves, toppings, fruit butters, as well as rhubarb chutney, orange marmalade, and Berry Blossom honey. Among the selection of preserves you'll find seedless black raspberry, tart cherry, blackberry, cherry berry, and more; toppings include Rum Cherry and Cherry Almondine; and fruit butters are made with peaches, cherries, and apricots. Gift selections are packed in white cedar boxes with Michigan motifs on the lids.

Free color brochure
Phone and mail orders, gift orders
MC, VISA

A Virginia jam and jelly factory—

Rowena's
758 West 22nd Street
Norfolk, VA 23517

800-627-8699
804-627-8699

This jam and jelly factory offers some unusual items—apricot ginger jam, cranberry nut conserve, lemon curd, pineapple curd, and carrot jam. (Suggestions for the carrot jam include mixing it with mustard to make a glaze for pork or chicken, enjoying it as an ice cream topping, or using it to make an easy carrot cake.) Rowena's also makes cooking sauces and puts together gift packs that include regional fare such as peanuts, hams, and other specialties.

Free color catalog
Phone and mail orders, gift orders
MC, VISA

From a California ranch—

Running Deer Ranch
P. O. Box 100
Paso Robles, CA 93447

800-ALL-PURE
805-239-1784

Growing up in the Black Forest region of Germany, Anneliese Baur Katz helped her mother and grandmother preserve food for the winter. Now, on a 70-acre ranch in California, she and her husband produce over thirty products, still using small-batch methods and the traditional high standards established early in her life. Running Deer Ranch makes preserves, marmalades, jellies, cordial preserves, and brandied fruits. A sampling of flavors includes fig and orange preserves, lemon marmalade, pomegranate jelly, brandied pears, and berry preserves with blackberry brandy. Condiments and baked goods are also made at the ranch.

Free price list
Phone and mail orders, gift orders
MC, VISA

From Sarabeth's Kitchen restaurants in New York—

Sarabeth's Kitchen
423 Amsterdam Avenue
New York, NY 10024

212-580-8335

In New York City, two Sarabeth's Kitchen restaurants feature fruit preserves that are also available by mail. Some products—Rosy Cheeks (strawberry-apple preserves), Plum Loco (plums, apples, and lemon), and Cranberry Relish—are available seasonally. Other preserves and butters, available year round, include Fruit Fantasy (peaches, raisins, almonds), Figgy (figs, pears, lemons, and spices), Lemon Pear Butter, Peach Apricot Preserves, and Chunky Apple Butter.

Free color brochure
Phone and mail orders, gift orders
AMEX, DC, MC, VISA

Sweet pickled fruits and spirited fruits—

Seyco Fine Foods, Inc.
25574 Rye Canyon Road, #E
Valencia, CA 91355-1109

800-423-2942

Seyco prepares what is perhaps the most complete line of sweet pickled fruits available—melons, peaches, watermelon rind, grapefruit peel, and a medley of fruits. A few highlights from the collection of specialty and spirited fruits are ginger or cinnamon pears, pickled kumquats, stuffed peaches in grenadine, stuffed prunes in sherry, apricots in rum, and peaches or cherries in brandy. Fruit toppings, preserves, jellies, and marmalade are also sold.

Color catalog, $2.00; 10 percent off first order
Phone and mail orders, gift orders
AMEX, DC, MC, VISA

Muscadine preserves, syrups, and juice—

Southern Specialty Foods Corporation
P. O. Box 2853
Meridian, MS 39302

800-233-1736
Fax: 601-483-1864

Paul Broadhead, founder of Southern Specialty Foods, oversees a 770-acre vineyard of native muscadine grapes in Mississippi. The harvest from this vineyard is made into an ever expanding line of products that includes jellies, jams, preserves, juice, and syrup. Other fruit preserves, honey, and Southern specialties are also featured.

Free color catalog
Phone, fax, and mail orders, gift orders
AMEX, DISC, MC, VISA

Organic preserves and canned fruit—

Walnut Acres
Penns Creek, PA 17862

800-433-3998
Fax: 717-837-1146

Walnut Acres' preserves, from organic, unsprayed fruit, are made with citrus pectin, alfalfa honey, and sometimes a little lemon juice. Choose blueberry, strawberry, wild elderberry, or black raspberry. Conserves, sweetened with fruit juice concentrates, are made from raspberries or a combination of strawberries and rhubarb. An apple spread called Apple Essence (the original Walnut Acres product) is also available. Canned fruits include peaches, whole cranberry sauce and applesauce, and there is a large selection of juices. For making your own fruit products at home, Walnut

Acres sells pectin, gelatin, and agar-agar.

Free color catalog
Phone, fax, and mail orders
MC, VISA

Wild huckleberry products—

Wilds of Idaho
1308 West Boone
Spokane, WA 99201

509-326-0197

The Wilds of Idaho pickers gather wild huckleberries in the mountains of northern Idaho each fall. These highly prized berries are used to make small batches of preservative-free jam, topping, syrup, and dessert filling.

Free price list
Mail orders, gift orders
MC, VISA

Cider jelly—

Wood's Cider Mill
RFD 2, Box 477
Springfield, VT 05156

802-263-5547

The Wood family has been making cider jelly and boiled cider since 1882. Cider jelly is concentrated over a wood fire from the juice of apples pressed on an original screw press. Each pound of cider jelly is made from the juice of about 30 to 50 apples. The Woods recommend using it with peanut butter for a delicious PB&J sandwich, on muffins, toast, or doughnuts, or as a condiment with meat dishes. (And try the following recipe for Cider Jelly Glaze.) You can also order cider syrup, maple syrup, and yarn from the fleece of the Woods' flock of sheep.

Free price list
Mail orders, gift orders
No credit cards

Cider Jelly Glaze

from Willis Wood of Wood's Cider Mill

  4 tablespoons butter
  ¼ cup Wood's Cider Jelly
  2 tablespoons brown sugar
  2 tablespoons brandy or Calvados
  2 tablespoons orange juice
  2 tablespoons cream (optional)

Melt butter and stir in jelly and sugar. Add the remaining ingredients and bring to a boil. Reduce heat and cook for 5 minutes. Cool slightly. Use to spread over cake, cheesecake, or apple tart, or as an accompaniment or glaze for pork chops or ham.

CHAPTER 21

RICE AND GRAINS

Rice and grains, among the simplest foods of all, provide some of our most satisfying and elegant dishes. In this chapter you'll find ingredients to make a perfect risotto or paella, as well as traditional polenta and kasha. Try some of the unusual kinds of rice you'll discover here—such as aromatic basmati and nutlike wehani. You'll also find wild rice, although it's not quite a true rice but an aquatic grass harvested from the lakes of Minnesota, Wisconsin, and Canada.

Wild rice—

Chuck & Earl's
P. O. Box 10786
Minneapolis, MN 55458

Contact by mail

Chuck & Earl's wild rice is harvested in the fall from the lakes of northern Minnesota, Wisconsin, and southern Canada, where it grows wild, free of pesticides and herbicides. Chuck & Earl's offers discounts for orders received before November 1, and savings on orders for large quantities.

Free price list
Mail orders, gift orders
MC, VISA

Imported and domestic rice and grains—

Dean & DeLuca, Inc.
Mail Order Department
560 Broadway
New York, NY 10012

800-221-7714
212-431-1691

Dean & DeLuca stock Italian arborio, a short-grained rice used for risotto; white and brown basmati rice; Riz Compleat, a French brown rice; Louisiana pecan rice; and wild rice from Minnesota. Grains include bulgar, coarse corn meal for polenta, grits, pearled barley, couscous, Irish oatmeal, and semolina.

Illustrated catalog, $2.00
Phone and mail orders, gift orders, and gift certificates
AMEX, MC, VISA

Wild rice from a Minnesota collective—

IKWE Marketing Collective
P. O. Box 183
Osage, MN 56570

218-573-3411

This wild rice is lake-harvested from natural stands by Anishinabeg ricers and hand-finished on the White Earth Reservation. You can order rice in packages or in handmade baskets, all with native recipes; bulk quantities also available. This collective also sells crafts —baskets, beaded jewelry, braided rugs, and quilts.

Free price list
Mail orders
No credit cards

Organic rice and grains—

Jaffe Bros., Inc.
P. O. Box 636
Valley Center, CA 92082

619-749-1133
Fax: 619-749-1282

Jaffe supplies long- and short-grain brown rice, in either 5- or 25-pound quantities. Grains include whole kernel corn, popcorn, millet, oats, wheat berries, rye berries, buckwheat groats, barley, quinoa, and amaranth. All are organically grown, unfumigated, and preservative-free.

Free catalog
Phone, fax, and mail orders, gift orders
MC, VISA

Cajun rice specialties from Louisiana—

Konriko Company Store
Conrad Rice Mill
307 Ann Street
New Iberia, LA 70560

800-551-3245
800-737-5667 (in LA)

The Conrad Rice Mill, American's oldest and on the National Register of Historic Places, supplies Konriko brand brown, white, and wild pecan rice. In addition, there are mixes for gumbo, pilaf, jambalaya, and artichoke rice. Other products include rice cakes, coffee, pralines, and Cajun seasonings. The catalog extends a warm invitation to visit southern Louisiana and includes a map and highlights of things to do and places to see.

Free color catalog
Phone and mail orders, gift orders
AMEX, MC, VISA

Brown rice and blends—

Lundberg Family Farms
P. O. Box 369
Richvale, CA 95974-0369

916-882-4551

Brown rice is the basis of this family enterprise in California. You can order premium or organic short- and long-grain brown rice, sweet brown rice, as well as specialty brown rice (wehani and California basmati), and blends of these varieties. Order in quantities of twelve 2-pound packages or a money-saving 25-pound package. Other rice products include syrup, flour, cereals, and cakes.

Free price list
Mail orders
No credit cards

Wild rice and aromatic rice—

Market Square Food Company, Inc.
1642 Richfield Avenue
Highland Park, IL 60035

800-232-2299
312-831-2228

Market Square Food Company's wild rice is harvested from the northern lakes of Minnesota and comes in bags or an attractive gift tin; recipes included. This company also sells A. B. Andy's brand Louisiana Extra-Fancy aromatic rice in 8-ounce and 2-pound quantities.

Free price list
Phone and mail orders, gift orders
MC, VISA

A variety of rice and grains—

G. B. Ratto & Company
821 Washington Street
Oakland, CA 94607

800-325-3483
800-228-3515 (in CA)
Fax: 415-836-2250

Ratto's international rice selection includes Italian arborio, Spanish "granza" type for paella, basmati from India or Thailand, and Japanese sushi rice. From California there is wehani, wild, and brown rice, and a wild rice mix. Take special note of Ratto's broken wild rice, available in 1- or 5-pound bags, which, besides being more economical, cooks a little faster, too. G. B. Ratto sells bulgur wheat, a product they've carried since 1897, in fine, medium, and coarse varieties, and will send you recipes for bulgur if you like. Other grains offered: buckwheat groats, popcorn, and mixes for tabbouleh and falafel.

Free illustrated catalog
Phone, fax, and mail orders, gift orders, and gift certificates
MC, VISA

Rice blends and samplers—

Select Origins, Inc.
Box N
Southampton, NY 11968

800-822-2092
516-924-5447
Fax: 516-924-5892

Select Origins has created its own blend of northern Ontario wild rice, California wehani, and long-grain brown rice. Wehani, developed from basmati seed and grown in the Sacramento Valley, turns bright russet when cooked and has a nutty aroma. You can buy wehani, Texas basmati, Italian arborio, and wild rice from Select Origins, as well as a rice sampler that comes with cooking tips and recipes. Try the following recipe for Lemony Chicken and Rice Salad developed by Tom and Kristi Siplon especially for serving in specialty food shops to introduce customers to their Select Origins rice blend. The wild rice in this Select Origins Blend gives the salad a nice crunchy texture.

Free illustrated catalog
Phone, fax, and mail orders, gift orders
AMEX, MC, VISA

American basmati-type rice—

Southern Rice Marketing
P. O. Box 880
Brinkley, AR 72021

501-734-1233

Southern Rice Marketing's Della Gourmet Rice is an American-grown aromatic rice, similar to Asia's basmati rice, with a nutty flavor and aroma. Grown on rich delta soil in Arkansas and Florida, it is available as white rice

Lemony Chicken and Rice Salad

from Select Origins, Inc.

You can complete this salad a day ahead, and it is actually tastier if you do. (Bring the salad back to room temperature before serving.) This dish always gets rave reviews and is excellent for a picnic, luncheon, or late night buffet.

1½ pounds boneless chicken breasts
 3 yellow onions
 3 cloves garlic
 2 lemons
 8 tablespoons good quality olive oil
 1 cup Select Origins Blend rice
 2 cups chicken broth
 ¼ teaspoon ground allspice
Salt and pepper to taste
 ½ cup chopped fresh parsley

Preparation: Cut chicken into small cubes. Mince the onions and garlic. Grate rind from one of the lemons and reserve. Squeeze both lemons; you should have about ⅓ cup juice. Heat 3 tablespoons of the olive oil in a large, wide pot. Sear chicken, in batches if necessary, over high heat until chicken is golden, about 5 minutes. Remove and set aside. Add onions and garlic to same pot. Cook over medium heat about 3 minutes or until onions are soft. Add rice and stir to coat well. Add broth and bring to a simmer. Season with salt and pepper, cover, and cook over low heat for 10 minutes.

Add the chicken and continue cooking, covered, until the rice is tender. Remove from heat and let stand, covered, for 15 minutes. Transfer to a large bowl and cool. Add the lemon juice, allspice, half the parsley, and remaining 5 tablespoons of olive oil to the rice. Mix gently, taste, and season with salt and pepper if needed. Refrigerate if not serving within the hour.

Serving: Bring salad back to room temperature. Just before serving toss the grated lemon rind and the rest of the parsley gently into the salad. Do not omit this step. It gives the salad its lovely lemony taste. Nice accompaniment might be crusty French bread and a wedge of your favorite cheese. Serves 4 to 6.

Almond Pilaf

from Southern Rice Marketing

½ cup sliced green onions, including tops
1 tablespoon butter or margarine
1 cup uncooked Della Gourmet Rice
½ teaspoon salt
2 cups chicken broth
⅓ cup sliced almonds, toasted
½ teaspoon pepper

In a large skillet or saucepan cook onions in butter until tender crisp. Add rice; cook 1 minute longer. Stir in the salt and broth. Bring to a boil, reduce heat, cover, and simmer 15 minutes or until rice is tender and liquid is absorbed. Add almonds and pepper, fluff lightly with a fork. Serves 6 to 8.

---

or organic brown rice. Try it in the recipe above for Almond Pilaf.

Free price list
Mail orders, gift orders
No credit cards

A selection of organic products—

Walnut Acres
Penns Creek, PA 17862

800-433-3998
Fax: 717-837-1146

Walnut Acres is a source for organic rice: long- and short-grain brown, wehani, basmati, wild rice, and wild pecan rice, as well as several rice and grain blends, including herbed bulgur, falafel, and kasha. Organic whole grains include spring and winter wheat, millet, barley, oat and buckwheat groats, and bulgur. Specialty grains include quinoa, a high-protein, gluten-free grain; amaranth seed; and Maskal Teff grains, an Ethiopian staple. In addition, you'll find over a dozen whole-grain cereals. Walnut Acres also sells a porcelain rice steampot.

Free color catalog
Phone, fax, and mail orders
MC, VISA

CHAPTER 22

SWEET SAUCES

The wonderful sauces in this chapter will turn a scoop of plain vanilla ice cream or a slice of ordinary pound cake into a spectacular dessert.

Four irresistible sauces—

Blanchard & Blanchard, Ltd.
P. O. Box 1080
Norwich, VT 05055

802-295-9200

Blanchard & Blanchard make four kinds of dessert sauces: Fudge (voted "The Best in New England" by the Boston *Globe*), Caramel Pecan, Mocha-Mountain Fudge, and Golden Caramel. You can find these sauces in specialty stores nationally, and Blanchard & Blanchard will be pleased to mail-order them for customers who can't find them locally— just ask for their retail price list. Try the following recipe from Blanchard & Blanchard for a Hot Apple Cake with Caramel Pecan Sauce.

Free price list
Mail orders
No credit cards

Several chocolate sauces—

Clearbrook Farms
5514 Fair Lane
Fairfax, OH 45227

800-888-3276
513-271-2053

In addition to fruit preserves, Clearbrook Farms make an enticing array of dessert sauces: Chocolate, Chocolate with Grand Marnier, Chocolate with Amaretto, Black Forest, Caramel Fudge, and Espresso Fudge. You'll find Clearbrook products in some specialty stores, or you can order directly from the company.

Free price list
Phone and mail orders
MC, VISA

Classic and unusual sauces—

Dearborn
1 Christopher Street
New York, NY 10014

212-691-9153

Dearborn's classic dessert sauces include chocolate, all-American milk chocolate, butterscotch, white chocolate and hazelnut, and toffee-caramel sauce. Listed in what they call the "wild and wonderful" dessert sauces are

Hot Apple Cake with Caramel Pecan Sauce

from Blanchard & Blanchard, Ltd.

2⅓ cups flour
2 teaspoons baking soda
½ teaspoon salt
1 teaspoon cinnamon
¼ teaspoon cloves
¼ teaspoon nutmeg
1 stick butter, softened
2 cups sugar
2 eggs
4 cups peeled, chopped apples
½ cup chopped walnuts
Blanchard & Blanchard Caramel Pecan Sauce
1 quart vanilla ice cream

Preheat oven to 325 degrees. Grease and lightly flour a 9×13-inch cake pan. Sift together flour, soda, salt, and spices in large bowl and set aside. Cream butter and sugar together. Add eggs, one at a time, beating well after each addition. Add sifted dry ingredients and beat at medium speed until well blended. Stir in apples and nuts. Pour into pan and bake 45 minutes, or until center of cake springs back when pressed lightly. Cool cake slightly.

Meanwhile, heat Caramel Pecan Sauce slightly in saucepan or microwave according to package directions. Serve cake warm topped with ice cream and Caramel Pecan Sauce. Serves 12.

Peppermint Reef, Mocha Rumba, and Bayou Crunch. You'll also find raspberry and blueberry syrups, and confections that include nuts and a chocolate truffle kit.

Free price list
Mail orders
No credit cards

Sweet Maine sauces—

Downeast Delicacies
Cape Porpoise Chutneys, Ltd.
P. O. Box 1281
Kennebunkport, ME 04046

207-967-5327

Jane Lamont's Downeast Delicacies include Magical Maine Wild Blueberry Delight, which she especially recommends for ice cream, pound cake, waffles, or French toast. The Honeyed Strawberry Sauce can be put to the same delicious uses, and also makes a quick glaze for chicken. Downeast Delicacies also makes several chutneys and a cranberry-apple relish.

Free illustrated brochure
Phone and mail orders, gift orders
MC, VISA

Southern specialties—

Gazin's
2910 Toulouse Street
P. O. Box 19221
New Orleans, LA 70179

800-262-6410

From this New Orleans purveyor of Cajun/Creole specialties you can order Vieux Carré brand chocolate topping, Amaretto chocolate sauce, or melba sauce, the classic raspberry sauce for peaches and ice cream. A sampler package will send one of each on its way to you. Other New Orleans treats include pecan-laced Gold Brick Sauce for sundaes and Bananas Foster Sauce for making the famous dessert that originated at New Orleans' Brennan's Restaurant.

Color catalog, $1.00 (credited on first order)
Phone and mail orders, gift orders
AMEX, MC, VISA

California temptations—

Grand Finale
200 Hillcrest Road
Berkeley, CA 94705

800-621-0851
415-655-8414

Barbara Holzrichter, proprietor of Grand Finale, suggests that you try her sauces on ice cream, fresh fruit, baked

goods—or simply the end of your finger. Chocolate flavors are triple chocolate fudge and crème de menthe fudge; caramel flavors are buttercream, bourbon pecan, Bailey's Irish Cream, macadamia, and Grand Marnier chocolate caramel. Her company also makes caramels and triple chocolate truffles; gift boxes that combine a sampling of products are available.

Free color brochure
Phone and mail orders, gift orders
AMEX, DC, MC, VISA

Traditional lemon curd and more sweet treats—

The Larder of Lady Bustle
P. O. Box 53393
Atlanta, GA 30355-1393

404-365-9679

Suggestions for using this company's traditional lemon jam include serving it on toast, croissants, ice cream, pound cake, angel food cake, and gingerbread, or using it as a filling for tarts. Additional treats from The Larder of Lady Bustle include tangerine sauce, minted butterscotch sauce, butterscotch sauce, brandied cranberries, and raisin sauce; the last two can also be served with various meats.

Free price list
Mail orders
No credit cards

Decadence sauces—

Narsai's
350 Berkeley Park Boulevard
Berkeley, CA 94707

415-527-7900

All of Narsai's dessert sauces are called Decadence, so you are forewarned!

Flavors include butter caramel, chocolate, orange chocolate, raspberry chocolate, and chocolate caramel. You will find them in specialty stores, or order direct from Narsai's. This company also makes jams and fruit conserves, mustards and dressings.

Free price list
Mail orders
No credit cards

Sweet endings—

The Silver Palate
274 Columbus Avenue
New York, NY 10023

212-799-6340

See if you can resist these Silver Palate sauces: fudge, fudge Grand Marnier, raspberry fudge, or mint fudge. If you haven't yet succumbed, try caramel pecan, wild blackberry cassis, or a mélange called It's the Berries. If you can't visit New York City's Silver Palate shop or find its creations in a local specialty shop, you can order directly from the source.

Free price list
Phone and mail orders
AMEX, MC, VISA

All natural, low-cal toppings—

Wax Orchards
22744 Wax Orchards Road S.W.
Vashon Island, WA 98070

800-634-6132
206-682-8251

Wax Orchards sweetens its sauces with concentrated fruit juice to create low-fat and low-calories treats—the fudge topping, for example, has only 16 calories per teaspoon. In addition to the original fudge flavor, there are Amaretto fudge, orange passion fudge, and peppermint fudge flavors. Ginger Sweet Topping is a combination containing fresh ginger and walnuts. Wax Orchards also makes preserves, conserves, fruit butters, chutneys, and Fruit Sweet syrups.

Free price list and nutritional information (please send two 25¢ stamps)
Phone and mail orders, gift orders
MC, VISA

CHAPTER 23

VEGETABLES, FRESH ONIONS AND GARLIC, SEA VEGETABLES, DRIED PEAS AND BEANS

You'll find a potpourri of produce in this chapter, which groups together every-thing from fresh sweet onions from Hawaii to dried fava beans from Egypt. Many will be familiar; others, such as colorful dried cranberry beans or pickled Maine fiddleheads, may be new. Read about the companies in New England that are harvesting nutritious local seaweed, long enjoyed in many countries and beginning to gain an audience here in the United States. To make a delicious dish similar to what you may have enjoyed in Japanese restaurants, try the recipe for Alaria Miso Soup.

Traditional bean dishes—

Bess' Beans
P. O. Box 1542
Charleston, SC 29402

800-233-2326

Bess' Beans, which originated in Charleston's Old City Market, come with recipes for down-home Old South dishes such as 13 Bean Super Soup, Charleston Black Beans, Low Country Red Beans, Lentil Salad, Hoppin' John, and more. There really is a Bess at Bess' Beans and her advice is that beans are rich in B vitamins and in protein, which can be enhanced for vegetarians and meatless meals by serving beans with rice or bread.

Free brochure
Mail orders
No credit cards

Vidalia onions—

Bland Farms
P. O. Box 506
Glennville, GA 30427-0506

800-843-2542

Vidalia onions, with more natural sugar than an apple, have a short and sweet growing season, too. Mature onions are available only from May 1 through June 1, although baby Vidalias are available from February to mid-April. During the rest of the year you can order Bland Farms' pickled onions and relishes, as well as mustards, dressings, and other products containing their famous Vidalia onions.

Free color catalog
Phone and mail orders, gift orders
AMEX, DISC, DC, MC, VISA

Sea vegetables—

Cape Ann Seaweeds Company
2 Stage Fort
Gloucester, MA 01930

508-283-9308

Linda Parker, proprietor of Cape Ann Seaweeds Company, likes to prepare seaweed as a satisfying simple meal and also finds that seaweed's flavor, texture, and affinity for other ingredients make it an interesting addition to curries, stews, and salads. From Cape Ann Seaweeds you can order alaria, nori, kelp, and dulse (see "A Sea Vegetable Primer" later in this chapter), and Linda will send recipes with your order. Try

the one she supplied for Alaria Miso Soup.

Free price list
Mail orders
No credit cards

Wild salad greens and exotic produce—

Fresh & Wild, Inc.
P. O. Box 2981
Vancouver, WA 98668

800-222-5578 (orders only)
206-254-8130
Fax: 206-896-8718

Fresh from the Pacific Northwest, this company ships seasonally available wild salad greens, edible flowers, baby white asparagus, and unusual produce that includes purple potatoes and pousse Pierre. Also known as salicornia, samphire, or glasswort, pousse Pierre is a crunchy, twiglike green that grows in salt marshes. It can be eaten raw or

Alaria Miso Soup

from Linda Parker, Cape Ann Seaweeds

¼ ounce dried alaria
1 cup sliced onion
3 carrots, sliced
Vegetable oil
1 tofu cake, sliced
3 tablespoons miso

Soak alaria in water a few minutes to make pliable. Save soaking water. Cut into 1-inch squares and sauté with onion and carrots in oil for 5 minutes, until seaweed is bright green. Add soaking water and extra water to make 6 cups. Add tofu and simmer 30 minutes. Cream miso with a little water or broth, stir into soup, and serve. Serves 4–6.

boiled and is delicious pickled in spiced vinegar. Fresh & Wild also supplies fresh wild berries and a wide variety of dried and fresh wild mushrooms and cultivated mushrooms (see details in Chapter 16, "Mushrooms and Truffles").

Free color brochure
Phone, fax, and mail orders
MC, VISA

Mountain-grown Pascal celery—

Green Brothers
P. O. Box 5284
Denver, CO 80217

303-296-3555

For more than seventy years Green Brothers have supplied their customers with mountain-grown Pascal celery, which they believe to be the world's finest. It's available seasonally for Thanksgiving and Christmas, and you can order in quantities of 6 or 12 stalks. Fruit baskets and gift items are also available.

Free illustrated catalog
Mail orders, gift orders
No credit cards

Kula-sweet Maui onions—

Ili Ili Farms
Box 150
Kula, Maui, HI 96790

800-367-8047, ext. 229

Although these onions are related to their more pungent varieties grown elsewhere, their sweetness is a result of the growing conditions of Kula—high altitude, year-round sunshine, ample rain, and quick-draining soil. Ili Ili Farms owner David Kapralik has

compiled a booklet of recipes for his onions that even includes several recipes for onion desserts! If you like Hawaii's rare and beautiful flowers, you can order these from Mr. Kapralik too.

Free color brochure
Phone and mail orders, gift orders
AMEX, MC, VISA

Organic peas and beans—

Jaffe Bros., Inc.
P. O. Box 636
Valley Center, CA 92082

619-749-1133
Fax: 619-749-1282

Jaffe's peas and beans, available in 5- or 25-pound quantities, include soy, mung, red kidney, pinto, adzuki, navy, black turtle, Great Northern, garbanzo, and baby lima beans; also black-eyed, whole sprouting, green split peas and lentils.

Free catalog
Phone, fax, and mail orders, gift orders
MC, VISA

Seaweeds, chips, and seasonings—

Maine Coast Sea Vegetables
Shore Road
Franklin, ME 04634

207-565-2907

This company was born over a pot of miso soup one early summer evening in 1971, and started with just two people harvesting, drying, packing, and shipping local seaweed. Today more than twenty people help produce more than thirteen tons of products that are shipped all over the United States and Canada. You can order six varieties of sea vegetables—alaria, dulse, kelp, nori, sea palm, and digitata. In addition, Maine Coast Sea Vegetables make Sea Chips, a seaweed-flavored tortilla chip; and several varieties of seasoning, including dulse with garlic, nori with ginger, and kelp with cayenne. A booklet of recipes is available for $3.00.

Free price list
Mail orders
No credit cards

Maine sea vegetables and information, too—

Maine Seaweed Company
Box 57
Steuben, ME 04680

207-546-2875

Larch Hanson and Cynthia Bullington harvest kelp, alaria, and digitata kelp and supply it in 1-pound packages. A family pack of more than 3 pounds of

A Sea Vegetable Primer
from Maine Coast Sea Vegetables

Eaten for centuries by coastal folks worldwide, sea vegetables are catching on with landlubbers everywhere in North America. These "marine greens" are nature's most complete source of minerals and trace minerals. While providing abundant vitamins, chlorophyll, enzymes, and vegetable protein, they are low in fat, contain no cholesterol, and have more total dietary and soluble fiber than oat bran.

Use them as a staple, as a side dish, or add in small amounts to salads, soups, grains, and vegetables. Here are the characteristics and some suggested uses for four popular wild Atlantic sea vegetables:

Alaria: Similar to Japanese wakame, this is the perfect choice for soups. Cooking for at least 20 minutes brings out its mild sweet taste and soft, chewy texture. Delicious raw in salads, either presoaked or marinated.
Dulse: Delicious as a raw snack with a distinctive strong sea flavor. After cooking for 5 minutes it adds a mild, sweet taste to soups, stews, chowders, salads, and sandwiches. Also pan-fries into tangy chips or bakes nicely with melted cheese.
Kelp: This all-around sea vegetable, similar to Japanese kombu, is delicious roasted, pan-fried, boiled, or marinated. It makes a great soup stock, imparting a richness usually associated with meat or fish.
Nori: This variety has a distinctive mild, nutty, salty-sweet taste. Best lightly roasted before use, it is delicious crumbled into soups, grains, salads, and popcorn.

assorted seaweeds plus recipes is also available. To help customers learn about sea vegetables, Larch Hanson sends a newsletter along with the price list. You can also order his collection of stories, poems, and recipes related to seaweed, as well as a forager's guide to sea vegetables. He and Cynthia offer summer camping experiences and travel in the fall and winter, presenting slide talks about their business.

Free price list
Mail orders
No credit cards

Seasonal Vidalia sweet onions and year-round pecans—

Mascot Pecan Company
P. O. Box 765
Glennville, GA 30427

800-841-3985
912-654-2195

Around Glennville, Georgia, it's estimated that over 15,000 acres of sweet onions are planted every year. In late May or early June the harvest is celebrated with the Glennville Onion Festival. Once the onion queen is elected, the local harvesting gets under way. You can order these sweet and delicious onions from the Mascot Pecan Company in May and June. Pecans are available year round.

Free price list
Mail orders
No credit cards

Exotic produce—

Melissa's Brand
P. O. Box 21407
Los Angeles, CA 90021

800-468-7111
213-588-0151

A Guide to Garlic Varieties and Storage Tips
from Mountain Meadow Farm

Elephant Garlic: Large ½-pound to 1½-pound bulbs with a mild garlic flavor. Bulb produces 3 to 8 large cloves. Excellent raw in salads and sandwiches or cooked whole in soups and sauces.
Silverskin: Strong flavor, medium size, and easy peeling qualities. Average bulb produces 7 to 12 cloves. Excellent keeping qualities.
Rocambole: The strongest flavor of all the garlics. A small purple bulb, producing 7 to 12 cloves. A special garlic for the adventurous cook.
Mountain Meadow Red Italian: A sweet-flavored Italian garlic. Bulb produces 6 to 10 cloves. One of our favorites because of its easy peeling qualities.
Storing Garlic: Store garlic in a cool, dry, well-ventilated place. Ideal temperature is 40 to 55 degrees. The long-keeping varieties should store well for 9 months.

Melissa's Brand is a wholesaler of tropical, Latin, oriental, and specialty produce—anything from Asian pears to yucca root. There is no minimum order and they can mail just about anything. Send for their seasonal list of produce or call with your request. Perishables can be shipped overnight by Federal Express.

Free seasonal price lists
Phone and mail orders
No credit cards

Organically grown garlic and shallots—

Mountain Meadow Farm
826 Ulrich Road
Prospect, OR 97536

503-560-3350

From Mountain Meadow Farm, located in the foothills of Oregon's Cascade Mountains, you can order several kinds of garlic in addition to shallots and pure garlic powder and oil. Fresh garlic varieties are elephant garlic, Silverskin, Rocambole, or Mountain Meadow Red Italian. Small, medium, and large garlic braids are made from the Silverskin variety. Mountain Meadow Farm has put together a combination package of 3 pounds of assorted garlic, especially for cooks who would like to experiment with different varieties.

Free illustrated brochure
Mail orders
No credit cards

Fresh and canned asparagus—

Mr. Spear
P. O. Box 1528
Stockton, CA 95201

209-464-5365

For more than ten years Chip Arnett has been shipping fresh white and green asparagus from the San Joaquin Delta to devotees all over the country. The season lasts from March to early June, and during the rest of the year you can order cans of colossal green spears. If you've ever wondered what makes white asparagus, Mr. Spear explains: "Soil is hilled up over the plant to prevent chlorophyll development by exposure to the sun. It is slightly more fibrous and stronger flavored than green asparagus and should be peeled before cooking. Exposure to the sun after cutting turns it red."

Free color brochure
Mail orders, gift orders
MC, VISA

Sweet Spanish onions from Oregon—

Ontario Produce Company, Inc.
P. O. Box 880
Ontario, OR 97914

800-848-7799
503-889-7500
Fax: 503-889-7823

Available from September through March, these jumbo, yellow, sweet Spanish onions are ideal for cooking and for holiday gifts.

Free price list
Phone, fax, and mail orders, gift orders
MC, VISA

Flageolets and other dried beans and peas—

G. B. Ratto & Company
821 Washington Street
Oakland, CA 94607

800-325-3483
800-228-3515 (in CA)
Fax: 415-836-2250

A rainbow of beans awaits you at G. B. Ratto: black beans, white canellini, red kidney, cranberry, and Swedish brown beans. In addition, you'll find Anasazi beans, madammas (small fava beans), garbanzo beans, American-grown flageolets, and mixed beans. Also shop for red and green lentils, and a selection of Southern specialty beans.

Free illustrated catalog
Phone, fax, and mail orders, gift orders, and gift certificates
MC, VISA

Preserved garden specialties—

Seyco Fine Foods, Inc.
25574 Rye Canyon Road, #E
Valencia, CA 91355-1109

800-423-2942

These special items are available from Seyco by the single tin or in cases of a dozen—artichoke hearts, giant mushroom buttons, green and white asparagus, hearts of palm, imported carrots, French string beans, petit pois, and flageolets.

Color catalog, $2.00; 10 percent off first order
Phone and mail orders, gift orders
AMEX, DC, MC, VISA

Organic fresh and canned vegetables, dried peas and beans—

Walnut Acres
Penns Creek, PA 17862

800-433-3998
Fax: 717-837-1146

Fresh organic root vegetables (potatoes, carrots, beets, and onions) can be ordered from Walnut Acres in 5- or 25-pound quantities. Walnut Acres also can vegetables that grow in organic fields adjacent to the cannery. They process tomatoes, corn, beets, pumpkin, green beans, peas, and sauerkraut. Canned beans include kidney, pinto, garbanzo, and Great Northern. Order two cans or money saving cases of twelve. Organic dried beans include navy, Great Northern, kidney, anasazi, adzuki, black, and garbanzo beans; also soybeans, sprouted green peas, red and green lentils. Many of these dried peas and beans are also used in Walnut Acres dried soup mixes.

Free color catalog
Phone, fax, and mail orders
MC, VISA

The source for canned fiddleheads, dandelion and beet greens—

W. S. Wells & Son
P. O. Box 109
Wilton, ME 04294

207-645-3393

This Maine cannery, founded in 1886, is the only company in the world canning dandelion greens and the only U.S. company canning fiddleheads and beet greens. You can also order pickled fiddleheads and dilly beans. Choose your favorites in 3-, 6-, or 12-can packs. The Wellses have put together a recipe pamphlet for their Belle of Maine brand products that includes family favorites such as fiddlehead quiche and dandelion spoon bread.

Free price list
Mail orders
No credit cards

You can order seasonal fresh shallots
from:

Herb Gathering, Inc.
5742 Kenwood Avenue
Kansas City, MO 64110

816-523-2653

and

Hickin's Mountain Mowings Farm
RFD 1
Brattleboro, VT 05301

802-254-2146

PART TWO

REGIONAL AND ETHNIC INGREDIENTS

CHAPTER 24

AMERICAN REGIONAL FOODS

This chapter is devoted to regional foods of the United States and highlights companies that offer a selection of products or ingredients for a specific kind of American regional cooking. When you are looking for specific foods and ingredients, it may be helpful to browse though previous chapters or consult the Index. Additional foods from New England, for example, will be found in Chapter 4, "Cheese and Dairy Products," and Chapter 14, "Maple Syrup and Maple Products." And in some chapters, such as Chapter 6, "Condiments and Savory Sauces," or Chapter 20, "Preserves," you'll find products that reflect the distinctive flavors of many regions.

A Spicy Taste of the Southwest

Natural foods from New Mexico—

Casados Farms
Box 1269
San Juan Pueblo, NM 87566

Contact by mail

Casados Farms, producers of chilies for more than four generations, is located on the banks of the Rio Grande in northern New Mexico where the climate is ideal for growing top-quality chilies. You can order caribe, molido, whole and crushed pequin, pods, seeds, and enchilada and taco sauce mix. Ristras, from 18 inches to 60 inches long, can be ordered from November to mid-April. Blue and white cornmeal, flours, beans, spices, peloncillo (coned brown sugar), and pine nuts are also available. You'll receive a free cookbook with the purchase of any five products.

Free color brochure
Mail orders
MC, VISA

Southwestern specialties from an Arizona orchard—

Country Estate Pecans
P. O. Box 7
1625 East Helmet Peak Road
Sahuarita, AZ 85629

800-327-3226
602-791-2062

In addition to pecans, pistachios, almonds, and dates, Country Estate Pecans stocks numerous spices and condiments for Southwestern cooking.

Besides such staples as tortilla chips and cornmeal, you can order from a selection of salsas, mixes, and ready-to-serve items. Unusual regional specialties include red pepper marmalade, jalapeño jelly, prickly pear barbecue sauce, mesquite honey, and papaya jam.

Free price list
Phone and mail orders
MC, VISA

A salsa to suit every taste—

Desert Rose Salsa Company
P. O. Box 5391
Tucson, AZ 85703

602-743-0450

Patti Swidler began making salsa on a small scale, as Christmas presents for friends. Now her Desert Rose brand salsas are highly regarded regional fare, and Patti and her husband are both involved with their expanding business. Desert Rose makes a salsa to please everyone—medium, hot, and conmemorativa (a blend of medium and green salsa), as well as medium and hot green salsa, and salsa enchilada. Two additional products are marinated cherry peppers and Salsa Barbacoa, a chunky and spicy barbecue sauce. You can find these products in specialty shops or order them directly from Desert Rose Salsa.

Free price list
Phone and mail orders
No credit cards

Everything for Southwestern cuisine—

The El Paso Chile Company
100 Ruhlin Court
El Paso, TX 79922

915-544-3434

Norma and Park Kerr's company, founded in 1981, grew out of a love for chilies and products of the El Paso area. You can order chili powder, chili fixings, canned chilies, dried beans, barbecue sauce, marinades, salsas (including a cactus salsa), spiced peanuts, tostados, and ready-to-serve chile con queso. Norma's decorative items include chili wreaths and ristras and cinnamon wreaths. Gift selections are packed in decorative boxes. Try the following recipe for Park Kerr's delicious Enchiladas Rojas en Rellados.

Free price list
Mail orders, gift orders
AMEX, MC, VISA

Traditional Southwestern ingredients—

Los Chileros de Nuevo Mexico
P. O. Box 6215
Santa Fe, NM 87502

505-471-6967

Tandy and Terrie Lucero, who run this New Mexico company, guarantee that all its spices and flours are freshly ground. Ground and whole chilies are available, as well as a blend of chilies and spices for making salsa. Blue corn products include whole kernels, meal, and flour, tortilla chips, popcorn, posole, and atole (roasted cornmeal to mix with milk and sugar for a traditional New Mexico breakfast). White corn products include posole, chicos (dehydrated sweet corn, can be cooked with pinto beans or pork); chaqueue (a white corn version of

Enchiladas Rojas en Rellados

*(Rolled, Red Baked Enchiladas) from Park Kerr
of The El Paso Chile Company*

1 dozen fresh corn tortillas
3 cups grated sharp cheese
2 cups chopped onion
2 cups chopped cooked beef or chicken
2 cups Basic Red Chili Sauce (recipe follows on next page)
1 cup sour cream
Fresh cilantro, chopped tomatoes, and lettuce for garnish

Fry tortillas slightly in hot oil until limp. Drain on paper towels. Place approximately 2 tablespoons cheese, 2 tablespoons onion, and 2 tablespoons chopped meat on one side of each tortilla. Roll and place seam side down in shallow baking dish. Continue using all the tortillas (reserving 1 cup cheese for topping). Pour Basic Red Chili Sauce over rolled tortillas. Spread thin layer of sour cream on top and sprinkle with the reserved cheese. Bake at 350 degrees until bubbly and hot, approximately 35 to 40 minutes. Before serving, garnish with chopped cilantro, lettuce, and tomatoes. Serve with refried beans and chile rellenos. Serves 4 to 6.

atole), and corn husks. Also sprouted whole wheat flour, piloncillo (coned brown sugar), and raw or roasted piñon nuts. Mexican chilies are available by the pound or package: arbol, ancho, cascabel, chipotle, guajillo, japones, negro, pasilla, serrano; you can also order chili or corn ristras, chili wreaths, and harvest arrangements.

Free price list
Mail orders
No credit cards

Chips and salsa from ski country—

Miguel's Stowe-Away
RR 2, Box 2086
Waterbury, VT 05676

800-448-6517
802-244-7886

Miguel's Stowe-Away Lodge and Restaurant, located near some of Vermont's best skiing, specializes in authentic Mexican foods. Some of Miguel's products, including salsa cruda (mild, regular, and hot) and blue and white tortilla chips (lightly salted and unsalted), are available in specialty stores and through mail order. Gift selections include a variety of products —the Red, White and Blue Pack is, naturally, a jar of salsa and a bag of each kind of tortilla chip.

Free illustrated brochure
Phone and mail orders, gift orders
MC, VISA

Salsa de Chile Colorado

(Basic Red Chili Sauce) from Park Kerr
of the El Paso Chile Company

12 dried medium red chili pods[1]
 3 cups water
½ teaspoon comino (cumin)
½ teaspoon oregano
 1 tablespoon flour
 1 teaspoon salt
 1 teaspoon vinegar
½ teaspoon brown sugar
½ teaspoon onion powder
¼ teaspoon garlic powder
Tomato sauce

Wash chili pods. Remove stems and as many seeds as possible. Bring chili pods
and water to a boil and simmer for 10 minutes, covered. Remove from heat,
cover, and let sit for 10 more minutes. Pour water and chilies into blender and
liquefy (do this in two batches, if necessary). Strain sauce through a colander
or large sieve. Pour back into saucepan. Add all remaining ingredients except
tomato sauce and simmer until thickened, about 20 to 25 minutes. Remove from
heat and cool. If sauce is too hot, add tomato sauce until it suits your taste.
Sauce is better if refrigerated for 24 hours.

[1]Choose mild or hot chili peppers, depending on your taste. Wash hands thoroughly
with soap and water after handling.

Jane Butel's recipes, and ingredients
too—

Pecos Valley Spice Company
1450 Heggen Street
Hudson, WI 54016

715-386-8832
Fax: 715-386-6731

Pecos Valley Spice Company offers
everything you'll need to create
authentic Southwestern feasts: ground
and crushed chilies, herbs and spices,
Chile Madness kits, yellow and blue
cornmeal, corn husks, posole (dried
hominy-type kernels), and sopaipilla
mix for making hollow, puffed pastry.
You can also order salsa, tostados, and
taco shells. All products are selected by
Jane Butel, a leading authority on
Southwestern cooking. Also available
are Jane's complete library of eight
Southwestern cookbooks and a video. If
you want to learn more about
Southwestern cooking, request
information about Jane Butel's cooking
classes in Santa Fe, New Mexico, and
Woodstock, New York.

Free catalog
Phone, fax, and mail orders
MC, VISA

Southwestern seasonings—

Pendery's, Inc.
304 East Belknap Street
Fort Worth, TX 76102

800-533-1870

The accent is decidedly on Southwestern flavors at this Fort Worth herb and spice company. Pendery's stocks many varieties of whole and ground dried chili peppers, herbs,

spices, and seasoning blends for spicy cooking. Special items include chili ancho cheese, chili pepper ristras and wreaths, and Texan and Mexican candies. (Southwestern aficionados will enjoy the gift items, too—cactus-inspired jewelry, hand-blown Mexican glassware, even bright gift wrap that features chilies or cactus.) Pendery's chili products are rated according to a color and heat scale, which is explained below in an excerpt from their informative catalog.

Free color catalog
Phone and mail orders, gift orders, and gift certificates
AMEX, MC, VISA

A Guide to Captivating Capsicums
from Pendery's, Inc.

A few quick definitions to assist in the jargon and selection of capsicum products:

Chili Pod: dried, whole fruit of the capsicum plant.
Chili Pepper: dried and ground whole chili pod.
Paprika: dried and ground mild red chili pod, high in vitamin C.
Red Pepper: dried and ground hot whole chili pod.
Chili Powder or Blend: blend of the ground chili pepper and other spices.

ASTA color unit: amount of extractable color from capsicum products. Extractable color is oil soluble, and is the color obtained through cooking.
SCAN color unit: standard to determine the different shades of capsicum products, determined by light-reflectance meter.
SCOVILLE heat unit (H.U.): standard to determine the pungency of capsicum products.

Varieties of dried chili pods:

Ancho: Dried poblano chili pod with rich color and sweet aroma of a giant raisin. Add to sauces, stews, and chile con carne. Stem. Seed. Add to simmering dish. Discard skin before serving. Very popular in Mexican cooking. 1500 to 3000 H.U.

Chili de Árbol: Chili pod with beautiful quality radiant red color. Use "as is" in stews, sauces, and oriental dishes. Try a few in cream of tomato soup for a brisk flavor lift. Discard before serving or give your guests fair warning. 20,000 to 30,000 H.U.

California Red: Large, sweet domestic California chili pod. Use in sauces, stews, and tomato dishes. Try in meat sauce and spaghetti. Stem. Seed. Add to simmering meat sauce. Discard skin and serve. 1000 to 1500 H.U.

Guajillo: Medium size, burgundy chili pod. Use in sauces, stews, and tomato dishes. Stem. Seed. Add to simmering sauce. Discard skin before serving. 2500 to 5000 H.U.

Chipotle: Whole jalapeño, smoke-dried, with marvelous aroma and flavor. Everyone from chefs of elite restaurants to masters of the outdoor grills covet these specialties. Try them in cream soups. Remove when flavor is just right. Wonderful! (Pungency of jalapeños varies, so H.U. can't be accurately assigned.)

Mirasol: Guajillo-type burgundy chili pod with flavor of its own. Use in sauces, stews, and Mexican dishes. Stem. Seed. Add to simmering sauce. Discard skin before serving. 2500 to 5000 H.U.

New Mexican Chili Pod: Large, burgundy-red domestic pod. Use in sauces, stews, and tomato dishes. The hot New Mexican chili pod is 3000 to 5000 H.U.; the mild variety is 1500 to 3000 H.U.

Pasilla Negro: Long, wrinkled, slender, mild, ebony pod. Use in stews, sauces, and many Mexican dishes. Stem. Seed. Add to simmering sauce. Discard skin before serving. 2500 to 3500 H.U.

Hot Red Oriental Chili Pods: Small, fiery chili pods. May be crushed or left whole. In many oriental dishes and stir frying, use "as is." Put some fire into that Sunday night special, toss in a few of these lively pods. Remove when your taste is satisfied. Once you start cooking with these easy additions, you will not be able to stop. Discard them before serving or give fair warning to your friends. They are reported to help cure sore throats and the common cold, a few of their myriad health benefits. Wash your hands carefully with soap and water after handling and *do not* put your hands to your eyes. Varieties of hot red oriental chili pods include:

Santaka: 2 to 2½ inches long, brick red.

Tientsin: 1½ to 3 inches long, bright orange-red.

Yunnan: 1½ to 3½ inches long, crimson.

Traditional tortilla products from Connecticut—

Severance Foods, Inc.
3476 Main Street
Hartford, CT 06120

203-724-7063

Just off Interstate 91 in Hartford there's a company dedicated to making traditional tortilla products from small batches of corn dough or *masa*. You can order regular or thick corn tortillas or blue corn tortillas; cut tortillas for chips; flour tortillas in four sizes; and round or triangular tortilla chips, either lightly salted or flavored with cheese.

Free price list
Mail orders
No credit cards

Tia Maria brand foods—

Seyco Fine Foods, Inc.
25574 Rye Canyon Road, #E
Valencia, CA 91355-1109

800-423-2942

You'll find a complete selection of Tia Maria Mexican food products from Seyco, including ground chili, enchilada sauce, several salsas, tins of whole or chopped green chilies, jalapeños, and pico de gallo verde (a blend of green chilies, onions, cilantro, and garlic).

Color catalog, $2.00; 10 percent off first order
Phone and mail orders, gift orders
AMEX, DC, MC, VISA

A directory from the Lone Star State—

A Taste of Texas
Texas Department of Agriculture
P. O. Box 12847
Austin, TX 78711

The marketing division of the Texas Department of Agriculture has put together a list of producers of authentic Texan food products. You'll find suppliers of fresh produce, candy, meats, and much more—and many will send their products right to your door. So, if you're a fan of Texas food, send for this booklet—it's free.

Cajun/Creole Specialties

A complete barbecue kit—

Carousel Spices
170 Highway 35
Red Bank, NJ 07701

201-741-3483

Carousel Spices offers Uncle Dutchie's Original Lousiana Style Cajun Barbecue Kit, which includes seasonings, a cast-iron blackening skillet, and a 24-page booklet with recipes for meat, poultry, seafood, vegetables, and sauces. The Cajun spice mix (in both hot and mild) and the skillet can also be ordered separately.

Free brochure
Phone and mail orders, gift orders
MC, VISA

Best from the bayou—

Community Kitchens
P. O. Box 2311
Baton Rouge, LA 70821-2311

800-535-9901
504-381-3900

Community Kitchens has all the makings for jambalaya, gumbos, and other Louisiana treats—Cajun-seasoned pork sausage, andouille sausage, seasoning mixes, and hot sauces. Menu suggestions and recipes are included with your order. You'll also find condiments, baking mixes, preserves, dessert sauces, and an excellent selection of coffees. There are many samplers to let you try a variety of products; also cookbooks and kitchen tools.

Free color catalog
Phone and mail orders, gift orders
AMEX, MC, VISA

From the heart of the French Quarter—

Creole Delicacies Company, Inc.
533 St. Ann Street
New Orleans, LA 70116

504-525-9508

This New Orleans shop, a supplier of
Creole and Cajun specialties for over
thirty years, stocks New Orleans coffee,
Cajun seasoning blends and main-dish
mixes, remoulade sauce, baking mixes,
pepper relishes, and smoked meats.
Tempting sweets include praline
topping, fruitcake, and confections such
as pralines and sugared pecans. Gift
assortments are packed in wicker
hampers and baskets.

Free color catalog
Mail orders, gift orders
AMEX, MC, VISA

Almost like shopping in New Orleans—

Gazin's
2910 Toulouse Street
P. O. Box 19221
New Orleans, LA 70179

800-262-6410

Find the basics—andouille sausage,
rice, and beans—for making soups and
gumbos. Also roux and starters for
gumbos, soups, and stews; and mixes
for beignets, grits, biscuits, and several
kinds of bread. If you'd like ready-to-
serve foods, Gazin's can send you tins
of turtle soup, seafood gumbo, or
crayfish bisque, and loaves of crusty
New Orleans French bread. Specialties
from Brennan's and Commander's, two
famous New Orleans restaurants, are
featured, as well as numerous sauces,
seasonings, preserves, confections, and,
to top it all off, coffee and chicory.

Color catalog, $1.00 (credited on first
order)
Phone and mail orders, gift orders
AMEX, MC, VISA

Quick fixings for Creole cooking—

Kajun Delicacies
P. O. Box 1494
Kenner, LA 70063

504-466-1198

The ingredients from Kajun Delicacies
make Creole cooking fast and easy.
There's a complete line of seasonings
and hot sauces, mixes for Cajun dinners
and soups, as well as ready-to-serve
gumbos and soups. Baking mixes
include buttermilk biscuit mix, corn
bread, and spicy cheese grits. A
collection of cookbooks and gift
packages completes the selection.

Brochure, $1.00 (credited on first order)
Mail orders, gift orders
No credit cards

Chef Paul Prudhomme's products—

K-Paul's Louisiana Enterprises
501 Elysian Fields
P. O. Box 770034
New Orleans, LA 70177-0034

800-4 KPAULS
504-947-6712

All of Chef Paul's popular cookbooks
are featured here, and he will be happy
to add his autograph before sending
them out. You'll find his Magic
Seasonings Blends™, andouille and
tasso, complete fixings for bean and rice
dishes, and specialties such as pickled
quail eggs, chowchow, and Cajun
popcorn. Sweet potato pecan pie,

Shrimp Jambalaya

from Gazin's

1 tablespoon shortening
1 tablespoon flour
¼ pound ham, cubed
¼ cup minced green pepper
1 bay leaf
¼ teaspoon thyme
⅛ teaspoon cayenne
1 sprig parsley, minced
1 onion, sliced
1 clove garlic, minced
    Salt and pepper to taste
2 cups tomatoes, chopped
1¼ cups tomato juice
1 pound shrimp, peeled
1 cup uncooked rice

Melt shortening in a heavy saucepan over medium heat. Add flour and stir until light brown. Add ham and stir for 3 minutes. Add all remaining ingredients except rice. Bring to a boil. Stir rice into liquid. Cover and simmer for 40 minutes. Serves 6.

smoked turkeys, and pecan pralines are also available. Jambalaya, etouffée, and shrimp Creole dinners for 6 to 8 are sent next-day air from K-Paul's Louisiana Kitchen.

Free color catalog
Phone and mail orders, gift orders
AMEX, DISC, MC, VISA

Easy-to-make Cajun/Creole foods—

Luzianne Blue Plate Foods
Box 60296
New Orleans, LA 70160

800-692-7895

With Luzianne Cajun/Creole dinners, even a novice cook can serve authentic New Orleans-style dishes. Add fresh meat, poultry, or seafood to make jambalaya, gumbo, shrimp Creole, or étouffée (a rich stew with a buttery sauce). This New Orleans establishment has been going strong since 1903 and specializes in coffee, coffee and chicory blends (also available as instant coffee), and teas.

Free illustrated catalog
Phone and mail orders, gift orders
MC, VISA

Creole and Cajun specialties—

Martin Wine Cellar
3827 Baronne Street
New Orleans, LA 70115

504-899-7411

This New Orleans wine cellar stocks a variety of Creole specialties, including gumbo filé, crab and shrimp boil, sauce and dip mixes, Cajun pickles and seasonings, instant roux, and K-Paul's products for blackened meat and fish.

Free price list
Phone and mail orders, gift orders
MC, VISA

Louisiana meats—

Poche's Meat Market & Restaurant
Route 2, Box 415
Breaux Bridge, LA 70517

318-332-2108

Looking for smoked andouille or tasso for making a gumbo? You can order these pork products from Poche's as well as cracklin's, boudin, fresh sausage, stuffed chaudin or tongue, pickled pork, hog lard, and other items. Poche's Meat Market & Restaurant will also ship its homemade roux, barbecue sauce, dried shrimp, and peeled crawfish in season.

Free price list
Phone and mail orders
MC, VISA

Authentic Creole foods—

Vieux Carré Foods Inc.
P. O. Box 50277
New Orleans, LA 70150

504-822-6065

Vieux Carré Foods, in New Orleans' historic French Quarter, carries a number of ingredients, condiments, and seasonings for Creole cooking: gumbo filé, roux, shrimp and crab boil, and Cajun/Creole seasonings. Sauces include shrimp remoulade, seafood, barbecue, and Louisiana hot sauce. On the sweeter side, you'll find praline and chocolate sauce. Vieux Carré also has a cookbook available.

Free price list
Mail orders
No credit cards

Favorite Fare from New England

Products from a Vermont general store—

F. H. Gillingham & Company
16 Elm Street
Woodstock, VT 05091

802-457-2100

The great-grandson of F. H. Gillingham now runs this Woodstock general store and mail order company that supplies traditional Vermont foods, including maple products, crackers, cheese, ham and bacon, baking mixes, preserves, and condiments. Cooks may be especially interested in the maple syrup baking and dessert cookbook and the kitchen accessories, which include soapstone griddles, a down-to-earth kitchen apron, and an old-fashioned apple parer, corer, and slicer.
Numerous gift selections and a monthly plan that ships Vermont specialties throughout the year are also offered.

Free color catalog
Phone and mail orders, gift orders
AMEX, MC, VISA

Fresh from a Vermont farm—

Hickin's Mountain Mowings Farm
RFD 1
Brattleboro, VT 05301

802-254-2146

The Hickin family must like to keep
busy. On their mountaintop farm in
Vermont they grow more than 100
kinds of fruits and vegetables and use
them to prepare dozens of products
that include preserves, fruit butters,
fruit syrups, pickles, sauces, and
chutney. Some are quite unusual:
yellow raspberry jam, maple tarragon
leeks, and dilled carrots, to name just a
few. Vermont favorites include cheese,
smoked meats, honey, fruitcake, maple
syrup, cream, and candy. If you visit
the farm, you can also buy fresh
produce, fruit, baked goods, and
plants.

Free brochure
Mail orders, gift orders
No credit cards

A taste of Vermont—

Maple Grove Farms of Vermont
167 Portland Street
St. Johnsbury, VT 05819

802-748-3136

You'll find a cornucopia of Vermont's
favorite country foods assembled by
Susan and Bill Callahan of Maple Grove
Farms. In addition to maple products
(syrup, spread, cream, sugar, candy,
and fudge), there are Vermont
preserves, relishes, canned wild
blueberries and syrup, baking mixes,
honey, nuts, cheese, and apples.
Maple-cured and smoked meats include
turkey, ham, duck, pheasant, and
bacon. Don't overlook the baked goods,

which include a maple fruitcake.
Among the numerous gift selections
you'll find one especially for cooks on
your list—a quart of flavorful grade C
maple syrup packed with *The Official
Vermont Maple Cookbook*.

Free color catalog
Phone and mail orders, gift orders
AMEX, MC, VISA

Carefully chosen New England treats—

New England Country Fare
378 Washington Street
Westwood, MA 02090

800-274-FARE
617-329-4874
Fax: 617-329-3884

Roberta Dehman Hershon, food writer,
former caterer, and the originator of
New England Country Fare, has
personally chosen the best of New
England's bountiful foods. Selections
are packed in charming hand-stenciled
baskets and include Yankee Samplers, a
Bountiful Breakfast selection, and
Chocolate Paradise and Ice Cream
Festival selections for the sweet-
toothed. The Cook's Collection
combines ingredients such as raspberry
vinegar and salad herbs with unique
regional treats like pickled fiddleheads
and dilly beans. Food items are all-
natural, and you can also order kosher
and sugar-free selections.

Free color brochure
Phone, fax, and mail orders, gift orders
AMEX, MC, VISA

Old-fashioned Vermont finds—

The Vermont Country Store
P. O. Box 3000
Manchester Center, VT 05255-3000

802-362-2400

This old-fashioned catalog offers a potpourri of goods, and tucked near the end you'll find traditional Vermont food favorites, including maple products, crackers, cheese, candy, cereals, flours, and baking mixes. Novel cook's aids include an 1880s potato masher and an old-fashioned crank flour sifter.

Free illustrated brochure
Phone and mail orders
MC, VISA

From the Sunshine States: California, the South, and Hawaii

A taste of the South—

Callaway Gardens Country Store
Pine Mountain, GA 31822

800-282-8181

Traditional Southern foods abound in this collection from Georgia. You'll find muscadine preserves, jelly, and sauce made from Georgia's muscadine grape crop; Southern-style condiments such as Georgia Vidalia Onion Relish, pepper jellies, and watermelon cubes; fruit butters made from peaches, apricots, and apples; as well as wild berry preserves. There are also Georgia-cured hams and bacon, sorghum syrup, smoked meats, and, of course, grits. Gift selections and *Country Cookin'*, a Callaway Gardens cookbook, are also offered. Muscadine grapes, native to the Southeast, were first grown at Callaway Gardens in 1944, and Muscadine Sauce was developed by Cason Callaway, who adapted it from his mother's treasured wild plum sauce recipe. Try it in the following recipe for Muscadine Bread.

Free color catalog
Phone and mail orders, gift orders
AMEX, MC, VISA

Traditional Southern favorites—

Early's Honey Stand
P. O. Box K
Spring Hill, TN 37174-0911

800-523-2015

Early's Southern-style meats include hickory-smoked pork sausage, bacon, ham, turkey, and summer sausage. They also provide preserves, baking mixes, and gift baskets that combine selections of Early's specialties.

Free color catalog
Phone and mail orders, gift orders
AMEX, DC, MC, VISA

Fresh from California—

Susan Green's California Cuisine
Quinn and Senter Road
P. O. Box 5083
San Jose, CA 95150-5038

800-527-4720

Think of your favorite California foods —fresh fruit, sourdough bread, Ghirardelli chocolate, creative condiments—and they're all available from this one source. You'll also find dried fruit and nuts, baked goods, and numerous gift items. Club plans supply you with seasonal fresh California fruit throughout the year.

Free color catalog
Mail and phone orders, gift orders
AMEX, MC, VISA

Muscadine Bread

from Callaway Gardens Country Store

½ cup butter
1 cup sugar
2 eggs
2 cups all-purpose flour
1½ teaspoons baking powder
½ cup milk
1 cup Callaway Gardens Muscadine Sauce
½ cup chopped pecans

Cream butter and sugar together until light and fluffy. Add eggs, beating in one at a time. Sift dry ingredients together and add alternately with milk and Muscadine Sauce. Stir in nuts. Bake in greased and floured loaf pan at 325 degrees for 50 to 60 minutes, until toothpick inserted in center tests clean. Makes 1 loaf.

Tropical treats from Hawaii—

Kalani's Hawaiian Catalog
1225 Alapai Street
Honolulu, HI 96813

800-545-8820

This collection features Hawaiian treats such as jams, jellies, honey, fruit syrups, condiments, tea and coffee, as well as baked goods and confections. Highlights include passion fruit jelly, papaya seed dressing, toasted Maui onion mustard, macadamia nuts, and dehydrated poi. You'll also find Hawaiian crafts, fragrances, musical recordings, and gift selections in baskets woven from dried leaves of the lauhala tree.

Free illustrated catalog
Phone and mail orders, gift orders
MC, VISA

Napa Valley specialties—

Oakville Grocery Company
P. O. Box 86
7856 St. Helena Highway
Oakville, CA 94562

707-944-8802

This shop, with locations in Oakville and Palo Alto, also offers a convenient mail order service to keep your pantry stocked with wonderful products from the Napa Valley. Individual products include wine vinegars, extra-virgin olive oils, pastas, preserves, sauces, and condiments. Gift baskets combine items to create the Pantry Stocker (a selection of basics), Basta Pasta (pasta products and accompaniments), a Taste of Napa Valley (an array of treats), and many more.

Free illustrated brochure
Phone and mail orders; gift orders
AMEX, MC, VISA

More Regional Treats

Celebrating the heartland—

American Spoon Foods, Inc.
P. O. Box 566
1688 Clarion Avenue
Petoskey, MI 49770-0566

800-222-5886
616-347-9030
Fax: 616-347-2512

This delightfully illustrated catalog features specialties native to northern Michigan, such as dried red tart cherries, cranberries, and wild blueberries. Other products include wild nuts (black walnuts, pecans, hickory nuts, and chestnuts); wildflower honey; preserves, jellies, and conserves made from hand-picked wild fruit; as well as mushrooms, maple syrup, teas, and a carefully chosen selection of additional American regional specialties. Gifts are packed in birch-bark baskets or in boxes decorated with charming folk art pictures.

Free seasonal catalogs
Phone, fax, and mail orders, gift orders
DISC, MC, VISA

A potpourri of regional treats—

Gourmet Treasure Hunters
10044 Adams Avenue, Suite 305
Huntington Beach, CA 92646

714-964-3355

Gourmet Treasure Hunters celebrates America's abundance by featuring a sampling of the best regional specialties. Some highlights: Vidalia onion relish, Tennessee Sunshine (a sauce made with hot crushed peppers), smoked rainbow trout pâté, California escargots, and many items from the Southwest and the New Orleans region. New items are constantly added, and Gourmet Treasure Hunters will be pleased to hunt for any regional specialty you would like to find.

Illustrated catalog (with newsletters for a year), $4.00
Phone and mail orders
AMEX

Favorites from New York State—

The Made in New York Store
P. O. Box 2000
Ithaca, NY 14851

607-272-2125

Chocolate syrup for making egg creams, Saratoga chips, a cookie cutter in the shape of the Chrysler Building—all these special New York State items can be ordered from this source. You'll also find Speidie Sauce for making "Speidies," marinated and broiled kabobs long popular among the ethnic communities in upstate New York. There's also a basket of the state's finest edibles, famous books by New York cooks, and even selections of New York State wines. There are also games, puzzles, and other items gathered from around the state.

Free illustrated catalog
Phone and mail orders, gift orders
AMEX, CB, DC, MC, VISA

Northwestern specialties—

To Market to Market
P. O. Box 492
West Linn, OR 97068

503-657-9192

Baskets from this company are filled
with such Northwestern treats as
Oregon hazelnuts, honey, apricot
marmalade, marionberry jam, and
smoked salmon. A crate of smoked
sturgeon and smoked salmon is also
available. Special gift baskets are packed
especially for teatime, or choose a
basketful of dessert treats or one
brimming with herb and spice blends.

Free illustrated catalog
Mail orders, gift orders
MC, VISA

Regional foods from an Ann Arbor
deli—

Zingerman's Delicatessen
422 Detroit Street
Ann Arbor, MI 48104

313-663-3400

Zingerman's prides itself on hunting
down good foods from around the
country to serve at the deli counter,
stock the shop, and send to mail order
customers. Their catalog offers just a
sampling of the 10,000 or so products in
the store, and you are invited to call
with special requests. It sounds like a
great place to stop for a sandwich next
time you find yourself in Ann Arbor.

Free catalog
Phone and mail orders, gift orders
MC, VISA

CHAPTER 25

THE INTERNATIONAL PANTRY

Here are sources for ingredients from around the world—your passport to adventurous cooking. Savor the subtle flavors of Thai cuisine, make your own sushi, or prepare an authentic Middle Eastern feast. You'll also find the cookbooks and special kitchenware you'll want for your culinary travels. This abundance and variety of international ingredients may inspire you to borrow from various national pantries to make exciting new versions of traditional American dishes or to harmoniously blend ingredients from around the globe to make your own cosmopolitan creations.

Asian Cuisines: Chinese, Japanese, Thai, Vietnamese, Korean, and More

Japanese foods and imports—

Anzen Importers
736 N. E. Union Avenue
Portland, OR 97232

503-233-5111

Although it would be impossible to inventory everything in Anzen's large Portland store, the company sends out a lengthy list of Japanese, Chinese, Thai, and Korean foods and invites you to write for ingredients you cannot locate elsewhere. Seaweed for sushi, wasabi (Japanese horseradish), fish flakes for soup stock, and fermented black beans are just a few of the items on their list. China and kitchenware are available, as well as materials for Japanese flower arranging and bonsai, and supplies for origami and sumi (ink painting).

Free price list
Mail orders
No credit cards

A mail order oriental pantry—

Joyce Chen Unlimited
423 Great Road (2A)
Acton, MA 01720

508-263-6922

Joyce Chen Unlimited has two retail stores (in Acton, Massachusetts, and Amherst, New Hampshire) and a mail order division called The Oriental Pantry. From there you can order Joyce Chen cooking sauces, which include soy sauces, stir-fry sauces, duck sauce, barbecue sauce, and a wide range of oriental ingredients. Cooking tools include cutting slabs, cookware, woks and accessories, cutlery, bamboo ware, and porcelain items.

Free price list
Mail orders
MC, VISA

Indonesian ingredients and traditional Dutch treats—

DeWildt Imports, Inc.
Fox Gap Road
RD 3
Bangor, PA 18013

800-338-3433

Since 1952 this family-run Pennsylvania company has provided an ever increasing range of Dutch-Indonesian ingredients. Hundreds of products are presented in a catalog that is spiced with recipes, tips, and excellent explanations of items that may be unfamiliar to many American cooks. Read the excerpt about sambals and krupuk below (DeWildt sells over a dozen kinds of each). You'll find essential but hard-to-find seasonings such as galanga root, lemon grass, and lime leaves; staples such as rice, beans, noodles, flour, and lentils. Also available: curry pastes for Thai cooking, coconut milk, numerous soy sauces, oils, condiments, chutneys, exotic fruits and juices. A well-chosen selection of cookbooks and kitchen tools is offered, too. Traditional Dutch items include cheese, baked goods, vegetables, chocolate, cocoa powder, and gift items. For friends who love to cook, the food baskets that assemble ingredients for a specific cuisine would be a perfect choice.

Free illustrated catalog
Phone and mail orders, gift orders
AMEX, MC, VISA

A potpourri of Asian ingredients—

Gourmet Treasure Hunters
10044 Adams Avenue, Suite 305
Huntington Beach, CA 92646

714-964-3355

This company has gathered many of the basics for Asian cooking, including five spice powder, star anise, hoisin sauce, and Szechuan peppercorns. There's also coconut milk, lemon grass, and powdered galanga, all used extensively in Thai cooking. Gourmet Treasure Hunters also carries Tu'on'g, a hot garlic sauce for Vietnamese cuisine. New items are added regularly, and if you don't find what you're looking for in the catalog, Gourmet Treasure Hunters will be glad to try to find it for you.

Illustrated catalog (with newsletters for a year), $4.00
Phone and mail orders
AMEX

Japanese foods from New York City—

Katagiri & Company, Inc.
224 East 59th Street
New York, NY 10022

212-755-3566

You can visit Katagiri in New York City and delight in their vast offering of oriental specialities, or you can order their catalog and browse at your leisure through pages of ingredients listed both in English and in Japanese. You may order canned goods, seasonings, sauces, pickles, miso, oils, vinegars, spices, and dozens of noodles, teas, and confections. Some particularly enticing items are pickled scallions, radish paste, and citron vinegar.

Chinese Noodle Soup with Pork and Winter Pickle

from David Bigge, The Spice Merchant

This is a popular style of noodle dish which is mostly noodles with less broth than a traditional "soup." The most interesting flavor here is the winter pickle, which is Chinese cabbage preserved with salt and garlic.

1 pound fresh or dried mein, boiled
4 cups soup stock, chicken or beef

Meat mixture:
2 tablespoons peanut oil
½ pound ground pork
2 teaspoons bean sauce
1 teaspoon soy sauce
¼ cup winter pickle, rinsed

Preparation:
Cook the noodles in plenty of boiling water until just done. They should retain some "bite" and not be mushy. This will take 4 to 10 minutes, depending on the type of noodle you use. Drain the noodles and keep warm.

Cooking:
Bring the stock to a boil in a large pot. Meanwhile, heat the oil in a frying pan or wok and add the ground pork. Cook over high heat until almost done, about 3 minutes. Add the bean sauce, soy sauce, and winter pickle. Stir-fry 1 minute longer.

Serving:
Transfer the cooked noodles to a large bowl and add the hot broth. Top with some of the meat mixture and serve. Serves 4.

Free catalog
Mail orders
No credit cards

Ingredients from a Chicago cooking
school—

**Oriental Food Market and Cooking
School**
2801 West Howard Street
Chicago, IL 60645

312-274-2826

Chu-Yen and Pansy Luke run a cooking
school in Chicago and also supply
cooks all over the country with essential
ingredients for oriental cooking. The
price list is alphabetical and has
hundreds of items, including
seasonings, vegetables (canned and
dried), herbs and spices, fruits and
nuts, seafood, and tea. Cooking utensils
also available (and if you order a new
wok you can request that they season it
for you!) as well as cookbooks, garden
seeds, and chinaware. Some highlights
from the product line include dried
lotus root, preserved jellyfish, boiled
gingko nuts, chrysanthemum tea, and
even X-rated fortune cookies.

Free price list (send business-size
stamped, self-addressed envelope)
Mail orders
No credit cards

Ingredients—and helpful
explanations—

Spice Merchant
P. O. Box 524
Jackson Hole, WY 83001

307-733-7811

David Bigge is the Spice Merchant and
his catalog promises "Oriental and

Asian condiments, spices, cookbooks,
gifts, and advice." You'll find all that he
promises and you'll appreciate the time
he's taken to explain each ingredient
and provide you with its alternate
names. (As he points out, fish sauce is
used in several Asian cuisines and is
also known as fish gravy, fish soy, nuoc
mam, ngan-pya-ye, nam pla, or patis. It
can be quite confusing.) Numerous
ingredients are available, including
fresh miso, nori (seaweed sheets for
making sushi), instant tamarind, curry
pastes, and much more. David has also
put together money-saving "shelf
stocker" packages of ingredients that
provide all the basics for Chinese, Thai/
Indonesian, or sushi preparation.
Cookbooks and cooking utensils are
well chosen and also carefully
explained. For anyone who wants to
learn more about Asian cuisines, the
Spice Merchant will be a source for
more than ingredients.

Free color catalog
Mail orders, gift orders
AMEX, MC, VISA

Everything for the oriental kitchen—

Tsang & Ma Wokery
P. O. Box 294
Belmont, CA 94002

415-595-2270

Tsang & Ma Wokery provides an
excellent variety of seeds for growing
oriental vegetables (more details in
Chapter 28, "Growing Your Own
Ingredients"), and a selection of
seasoning oils, soy sauces, stir-fry
sauces, traditional sauces, and regional
seasonings. Equipment for the oriental
kitchen includes woks and covers,
steamers, cleavers, and miscellaneous
tools.

An Introduction to Sambals and Krupuks

from DeWildt Imports

Sambal is a paste made of hot chili peppers, with some salt and other seasonings, fresh or fried, which is used to flavor the many dishes that make up Indonesian cuisine and many delectable oriental specialties. Sambals are used both as condiments on the dinner table and as ingredients for cooking, and no Indonesian Rijsttafel (Rice Table) is complete without sambals. Some of the more popular sambals are:

Sambal Ulek: a fresh hot pepper paste, lightly salted. A basic ingredient to any spiced vegetable or meat dish.

Sambal Badjak: a fried mixture of Sambal Ulek, made with onions and other spices; used as a condiment.

Sambal Djeroek: a popular mixture of fresh hot pepper paste, with spices and onion. What makes it different? A fresh Indonesian lime leaf is blended through the paste, making it delightful and unique.

Sambal Nasi Goreng: one of the ingredients of the well-known Nasi Goreng, the Indonesian fried rice dish; also served separately with the meal.

Krupuk is one of the most addictive delectables to come out of Asia. These "wafer chips," native to Indonesia, Malaysia, Thailand, and China, come in a variety of flavors, shapes, and sizes, and they can be reddish-pink, orange, yellow, or pale white. Use Krupuk to accompany meals, cocktails, or as a snack for friends and family.

Krupuk Udang, made of shrimp, egg white, and tapioca, is the most popular Krupuk and comes in small, medium, and large sizes. Tangy Cassava is made from sweet potato starch and speckled with chili, paprika, and other spices. Other Krupuks are made with fish, soy beans, and egg noodles.

Krupuks should be deep fried in hot oil for a few seconds, causing them to puff up many times their size. Remove with a slotted spoon and drain on paper towels before serving.

Free illustrated catalog
Phone and mail orders
MC, VISA

Asian ingredients from a Northwestern purveyor—

Uwajimaya, Inc.
519 Sixth Avenue S.
P. O. Box 3003
Seattle, WA 98104

206-624-6248

You'll find a fine selection of Asian groceries and gifts available from this Seattle supplier—canned goods, pickled vegetables, dried seafood, tea, spices, and sauces, as well as rice, flour, and noodles. Philippine, Chinese, and Korean food specialties are offered. Uwajimaya, which celebrated its sixtieth anniversary in 1988, has three shops in the Northwest in addition to its mail order business.

Free catalog
Mail orders
No credit cards

Flavors from Around the World

From Hungary

It all began with paprika—

Paprikas Weiss
1546 Second Avenue
New York, NY 10028

212-288-6117

Paprikas Weiss has been doing business for almost a hundred years at its location in the heart of New York's Upper East Side. The shop and the mail order business are excellent sources of Hungarian specialties such as spices, meats, and cheese, baking ingredients,

imported preserved fruits, and a cornucopia of ingredients from Poland and Rumania. There's even a chef's apron with a message—"Kiss me, I'm Hungarian."

Seasonal catalogs, $3.00 annual subscription
Phone and mail orders, gift orders, and gift certificates
AMEX, MC, VISA

From India

Bringing Indian cuisine to the United States—

Cinnabar Specialty Foods
214 Frontier Drive
Prescott, AZ 86303

800-824-4563
602-778-3687

When Neera Tandon moved to the United States from India in 1972, she began a catering business and taught cooking classes to share the wonderful foods of her homeland. Cinnabar Specialty Foods, launched in 1985, produces chutneys (tomato, tomato-mint, mango, pear-cardamom, and peach); Kashmiri marinade (a combination of fresh garlic, ginger, and spices); and tandoori grilling paste. Other products include a Thai seafood marinade, Barbados honey pepper sauce, and Asian tamarind sauce. The Cinnabar sampler pack lets you choose four products you'd like to try.

Free illustrated brochure
Phone and mail orders, gift orders
MC, VISA

From Italy

Traditional Italian foods—

Balducci's
Mail Order Division
11-02 Queens Plaza South
Long Island City, NY 11101-4908

800-822-1444
800-247-2450 (in NY State)
718-786-9690 (special requests)

The Balducci family provides food from around the world with a special accent on Italian specialities. In addition to a selection of imported Italian meats, cheeses, vinegars, oils, and condiments, the company's kitchens turn out specialties such as traditional panettone, homemade focaccia, and numerous ready-to-serve dishes such as veal rollatini and frittatas. Gift baskets are also available.

Free seasonal catalogs
Phone and mail orders, gift orders
AMEX, MC, VISA

From a landmark Italian grocery—

Central Grocery
923 Decatur Street
New Orleans, LA 70116

504-523-1620

This historic grocery, located at the same site in New Orleans since 1906, carries hundreds of domestic and imported food specialties. They will send you a price list that provides a sampling of their pastas, oils and vinegars, cheeses, baked goods, and condiments, and you may call for other items. Ingredients for Cajun/Creole cooking are also featured, as are New Orleans coffees with chicory.

Free price list
Phone and mail orders
No credit cards

From a historic New York City Italian grocery—

Manganaro Foods
488 Ninth Avenue
New York, NY 10018

800-472-5264
212-563-5331

Manganaro's stocks a fine selection of imported Italian foods—everything from antipasto to espresso beans. You'll find imported meats, cheeses, oils and vinegars, pastas, and baked goods such as panettone and biscotti. This shop, located on the West Side of New York City for almost a hundred years, also offers its own Italian family cookbook. You are invited to call about items not featured in the catalog. If it's Italian, Manganaro's probably has it—or will know where to get it for you.

Free color catalog
Phone and mail orders, gift orders
AMEX, DC, MC, VISA

Italian foods from fresh, natural ingredients—

Providence Cheese and Tavola Calda
407 Atwells Avenue
Providence, RI 02909

401-421-5653

Providence Cheese and Tavola Calda has a long list of local and mail order customers who are devoted to the shop's original and completely fresh food operation. Everything is made from natural ingredients without fats, shortenings, salt, honey, or sugar. ("No

freezers and not even a can opener,"
says proprietor Ginny Wheatley
proudly.) Ingredients include
organically grown, stone-ground durum
wheat flour, fresh eggs and cow and
goat milk for cheeses, and fruit
concentrates as sweeteners. Breads,
focaccia, pizza, calzone, pastas, and
sauces are all made fresh in the shop. A
variety of desserts are sweetened with
fruit and fruit concentrates to the
European level of sweetness. Because
the product list changes frequently, it's
best to call Ginny to discuss your needs
and find out what's available.

Free product list
Phone and mail orders
No credit cards

Call for Italian groceries—

Todaro Bros.
555 Second Avenue
New York, NY 10016

212-679-7766

This New York grocery specializes in
imported Italian items such as cheese,
oil, and condiments. Although the
company does not currently have a
catalog, you may call Todaro with your
shopping list and the mail order
department will ship what you request.

No catalog
Phone and mail orders
AMEX, MC, VISA

From the Middle East

Fresh baked goods and Mid-East
ingredients—

Ghossain's Mid-East Bakery
2935 Market Street
Youngstown, OH 44507

800-544-2415
216-782-9473

In addition to traditional baked
products such as lahvosh, pita, and
baklava, Ghossain's Mid-East Bakery
supplies a variety of imported foods
and ingredients including essentials
such as bulgur, lentils, beans, and
spices, as well as grape leaves, tahini,
Turkish coffee, roasted chickpeas,
tamarind syrup, and pomegranate juice.
You can call to inquire about items not
specifically mentioned on the list, and
the staff will try to find them for you.

Free price list
Mail and phone orders
MC, VISA

Everything for Middle Eastern cuisine—

Sultan's Delight
P. O. Box 253
Staten Island, NY 10314

718-720-1557

This is a complete source of ingredients
for Middle Eastern cooking. Basics
include peas, beans, semolina, cereals,
oils and tahini, nuts, seeds, and spices.
There's also a fine variety of olives and
pickles, cheeses, doughs, pastries, and
confections. Ready-to-serve delicacies
include stuffed vine leaves and
hummus. A selection of Turkish
coffees, coffeepots, and cups is also
available—as well as music and
costumes for belly dancing.

Free illustrated catalog
Mail orders
MC, VISA

From Portugal

Portuguese sausage and other specialties—

Lisbon Sausage Company, Inc.
Amaral's Linguica
433 South Second Street
New Bedford, MA 02740

508-993-7645

Although this company specializes in meats such as linguica, chourica, and salpicao, it stocks other Portuguese specialties, including ceci nuts, pickled eggs, lupini beans, and hot mixed pickles. Call or write and they will also try to get Portuguese items not mentioned on the price list.

Free price list
Mail orders
MC, VISA

From Scandinavia

Tre Kronor Scandinavian Center
248 Main Street
Farmington, CT 06032

203-677-1881

Carl Dahlberg is continually adding new items to his list of Scandinavian foods, which includes such specialties as glogg spices, dilled caviar paste, berry preserves, Swedish pancake mix, and reindeer meatballs. You may also order gift selections of these foods. If you visit the Center you'll be able to browse among Scandinavian crystal, china, flatware, and linens, as well as traditional crafts and clothing. There's also a bakery where you can relax over coffee and freshly made pastries.

Free price list
Phone and mail orders
MC, VISA

More International Ingredients

These companies are good sources for a range of international ingredients:

Dean & DeLuca, Inc.
Mail Order Department
560 Broadway
New York, NY 10012

800-221-7714
212-431-1691

Among Dean & DeLuca's imported and domestic specialty foods you'll find a selection of international ingredients specifically for Italian, Mexican, Chinese, Japanese, Indonesian, and Indian cooking. Gift baskets that combine ingredients for French or Italian cuisine are also offered.

Illustrated catalog, $2.00
Phone and mail orders, gift orders, and gift certificates
AMEX, MC, VISA

Gourmet Treasure Hunters
10044 Adams Avenue, Suite 305
Huntington Beach, CA 92646

714-964-3355

As well as carrying a great selection of cooking essentials and North American specialties, this company has hunted down delicacies from around the world. Some highlights for Mexican cooking include mole (a sauce of spices, nuts, seeds, and chocolate for poultry), epazote (a pungent herb), and annatto seed (a subtle-flavored seed also known as achiote). You'll also find sauces from Jamaica and Barbados; herbs, spices, and condiments for Indian and Middle Eastern cooking; and a selection of hard-to-find items such as potato flour and pearl sugar. Call Gourmet Treasure Hunters for anything you don't see in their stock.

Illustrated catalog (with newsletters for
a year), $4.00
Phone and mail orders
AMEX

G. B. Ratto & Company
821 Washington Street
Oakland, CA 94607

800-325-3483
800-228-3515 (in CA)
Fax: 415-836-2250

G. B. Ratto has been a provisioner of
ethnic foods since 1897, and you'll find
Ratto's pantry divided into specialty
"shelves" of Indo-Asian, Spanish, and
French ingredients. For Anglophiles,
there's even a shelf of specialties from
the British Isles, including oatcakes
from Scotland and porridge from
Ireland. The international shelf is a
potpourri of German, Greek, and other
specialties such as aspic jelly powder
and stuffed vine leaves. If you are
looking for something that isn't in the
catalog, send a note to Ratto's and
they'll search the store inventory for
you.

Free illustrated catalog
Phone, fax, and mail orders, gift orders,
and gift certificates
MC, VISA

Savories, Ltd.
1450 Heggen Street
Hudson, WI 54016

715-386-8832
Fax: 715-386-6731

Savories, Ltd., offers a wide variety of
hard-to-find food products from around
the world, including coffee beans, wild
rice blends, seasonings, and spices.
Upon request, Savories, Ltd., will help
you locate almost any hard-to-find food
product.

Free catalog
Phone, fax, and mail orders
MC, VISA

Zabar's
2245 Broadway
New York, NY 10024

212-496-1234
Fax: 212-580-4477

Zabar's is a large New York City food
emporium that makes many
international products available through
its mail order catalog. You'll find
imported specialties such as cheeses,
meats, pastas, coffee and teas,
preserves and condiments. They also
offer a wide selection of cooking
equipment and tools. Try to visit the
store on Broadway next time you're in
New York—selecting a loaf from among
the more than sixty kinds of bread is an
experience all food lovers will enjoy.

Free color catalog
Phone, fax, and mail orders, gift orders
AMEX

Zingerman's Delicatessen
422 Detroit Street
Ann Arbor, MI 48104

313-663-3400

Zingerman's imports staples and special
foods for many cuisines. If, for
example, you'd like to have an English-
style afternoon tea, ring Zingerman's
for British biscuits (cookies to us),
cheeses and crackers, smoked fish,
preserves, and, of course, the best
British tea. Gift baskets include
ingredients for a paella feast, a pasta
lover's selection, and foods for a perfect
picnic. Custom gift selections are also
available. Call for special items that may
not be in the catalog—the store stocks
about 10,000 products.

Free catalog
Phone and mail orders, gift orders
MC, VISA

You'll find more ingredients for international cooking in Chapter 12. "Herbs and Spices."

Find seeds to raise your own oriental vegetables in Chapter 28, "Growing Your Own Ingredients."

PART THREE

SPECIAL SOURCES FOR COOKS

CHAPTER 26

BOOKS FOR COOKS

Those of us who read cookbooks the way other people read novels can never have too many of these wonderful diversionary volumes. Here are sources for cookbooks that may be difficult to find in your local bookshop, as well as some introductions to individuals who deal especially in rare and out-of-print books about food and wine.

Regional community cookbooks—

The Cookbook Collection, Inc.
2500 East 195th Street
Belton, MO 64012

816-322-2122

The Cookbook Collection presents a selection of America's community and Junior League cookbooks by region— the Midwest, Florida, the West-Pacific, etc. Additional special sections are devoted to cookbooks dealing with diet, health, and nutrition; microwave cooking; and special interests and occasions. Highlights include *The Garlic Lovers' Cookbook* (Volumes I and II) from the Gilroy Garlic Festival; *A Culinary Visit to Historic Sonoma*, which tours California's wine country with some of its best-known cooks and includes recipes from some of its finest restaurants; and *The Shaker Cookbook* from the Shaker Historical Society in Ohio, a classic that has enjoyed 13 printings in twenty-five years.

Free color catalog
Mail orders
No credit cards

One-of-a-kind books on wine and food—

Household Words
P. O. Box 7231
Berkeley, CA 94707

415-524-8859

Kay Caughren offers this engrossing collection of out-of-print cookbooks and books about wine, including some unusual volumes. All are in good or very good condition and any defects are candidly described; most books are reasonably priced under $25. Among the numerous categories from basic cookbooks to the quaint and curious, Kay feels some of the most interesting are the fund-raising cookbooks issued by churches and ladies' groups. She explains: "The first ones were issued during the Civil War. They are usually well thumbed; many have the owner's favorite recipes written in, and often contain local advertising. These books are an important source for social historians and a record of regional and ethnic cooking. Women *trusted* these recipes. They are usually signed and certainly were kitchen-tested!"

Catalog, $3.00
Mail orders
No credit cards

Hundreds of cookbooks, many discounted—

Jessica's Biscuit
The Cookbook People
Box 301
Newtonville, MA 02160

800-225-4264
800-322-4027 (in MA)
617-965-0530 (metro Boston)

Over 400 cookbooks are offered in the Jessica's Biscuit catalog, including some new releases and many best-sellers. Each entry includes a brief description to let you know the scope of the book and the number of pages and/or recipes included. Many books are offered at substantial savings over their cover prices.

Free color catalog
Phone and mail orders, gift orders
MC, VISA

Out-of-print books for the collector—

MCL Associates
Box 26
McLean, VA 22101-0026

Contact by mail

MCL Associates are dedicated to their clientele of cookbook collectors. Phyllis King, who directs the used book division of the company, describes

cookbook collecting as a hobby that keeps us in touch with our own rich heritage and allows us to share those of people around the world. The descriptive catalog includes categories such as celebrations, holidays, and entertaining; baking and breads; celebrating with children; and restaurants and their recipes. In addition, MCL will conduct a search if you are looking for a particular cookbook that may no longer be in print.

Catalog, $3.50
Mail orders
No credit cards

A search service for out-of-print cookbooks—

Ms. Charlotte Safir
Out-of-Print Books
1349 Lexington Avenue, Apt. 9B
New York, NY 10128

212-534-7933

Although Charlotte Safir will conduct a search for any out-of-print book, she specializes in cookbooks and children's books and, naturally, has a particular interest in cookbooks written for children. Although she does not maintain a shop or offer a catalog, you may let her know about your particular interest and she will send a list of what's available in her large stock of out-of-print books. She will search for any book you might need and also compiles a want list of books she is currently seeking. Charlotte particularly enjoys helping clients put together subject collections. She has, for example, helped a California man, originally from New England, assemble a remarkable collection of Cape Cod cookbooks. For a black woman lawyer in Virginia who avidly collects books by black authors on soul food and early Southern cooking, she has found titles that the collector didn't know existed. And, for an author who is compiling a comprehensive book about tea, she has recently provided some invaluable research.

No catalog; please write with request

More regional cookbooks—

Simmer Pot Press
Route 3, Box 973-A
Boone, NC 28607

704-262-3289

Simmer Pot Press offers a potpourri of books including regional and special interest cookbooks such as Jack Daniel's *The Spirit of Tennessee Cookbook* and *The American Country Inn Bed & Breakfast Cookbook*. In their noncookbook collection you'll find books dealing with American traditions and country life.

Illustrated catalog, $1.00
Mail orders
No credit cards

Cookbooks from clubs and organizations—

The Wendopher Company
1920 Jamestown-Gunnersville Road
Jamestown, OH 45335

Contact by mail

Linda Whealdon has assembled this collection of cookbooks from clubs, organizations, and churches across the United States. She provides a very

complete description of each book and gives a sampling of their recipes. Some highlights include *Historic Virginia Inns: A Cook's Tour*, and *Spa Specialties* from the kitchen of Lake Austin Resort in Texas.

Illustrated catalog, $1.00
Mail orders, gift certificates
MC, VISA

Antiquarian cookbooks—

The Wine and Food Library
1207 West Madison Street
Ann Arbor, MI 48103

313-663-4894

The Wine and Food Library is an antiquarian bookshop founded by Jan Longone in 1973. An ever changing stock of about 15,000 items includes books by and about great chefs; cookbooks from every continent and culture; books about famous hotels, resorts, and restaurants; books about single food subjects (from abalone to zucchini); and encyclopedic works. The catalog lists 500 individual items as well as numerous specialty lists and special offers. A separate catalog of rare books from 1600 to 1972 is fully annotated with complete historic and bibliographic information. Among Jan's clients are cooks, chefs, bakers, restaurateurs, authors, culinary historians, and museums. Her pleasure, she says, is in matching the right books with the right people.

Catalog, $3.00; rare catalog, $5.00
Mail orders
No credit cards

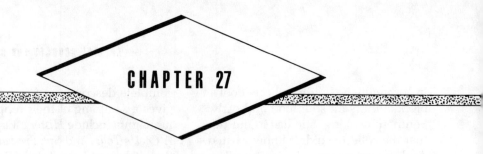

CHAPTER 27

EQUIPMENT AND TOOLS

Remember the colorful Christmas catalogs that were our "wishbooks" when we were children? Well, for grown-ups who love to cook, the catalogs offered by these suppliers are today's answer to those magical pages of years ago. Here you'll find everything from the finest imported French copper cookware to small and well-designed kitchen tools that can make food preparation a joy. You'll have fun discovering cookie and chocolate molds based on lovely antique originals and finding old-fashioned tools you thought existed only in antique shops. It's time to start making that wish list!

Beautiful ceramic cookie molds—

Brown Bag Cookie Art
7 Eagle Square
Concord, NH 03301

800-228-4488
603-226-1984

Brown Bag Cookie Art produces a charming collection of ceramic cookie molds in whimsical shapes—animals, hearts, angels and other Christmas favorites. There are also shortbread pans inspired by antique butter molds and plaques. Each comes with a booklet of cookie recipes; some of the shortbread recipes, such as ginger shortbread and orange spice shortbread, sound like delicious variations on a favorite theme.

Free illustrated catalog
Phone and mail orders, gift orders
MC, VISA

Calphalon and Chaudier cookware at a discount—

Chattanooga Cookery
725 East Eleventh Street
Chattanooga, TN 37403

615-266-6112

This restaurant supplier also sells cookware to home cooks and offers increasing discounts for larger orders. A complete line of Chaudier and Calphalon cookware is available as well as commercial aluminum cookware.

Free color brochure
Phone and mail orders
MC, VISA

Professional quality for the home cook—

The Chef's Catalog
3215 Commercial Avenue
Northbrook, IL 60062-1900

800-338-3232 (orders)
312-480-8305 (customer service)

The Chef's Catalog has been providing professional-quality cooking equipment for the home chef since 1979. You'll find appliances by companies like KitchenAid, Cuisinart, and Krups; Henckels knives and kitchen tools; Calphalon and Le Creuset cookware. Books from Frugal Gourmet Jeff Smith are featured, as well as a selection of items chosen by him that range from a handsome brass pepper mill to a practical wooden citrus juicer. You'll also find foods such as garlic braids and dessert sauces, and unusual items like hand-molded Spanish bottles for your homemade vinegars.

Color catalog, $3.00
Phone and mail orders, gift orders
AMEX, DISC, MC, VISA

Good prices on quality equipment—

A Cook's Wares
3270 37th Street
Beaver Falls, PA 15010-1263

412-846-9490

Byron and Gail Bitar, owners of A Cook's Wares, promise substantial savings on Cuisinart food processors and accessories, Henckels cutlery, Krups appliances, Le Creuset pans, KitchenAid mixers, and more. In addition to these well-known items, they offer an array of bakeware and accessories, cooking utensils, hard-to-find and practical items. There's a

particularly nice selection of imported French porcelain cookware, including hand-painted game-head terrines. Food items include imported chocolate, spices, preserves, oils, and vinegars.

Illustrated catalog, $1.00
Phone and mail orders, gift orders
AMEX, MC, VISA

From a Tennessee general store—

Cumberland General Store
Route 3, Box 81
Crossville, TN 38555

800-334-4640
615-484-8481

If you enjoy browsing through thick, old-fashioned catalogs you'll love the one put out by Cumberland General Store. They claim to have "goods in endless variety for man and beast," and no one could argue with that; in fact, you'll find things you were sure hadn't been made for years. Cooks will be especially interested in the cast-iron utensils, enamelware, copper cookware, stainless steel items (including four big stock pots), rolling pins, and cookie molds. You'll also find old-fashioned blue and white stoneware bowls and crocks as well as pages of useful kitchen tools that have stood the test of time. Wood-burning kitchen stoves are also available.

Illustrated catalog, $3.00
Phone and mail orders, gift orders
DISC, MC, VISA

Essential tools, large and small—

Dean & DeLuca, Inc.
Mail Order Department
560 Broadway
New York, NY 10012

800-221-7714
212-431-1691

Dean & DeLuca sell Italian stainless
steel and French copper cookware and
heavy-gauge steelware. In addition,
there's metal bakeware, ceramic ware,
pastry tools, graters and grinders, and
many small but essential kitchen tools.
Highlights include a couscousière for
making classic couscous, black steel
baguette pans, timbale molds, baking
stones for bread and pizza, and
handsome Pillivuyt dinnerware. There's
also a tantalizing array of specialty
foods and international ingredients. Gift
baskets are available, and you can make
custom selections.

Illustrated catalog, $2.00
Phone and mail orders, gift orders and
gift certificates
AMEX, MC, VISA

Brand names for the kitchen—

European Home Products
236 East Avenue
Norwalk, CT 06855

800-225-0760
203-866-5165

Tools for the chef range from a feather
pastry brush to a complete line of
KitchenAid and Le Creuset products.
There's a good selection of Peugeot
pepper mills, Sabatier knives, and
Pillivuyt porcelain, as well as decorative
canisters, novelty oven mitts, and gift
items.

Free color catalog
Phone and mail orders
AMEX, MC, VISA

Chocolate molds from antique casts—

Holcraft Collection
P. O. Box 792
Davis, CA 95616

916-756-3023

Among the delightful collection of quilts
and crafts assembled by Adrienne
Trouw, you'll find some unusual
chocolate molds made in Holland from
the original antique casts. Although
beautiful as decorative pieces, they are
professional-quality, heavy-gauge molds
that give clear definition to molded
chocolates. Choose from Christmas
favorites, a barnyard of animals, hearts,
and Dutch themes. Adrienne includes
instructions for using the molds to
make chocolates, candles, or papier-
mâché or chalkware figures.

Free illustrated catalog
Phone and mail orders, gift orders
MC, VISA

Shop at home for your kitchen—

Kitchen Collection
71 East Water Street
Chillicothe, OH 45601

800-292-9150

The Kitchen Collection has almost 50
stores from coast to coast, and if you
don't have one close by, the crammed
color catalog will bring its products to
your door. As well as mixers, coffee
makers, toasters, pasta and ice cream
makers, you'll find cookware, cutlery,
and baking pans of all descriptions. The
selection of cast-iron cookware includes
pans for muffins, breadsticks, skillet
corn bread, and cornsticks. It's fun to
browse through the selection of more
than 30 "handy helpers" priced under
$5.00.

Free color catalog
Phone and mail order, gift orders
DISC, MC, VISA

Baking equipment—

Kitchen Krafts
P. O. Box 805
Mount Laurel, NJ 08054

609-778-4960

Kitchen Krafts specializes in baking
supplies, including cake and muffin
pans, cake-decorating supplies, and
equipment for canning and drying food.
You'll find many novelty cake pans,
parchment paper, and a tool for making
homemade sugar ice cream cones.
There's also a selection of specialty
sugars, flavorings, baking chocolates,
and cookbooks for cake and candy
making.

Free illustrated price list
Mail orders
No credit cards

An equipment catalog with newsletter
updates—

La Cuisine
323 Cameron Street
Alexandria, VA 22314

800-521-1176
703-836-4435

La Cuisine features copper cookware in
both hotel weight and lighter
presentation weight. A handy copper
item here is a KitchenAid bowl liner
that allows you to produce high-volume
beaten egg whites with the convenience
of a mixer. They also offer aluminum,
stainless steel, cast-iron, and carbon
steel cookware. Additional equipment
includes metal and ceramic bakeware,
molds, cookie cutters, knives, specialty

tools, and small kitchen essentials.
You'll find many wonderful items here
—a yule log mold for baking *bûche de
Noël*; a poppy seed grinder; French wire
baskets for salad, parsley, and garlic;
even a children's pasta machine. In
addition to equipment, there's a
selection of teas, preserves, herbs and
spices, and ingredients for baking.
Because many items are imported and
prices fluctuate, you are invited to call
for information about availability and
price. The catalog is supplemented by
regularly published newsletters.

Catalog and supplements, $3.00
Phone and mail orders
MC, VISA

Tools for food garnishes—

Lieba, Inc.
405 West Franklin Street
Baltimore, MD 21201

301-727-7333

If you've ever admired cleverly crafted
food garnishes—onions transformed
into chrysanthemums or apples made
into perky birds—and wondered how it
was done, this collection of five tools
and the accompanying instruction book
will show you how.

Free price list
Mail orders
No credit cards

Baking and candy-making supplies—

Maid of Scandinavia
3244 Raleigh Avenue
Minneapolis, MN 55416

800-328-6722
800-851-1121 (in MN)
925-9256 (Twin Cities metro area)

Maid of Scandinavia specializes in ingredients and equipment for bakers and candy makers, and its catalog of almost 200 pages is crammed with hundreds of items. Of special interest are baking pans—for éclairs, madeleines, tarts, and tea cakes—as well as pie pans, bread pans, and numerous springform pans. Also pastry forms, cookie cutters, cake-decorating supplies, and a selection of general-purpose kitchen tools such as thermometers, spatulas, and no-nonsense graters. Baking chocolates and other ingredients are also offered. You may enjoy Maid of Scandinavia's *Mailbox News*, a monthly magazine for candy makers and bakers.

Color catalog, $1.00
Phone and mail orders
DISC, MC, VISA

Handcrafted items from a nonprofit group—

Oak & Iron
2700 Commerce Street
LaCrosse, WI 54601

800-356-5432
800-362-6060 (in WI)

A sturdy bagel cutter was the first item made by Oak & Iron, a nonprofit workshop for the handicapped, and it launched an exciting success story. The workshop now makes dozens of items and sells products to mail order customers around the world. Among the carefully crafted red oak items you'll find useful things for the kitchen—lazy Susans, spice racks, canister sets, pot racks, and recipe boxes. There are also ice buckets, TV trays, clocks, and several versions of the original bagel cutter.

Free color catalog
Phone and mail orders, gift orders
AMEX, MC, VISA

A well-designed baking cloth—

Pantry Products
1605 East Lincoln
Fort Collins, CO 80524

303-484-6692

Pantry Products' patented baking cloth uses suction cups to keep the Stay-Put Pastry Cloth in place and comes with a knitted rolling pin cover. The cloth will let you roll out dough quickly without sticking and without absorbing excess flour. It's made of heavy cotton duck cloth and both the cloth and cover are machine washable.

Free information
Phone and mail orders
MC, VISA

Cookie cutters galore—

Patti Deer
5620 Bonnie Street
San Bernadino, CA 92404

Contact by mail

Among dozens of fanciful cookie cutters in this collection you'll find aardvarks, sea horses, chess pieces, and dinosaurs, as well as cutters based on Bible stories, Mother Goose tales, and astrological signs. There are also lots of choices for Christmas, Halloween, and other holidays.

Illustrated catalog, 50¢
Mail orders
No credit cards

Pottery bakeware—

Planned Pottery
2594 Portland Street
P. O. Box 5045
Eugene, OR 97405

503-345-2471

June Knori's Planned Pottery bakeware is made of unglazed stoneware to give breads and other bakery items the characteristics of goods baked in traditional brick ovens. There are pans for breads, pies, and pizzas, as well as rectangular and square bakers. Bun warmers are prettily decorated with a design of fernlike Oregon foliage. June has prepared a cookbook, now in its third edition, with dozens of recipes for yeast breads, quick breads, desserts, and main dishes.

Free illustrated brochure
Phone and mail orders, gift orders
MC, VISA

Cooking equipment selected by a former chef—

Pour Le Chef
P. O. Box 12269
Portland, OR 97212

800-543-3177

Curtis Johnson, a former chef, started Pour Le Chef to bring quality cookware and equipment to home cooks all over the country. He carries Le Creuset cookware; a selection of coffee makers, espresso and cappuccino machines; tableware; cookbooks; and a variety of coffee beans. Curtis emphasizes customer service and will be pleased to try to find any item of equipment or special cookbook you may be seeking.

Catalog, $1.00 (refundable with order)
Phone and mail orders, gift orders
No credit cards

Grain mills, dehydrators, kitchen tools—

R & R Mill Company, Inc.
Smithfield Implement Company
45 West First North
Smithfield, UT 84335

801-563-3333

R & R Mill, a seventy-five-year-old Utah business, supplies both hand- and motor-driven grain and corn mills and several kinds of food dehydrators. You'll also find yogurt makers, ice cream freezers, cast-iron cookware, and useful kitchen tools such as cherry stoners, kernel cutters, graters, steamer baskets, and an old-fashioned corn popper.

Free illustrated brochure
Mail orders
MC, VISA

Everything for sausage making—

The Sausage Maker
26 Military Road
Buffalo, NY 14702

716-876-5521
Fax: 716-875-0302

This is a source for everything you'll need to make your own sausages—equipment, seasonings, cures, and casings. Starter kits contain seasonings and equipment for making breakfast, Polish or summer sausage, or smoked pepperoni, and there's also a kit to smoke turkey, chicken, or game in your oven. Order *Great Sausage Recipes and Meat Curing*, to get over 175 recipes.

Free illustrated catalog
Phone, fax, and mail orders
AMEX, MC, VISA

Wooden kitchen accessories from
Vermont—

Weston Bowl Mill
P. O. Box 218
Weston, VT 05161

802-824-6219

This selection of Vermont-made
woodenware includes many kitchen
items—rolling pins, knife holders, cake
racks, a cookbook holder, meat
tenderizers, a butter mold, scoops, over
a dozen different cutting boards, and
much more. You'll also find bowls
(from 6 inches up to 20 inches), wine
racks, condiment jars with wooden
tops, paper towel holders, peg racks,
and a selection of old-fashioned
wooden toys and gift items. You can
order wooden items unfinished, or
choose one of the three finishes offered
by the mill.

Free illustrated catalog
Phone and mail orders, gift orders
MC, VISA

Items for cooks from around the
world—

Williams-Sonoma
P. O. Box 7456
San Francisco, CA 94120-7456

415-421-4242 (orders)
415-421-4555 (customer service)
Fax: 415-421-5153

When this catalog arrives in the mail,
the response of some cooks is to drop
their whisks and see what wonderful
new items Chuck Williams has found
on his travels. In addition to fine

cookware (Calphalon, Chantal, Le
Creuset) and top-quality tools
(KitchenAid, Cuisinart, Krups), you can
count on finding unusual items like
Viennese glass cookie stamps, pretty
porcelain rice bowls, or a rare imported
tea. Food items and recipes are always
part of the catalog. Williams-Sonoma
now has more than 60 shops across the
country.

Bimonthly catalogs, $2.00 for 12 issues
Phone, fax, and mail orders, gift orders
AMEX, MC, VISA

Especially for cake decorating—

Wilton Enterprises
2240 West 75th Street
Woodridge, IL 60515

312-963-7100

The Wilton Yearbook, now in its
twentieth year, combines cake-
decorating equipment and supplies with
recipes and illustrated step-by-step
instructions for techniques such as
piping and tinting icings. The amazing
variety of cake pans includes animals,
characters, holiday pans, and tier pan
sets—and there are ornaments for every
occasion.

Color catalog/instruction book $4.99
Phone and mail orders, gift orders
MC, VISA

From A to Z (almost)—

The Wooden Spoon
Route 145
Heritage Park
P. O. Box 931
Clinton, CT 06413-0931

800-431-2207
203-664-0303

This catalog contains everything from apple parers to whisks. In addition to cook's basics such as pepper mills and cookie pans, you'll find lots of clever items—an acrylic cookbook holder that folds flat, barbecue baskets for grilling many kinds of foods, and commercial-quality roasting racks. Foods include garlic, shallots, dried cherries, oils, and specialty peppercorns.

Color catalogs, $2.00 for a one-year subscription
Phone and mail orders, gift orders
AMEX, DISC, MC, VISA

Housewares from around the world—

Zabar's
2245 Broadway
New York, NY 10024

212-496-1234
Fax: 212-580-4477

At Zabar's, a large food emporium in New York City, the mezzanine features hundred of items of equipment for the cook. Their catalog offers a selection of these products ranging from large items (bread makers, toaster ovens, espresso and cappuccino machines) to smaller tools (Italian stainless steel strainers and popular Mouli graters). You'll also find knives, cookware, kitchen scales, special items like soda syphons, as well as coffee and specialty foods.

Free color catalog
Phone, fax, and mail orders, gift orders
AMEX

And for Outdoor Cooking

Barbecue woods for special flavor—

American Wood Products
9540 Riggs
Overland Park, KS 66212

913-648-7993

Wood chips can be ordered in these varieties: hickory, mesquite, sweet & smoky (apple and hickory), apple, cherry, and sassafras. Wood chunks and mesquite lump charcoal are also available, as well as Wicker barbecue sauces and spices for game and barbecue.

Free price list
Mail orders
No credit cards

An outdoor cooker and smoker—

Henkel, Inc.
P. O. Box 1322
Hammond, LA 70404

504-345-1016

Henkel's Smokey Bayou Outdoor Cooker uses convection heating to broil, bake, roast, and smoke foods. It's available in 7 sizes and can be adapted to use liquid propane or natural gas.

Free illustrated catalog
Phone and mail orders
MC, VISA

Hardwood charcoals and specialty cooking woods—

Peoples Charcoal Woods
55 Mill Street
Cumberland, RI 02864

800-729-5800
401-725-2700

To liven up your barbecues you can order logs, chunks, and chips of mesquite, hickory, apple, cherry, pecan, ash, maple, sweet birch, and oak. Chips are also available in alder, maple, and cob, walnut, nectarine, peach, almond, plum, fig, and olive, and you can order Pinot Noir grapevines. (Additional specialty woods, including sassafras and eucalyptus, are available seasonally.) Charcoal is available in maple, mesquite, Canadian maple, and various native American hardwoods. Ask for Peoples' retail price list when you write or call.

Free price list
Mail orders
No credit cards

For more sources of tea- and coffee-making equipment, check the selection available from the companies in Chapter 5, "Coffee and Tea."

Many of the suppliers in the "Asian Cuisines" section of Chapter 25, "The International Pantry" offer tools for oriental cooking.

GROWING YOUR OWN INGREDIENTS

It's hard to beat the flavor and freshness of home-grown produce. And for vine-ripened tomatoes, tender baby zucchini, crispy-fresh oriental vegetables, your own backyard may be your best source. A modest back-door herb garden can supply you with fresh herbs throughout the growing season and home-dried herbs to take you through the winter. Even if you only have room for a container garden on a city terrace, you can enjoy fresh herbs and some unusual vegetable varieties.

If you're more adventurous, try growing a supply of fresh mushrooms, shallots, fiery horseradish, or elephant garlic. You can even harvest your own saffron, the world's rarest and most expensive spice, by collecting the stigmas from fall-flowering saffron crocus bulbs.

Creative cooks who like to garden and dedicated gardeners who also enjoy cooking find that the two pursuits become interdependent after a while, each making the other more rewarding. And whether you're an experienced gardener with a large backyard plot or a beginner with a windowsill garden, here are some excellent sources of seeds and plants for vegetables and herbs that will bring variety and just-picked flavor to all of your cooking.

Herb plants from Cape Cod—

Cape Cod Herb Company
9 Childs Homestead Road, Box 1058
Orleans, MA 02653

508-240-0433

You may wish to add some of the Cape Cod Herb Company's unusual varieties to your herb garden. Here is a sampling from their list of dozens of plants: chocolate mint, tricolor sage, cinnamon basil, French fringed lavender, and caraway thyme. Herb plants are available in 4-inch pots for spring shipment, and most varieties have several plants in each pot, ready for division. Dried herb blends and potpourri are also available.

Free information
Mail orders
No credit cards

Herbs from a historic farm—

Caprilands Herb Farm
534 Silver Street
Coventry, CT 06238

203-742-7244

Visitors to Caprilands Herb Farm can have lunch or tea in an eighteenth-century farmhouse and browse through a bookshop, a basket shop, a greenhouse gallery for seeds and plants, and a restored barn for dried herbs, greeting cards, and prints. In addition, there are 31 different gardens growing over 300 varieties of herbs. Herbs and plants are available by mail, and Caprilands features a special collection for the beginning gardener. The catalog also includes an array of gardening accessories and books that will appeal to both cooks and gardeners.

Free illustrated catalog
Mail orders
No credit cards

Herbs and garden plants—

Carroll Gardens
444 East Main Street
Box 310
Westminster, MD 21157

800-638-6334
301-848-5422

The Carroll Gardens catalog provides descriptions of the herbs offered, as well as tips for use and storage. There are increasing discounts for ordering 3, 6, or 12 plants. The catalog also offers perennials, roses, vines and woody plants, books and gardening aids.

Illustrated catalog, $2.00
Phone and mail orders, gift orders, and gift certificates
MC, VISA

Vegetables and herbs—

Comstock, Ferre & Company
263 Main Street
Wethersfield, CT 06109

800-346-6110
203-529-3319

Comstock, Ferre & Company, which celebrates its one hundred and seventieth anniversary in 1990, offers a fine selection of vegetables and herbs, each well described and with planting tips. One unusual vegetable is Butterblossom squash, which produces numerous flowers for dipping in batter and frying. You are invited to visit the company's farm during early August to view new and current varieties of vegetables and flowers. The catalog also offers a selection of seeds for annual, biennial, and perennial flowers.

Free illustrated catalog
Phone and mail orders
MC, VISA

Rare lettuce, vegetables, and herbs—

The Cook's Garden
P. O. Box 65
Londonderry, VT 05148

802-824-3400
Fax: 802-824-3027

Experienced market gardeners Ellen and Shepherd Ogden offer an extensive selection of lettuces and hard-to-find salad greens: 50 lettuces; 20 chicories; 40 special salads; plus crudité vegetables, drying tomatoes, baby vegetables, and many herbs. You'll also find special seed collections (for example, Year-round Lettuce Garden, Windowsill Greens Garden, Crudité Garden), books, and supplies. The catalog is seasoned with friendly tips, growing advice, and recipes.

Illustrated catalog, $1.00
Phone, fax, and mail orders, gift orders
MC, VISA

Seeds for oriental vegetables—

Evergreen Y. H. Enterprises
Box 17538
Anaheim, CA 92817

Contact by mail

In addition to offering seeds for more than 70 kinds of Chinese and Japanese vegetables, this catalog will provide you with a thorough introduction to Asian produce. There is a photograph of each vegetable and a list that cross-references oriental vegetable names. Did you know, for instance, that coriander is also known as Chinese parsley, cilantro, yuen sei and shian choy? Combination packages of popular seeds are offered at a 10 percent discount.

Illustrated catalog, $1.00 (refunded with order)
Mail orders
No credit cards

Hundreds of herb products from Michigan—

Fox Hill Farm
440 West Michigan Avenue
Box 9
Parma, MI 49269-0009

517-531-3179

Fox Hill Farm is a family-owned herb farm located in the gently rolling Michigan countryside. They grow 450 varieties of herbs, fragrant plants, scented geraniums, and specialty vegetables, and offer herb plants plus a variety of culinary herbs and herb products through mail order. The Fox Hill Farm gardens are open for tours from mid-April to mid-October.

Free illustrated brochure
Mail and phone orders, gift orders
MC, VISA

A complete source for mushroom-growing supplies—

Fungi Perfecti
P. O. Box 7634
Olympia, WA 98507

206-426-9292

Although Fungi Perfecti offers complete equipment and supplies for growing mushrooms on an ambitious scale, beginners may be most interested in the kits for growing oyster and shiitake mushrooms indoors or for starting a mushroom patch in the backyard. This catalog is well illustrated, with clear explanations, and is a good place to begin to learn about mushroom growing. Books for beginners and advanced cultivators are offered.

Illustrated catalog, $3.00
Phone and mail orders
MC, VISA

Herbs and friendly advice—

Herb Gathering, Inc.
5742 Kenwood Avenue
Kansas City, MO 64110

816-523-2653

Seeds for *herbes de cuisine* are conveniently offered in small, medium, and large packets, and each listing includes lively and informative tips. For example, Borage: "Bushy—tends to get heavy and fall over—so stake for best results. The Madonna blue, star-shaped flowers droop, so plant high to look upward at these jewels. A good bee plant! Edible flowers—float in punch, sprinkle in salads, freeze in decorative ice." In addition to herbs, Paula Ann Winchester offers a carefully chosen selection of seeds for French vegetables and edible flowers, and the catalog describes the cultivation and characteristics of each. A book nook and gift selection complete this catalog.

Illustrated catalog, $2.00
Mail and phone orders, gift orders, and gift certificates
MC, VISA

Over 50 kinds of oriental seeds—

Kitazawa Seed Company
1748 Laine Avenue
Santa Clara, CA 95051-3012

408-249-6778

Here is a selection of seeds for more than 50 kinds of oriental vegetables, including beans, cabbage, eggplant, Japanese greens, mustard greens, squash, peas, and radishes.

Free price list
Mail orders
No credit cards

Shallots, leeks, and more for the cook—

Le Jardin du Gourmet
Box 75
St. Johnsbury Center, VT 05863

802-748-5646

Raymond Saufroy has been selling shallots since 1954 and offers several varieties for spring or fall planting. In addition, he sells leeks, garlic, and over 200 varieties of American and French vegetable, herb, and flower seeds. Also some special items such as wild strawberries, miniature pumpkins, and miniature corn.

Free catalog
Mail orders, gift orders
MC, VISA

Seeds especially for city dwellers—

Manhattan Farms Ltd.
P. O. Box 33972
Station D
Vancouver, BC V6J 4L7
Canada

604-253-0916

Manhattan Farms was started by two avid urban gardeners, and the resulting seed collections have been designed with the special needs of the city farmer in mind. Seeds come with an illustrated guide that will introduce you to the how-tos of container growing and small plot gardening. The ten seed collections include: edible flowers; northern European herbs; Mediterranean herbs; basil (five varieties); tomatoes (five varieties); gourmet greens (Belgian endive, radicchio, arugula, mâche, rhubarb chard); salsa (tomato, cilantro, tomatillo, ancho and jalapeño peppers); ratatouille (tomato, bell pepper, eggplant, basil, zucchini); and peppers (five varieties, described as "mild to challenging"). All seeds are open-pollinated varieties (unlike hybrids, you can collect these seeds from your plants for use in your garden the next year). The collections are beautifully packaged and would make welcome gifts for friends who enjoy gardening and cooking. When writing Manhattan Farms, remember that postage for a letter to Canada is 30¢.

Free information
Mail orders
No credit cards

A Guide to Using Edible Flowers
from Manhattan Farms

While edible flowers bring subtle new flavors to the kitchen, their most important contribution is decorative. They add a festive touch to salads and make interesting garnishes for soups and other dishes.

Always handle flowers very gently; they are delicate and can be easily bruised. It is best to pick flowers on the same day you plan to use them, gathering them early in the morning before it gets too hot. Those with stems can be stored in a vase; single blossoms can be placed gently between damp paper towels and kept in the fridge.

Before use, carefully check the flowers to make sure there are no little insects hiding in them. Wash and pat dry carefully. It's a good idea to taste your flowers before adding them to any dish to make sure they will enhance the flavor. If you find some of them bitter, trim the white portion off the base of the petal and taste again.

Here are some suggestions for using the edible flowers you can grow from Manhattan Farms seeds:

BERGAMOT (also known as bee balm): This very aromatic flower is delightful in salads and as a garnish. Dried bergamot leaves are a good seasoning for duck, sausage, pork, and curries.

BORAGE: Both the leaves and the flowers of borage can be eaten. The leaves and stems taste like cucumbers and can be used in salads. Float flowers in drinks or use them to decorate salads. Flowers can be candied by dipping them in egg white, then sugar, and then allowing them to dry.

CALENDULA (also called pot marigold): A pleasant peppery flavor and rich color makes calendula an interesting addition to salads, stews, and herb butters. Dried petals can be used as a saffron substitute.

CORNFLOWER (also known as Bachelor Button): Mild-flavored cornflowers are used primarily for their decorative qualities. Use petals in salads and whole flowers as a garnish. Because they do not lose their color when dried, these flowers are a good choice for dried arrangements, pressing, and potpourri.

DIANTHUS (commonly known as pink): The spicy, clovelike flavor of dianthus is good in wines, syrups, and butters. Try it as a garnish for soups and salads or candy them and use as a decoration on cakes.

GARLIC CHIVE: The delicious garlicky taste of this chive blossom is excellent in salads; the leaves can be used in the same ways as regular chives. This perennial plant takes a little patience to establish during the first year, but your patience will be rewarded for many years to come.

HOLLYHOCK: A mild, floral flavor makes this flower a delicious substitute for lettuce in sandwiches. And if you remove the center part from this flower, it makes a pretty little bowl for serving dips and savory snacks.

JOHNNY-JUMP-UP (also known as heartsease and love-in-idleness): This wild pansy has a rather bland flavor but is lovely as a garnish or an addition to salads. They can also be candied in the same way as borage flowers.

LEMON GEMS (part of the marigold family): While all marigolds are edible, few are palatable. However, this old-fashioned variety has a delicious, slightly bitter, lemony flavor. Use the petals in salads, the whole flowers as garnishes, or dry the blossoms and add to soups and stews for extra color and flavor. A beneficial companion plant for vegetables, this plant helps deter garden pests.

NASTURTIUM: The flavorful flowers, leaves, and seeds of this colorful plant are all edible. Add leaves and flowers to salads and sandwiches; use flowers in soups, stuffings, or as a vibrant garnish. Try making nasturtium butter by blending chopped flowers with butter. The seeds can be pickled and used as a substitute for capers.

A source for seeds and herbal products—

Meadowbrook Herb Garden
Route 138
Wyoming, RI 02898

401-539-7603

Meadowbrook sells seeds for more than 100 herbs, many of which are offered in several varieties. There are 8 varieties of basil, for example, and 4 kinds of yarrow. There is also a good assortment of dried herbs, herb mixtures, herbal teas, vinegars, and jellies. If you enjoy herb-based soaps and toiletries, Meadowbook's line is very complete.

Free illustrated catalog
Mail orders
MC, VISA

Herbs and plants from Maine—

Merry Gardens
Camden, ME 04843

Contact by mail

Ervin and Mary Ellen Ross have been running Merry Gardens since 1947, and they offer an extensive collection of herbs, house and conservatory plants. If you enjoy scented geraniums, peruse their amazing variety. They also specialize in ivies and fuchsias. In addition to the catalog, the Rosses offer numerous informational leaflets and articles for 35¢ and 50¢.

Illustrated catalog, $2.00
Mail orders
No credit cards

Preserving traditional Southwestern crops—

Native Seeds/SEARCH
2509 North Campbell Avenue, #325
Tucson, AZ 85719

Contact by mail

Native Seeds/SEARCH, a nonprofit seed conservation organization, was founded in 1983 to preserve the traditional native crops of the American Southwest and northwestern Mexico. It offers a great variety of seeds for beans, peas, chilies, corn, gourds, herbs, tomatoes, tomatillos, and more. The catalog also features cookbooks, a selection of reasonably priced handmade Indian baskets, as well as food items, herbs, and spices.

Illustrated catalog, $1.00
Mail orders
No credit cards

Vegetables and herbs from Oregon—

Nichols Garden Nursery
1190 North Pacific Highway
Albany, Oregon 97321

503-928-9280

This is a family business that has been around for more than fifty years and now keeps two generations of the family busy. They bring you vegetable seeds, elephant garlic, shallots, saffron crocus bulbs, culinary and ornamental herb plants and seeds. There are also tools, books, potpourri ingredients, and food items including herb and spice blends, teas, yogurt cultures, and more.

Free illustrated catalog
Mail order
MC, VISA

Special vegetable seeds for international cuisines—

Pinetree Garden Seeds
New Gloucester, ME 04260

207-926-3400

This Maine company was founded in 1979 specifically to meet the needs of home gardeners with limited space and therefore less need for large seed packets. The interests of gardening cooks are met with special sections on vegetables for Italian, oriental, Continental, and Latin American cooking. The Pinetree catalog is ideal for settling down with on a winter night—over 600 varieties of seeds are described by people who know them well. A few volumes from the well-chosen selection of gardening books (which includes books for children, too) will also help pass the winter months until it's time for planting.

Free illustrated catalog
Phone and mail orders
MC, VISA

Traditional and modern vegetables and herbs—

Plants of the Southwest
1812 Second Street
Santa Fe, NM 87501

505-983-1548

This company is dedicated to preserving the variety of plants native to the American Southwest. Cooks will be especially interested in listings of herbs, ancient American vegetables, and modern vegetables. For example, along with varieties of well-known herbs, you'll discover chia, a traditional Mexican herb for seasoning poultry and meat (and the tip that sprouted chia gives salads a peppery boost). Also you'll find cota (Navajo tea) and epazote, often used in Mexican cooking to flavor beans, and an excellent selection of seeds for beans, chili peppers, corn, and squash.

Color catalog, $1.50
Mail orders, gift certificates
MC, VISA

Vegetable and herb seeds—

Redwood City Seed Company
Box 361
Redwood City, CA 94064

415-325-7333

The carefully described vegetable and herb seeds from Redwood City Seed Company are open-pollinated. The company offers many books and booklets that will be of interest to both gardeners and cooks. You may also subscribe to catalog supplements (published in February, June, and October) that list recent additions and scarce and unusual seeds.

Illustrated catalog, $1.00
Mail orders
No credit cards

Herbs from A to Z—

Rosemary House
120 South Market
Mechanicsburg, PA 17055

717-697-5111
717-766-6581

The Rosemary House seed list begins with aconite and ends with yucca; the plant list begins with aloe and concludes with zebrovka, a sweet grass used to flavor vodka. Rosemary House also sells rare saffron bulbs, which are imported from Holland every fall. With saffron worth $2000 per pound, it definitely pays to grow your own! This catalog also offers dried culinary herbs, seasoning mixes, imported bouquets garnis, teas, gift items, kitchen accessories, and cookbooks.

Illustrated catalog, $2.00
Mail orders, gift orders
No credit cards

Herb plants and seeds plus advice and recipes—

Sandy Mush Herb Nursery
Route 2
Surrett Cove Road
Leicester, NC 28748

704-683-2014

Sandy Mush Herb Nursery sounds idyllic: "We live and work on a high mountain farm near Asheville in western North Carolina, where, in addition to our large collection of herb plants, we raise long-haired Angora goats whose mohair keeps many people warm! We have four greenhouses and an ever-increasing number of rock-walled herb gardens. Our main greenhouse is flanked by rock retaining walls filled with creeping herbs and topped by seasonal bulbs, heathers and flowers." The charmingly illustrated catalog is written in graceful calligraphy and offers herb plants and seeds, books and note cards, in addition to lots of helpful advice, recipes, and suggestions for laying out attractive herb gardens. Best of all, you may visit the nursery by calling or writing Kate Jayne to make an appointment.

Illustrated catalog, $4.00
Mail orders
MC, VISA

A source for heirloom seeds—

Seeds Blum
Idaho City Stage
Boise, ID 83706

Contact by mail

Jan Blum—appropriately pronounced "Bloom"—founded Seeds Blum in 1981 to specialize in "heirloom" seeds that are seldom or never seen in commercial seed catalogs. When Jan experienced gardening success with seeds given to her by an aging neighbor, she discovered that many "handed down" seeds are superior for home gardeners who grow for flavor and wish the harvest to extend throughout the growing season. Included are seeds for vegetables, grains, edible flowers, herbs, fall and winter gardens, as well as suggestions for planting gardens with an Asian, Southwestern, or Italian flavor. There's also a nice selection of books and gifts.

Color catalog, $3.00
Mail orders, gift orders, and gift certificates
No credit cards

Carefully chosen seeds—

Shepherd's Garden Seeds
6116 Highway 9
Felton, CA 95018

408-335-5311

Renee Shepherd works closely with French, Dutch, Italian, English, Japanese, and American seed houses and selects vegetable and herb varieties for their flavor, tenderness, and texture, as well as disease resistance and easy culture. Special seed collections include small-space gardens, a French garden, an Italian garden, baby vegetables, and

more. A child's garden collection features big-seeded varieties that are easy to plant and grow, along with charmingly illustrated instructions written for children. Ms. Shepherd has also written a wonderful cookbook which is available from her company. Both the book's introductory description of her love for gardening and her recipes are inspiring. The recipe for Tomato Lemon Chutney is borrowed with thanks from *Recipes from a Kitchen Garden*.

Illustrated catalog, $1.00
Mail and phone orders; gift orders
AMEX, MC, VISA

Heirloom vegetables, herbs, and flowers

Southern Exposure Seed Exchange
P. O. Box 158
North Garden, VA 22959

Contact by mail

This company specializes in open-pollinated, heirloom, and traditional varieties of vegetables, sunflowers, flowers, and herbs. There are also heirloom fruit trees, rare perennial multiplier onions, top-set onions, and garlic. The company's larger goal, insightfully explained in the catalog, is to foster cooperative self-reliance in the Mid-Atlantic region by encouraging increased reliance on locally adapted varieties and regional food production. The catalog also contains books and gardening supplies, with special supplies for seed savers.

Illustrated catalog, $3.00
Mail orders
No credit cards

Tomato Lemon Chutney

from Renee Shepherd, Shepherd's Garden Seeds

An excellent chutney with a complex, not too sweet flavor. It makes a fine gift.

 1 tablespoon oil
 1 small whole fresh or dry chili pepper, crumbled
½ teaspoon cumin seed
¼ teaspoon nutmeg
¼ teaspoon mustard seed
 4 large tomatoes, sliced very thin
½ fresh lemon
⅓ cup raisins or currants
½ cup sugar

Heat oil in a saucepan. Add the crumbled chili pepper, cumin seed, nutmeg, and mustard seed. When the seeds start to jump in the oil, add the tomatoes. Quarter the lemon half, removing any seeds, and lay it on top of the other ingredients in the pan. Simmer, stirring as needed to keep from sticking, for 15 minutes. Stir in the raisins or currants and the sugar. Continue to simmer, stirring frequently, until the mixture thickens, about 30 minutes. Cool and transfer to jars. Store chutney in the refrigerator. Makes about 2 cups.

Herbs with garden plans—

Sunnybrook Farms Nursery
9448 Mayfield Road
P. O. Box 6
Chesterland, OH 44026

216-729-7232

Sunnybrook Farms Nursery has been in the business for more than sixty years, and it seems to have cooks' interests high on its list. Almost half the attractive catalog is devoted to herbs, and there is a reasonably priced Cook's Garden of 20 popular culinary herbs that comes with an 8-page booklet of design, planting, care, and harvesting instructions for a 9′ × 12′ herb garden.

A lovely selection of scented geraniums, perennials, hostas, and ivies completes the catalog.

Illustrated catalog, $1.00
Phone and mail orders
MC, VISA

Oriental vegetables and a starter kit—

Sunrise Enterprises
Box 10058
Elmwood, CT 06110

Contact by mail

This catalog offers more than 100 kinds of oriental vegetables, including 17 varieties of Chinese cabbage. The proprietors of Sunrise Enterprises have thoughtfully put together a kit for beginners that includes an instruction book, 10 packets of oriental vegetable seeds, and garden supplies. A selection of books about gardening, cooking, herbs, bonsai, and traditional Chinese exercise is also offered.

Illustrated catalog, $1.00
Mail orders
No credit cards

Everything for the oriental kitchen—

Tsang & Ma Wokery
P. O. Box 294
Belmont, CA 94002

415-595-2270

In addition to a selection of seasonings, sauces, and equipment for oriental cooking, Tsang & Ma Wokery offers an excellent variety of seeds for growing oriental vegetables, including several varieties for each of the following: Chinese cabbage, mustard greens, leafy greens, radishes, edible gourds, eggplant, and herbs. Varieties are illustrated and well described, and general planting information about oriental vegetables is provided.

Free illustrated catalog
Phone and mail orders
MC, VISA

Herb plants and seeds—

Well-Sweep Herb Farm
317 Mount Bethel Road
Port Murray, NJ 07865

201-852-5390

This farm provides a complete selection of culinary herb plants, including 21 kinds of basil and a dozen different chives. For scented geranium enthusiasts, there are over 80 different kinds, although some are available at the farm only. Plants are shipped well rooted in 2- to 3-inch pots. The Well-Sweep catalog also offers herb seeds, dried flowers, potpourri, and gift items. *Favorite Recipes From Well-Sweep Herb Farm* was published in 1989 and is available by mail. The farm hosts June and September open houses, a special Christmas event, and year-round workshops.

Illustrated catalog, $1.00
Mail orders
No credit cards

And for Gardening Equipment—

Gardener's Eden
P. O. Box 7303
San Francisco, CA 94120-7307

415-421-4242

If you like Williams-Sonoma's catalog for cooks, you'll enjoy its garden catalog, too. In addition to gardening furniture, tools, and supplies, you'll find carefully chosen items such as French wire baskets, herbal steppingstones, vases, and cachepots.

Free color catalog
Phone and mail orders, gift orders
AMEX, MC, VISA

Gardener's equipment and mushroom-growing kits—

Gardener's Supply
128 Intervale Road
Burlington, VT 05401

802-863-1700

This supply company has a full range of products from greenhouses and shredders to organic fertilizers and composting supplies. Helpful and ecologically sound items include safe and natural pest controls and nontoxic wood preservatives. Try growing your own Belgian endive or mushrooms from the various kits offered. Will Rapp, president of Gardener's Supply, has been active in getting a leaf composting program under way in Burlington, and he will be happy to share information with you about composting on an individual or community basis.

Free color catalog
Phone and mail orders, gift orders
MC, VISA

High-quality tools—

Smith & Hawken
25 Corte Madera
Mill Valley, CA 94941-1829

415-383-2000
Fax: 415-383-7030

A delightful catalog of tools of the trade, garden wear, furniture, planters, and accessories. The emphasis is on high-quality, specialized tools that handle garden chores efficiently. Everything is completely guaranteed.

Free color catalog
Phone, fax, and mail orders, gift orders
AMEX, DC, MC, VISA

Additional sources—

You may also wish to contact these companies for their all-purpose gardening catalogs, which offer a good selection of vegetable seeds as well as fruit trees, berry bushes, flowers, and gardening supplies:

W. Atlee Burpee & Company
300 Park Avenue
Warminster, PA 18974

800-888-1447

Henry Field's Seed & Nursery Company
407 Sycamore Street
Shenandoah, IA 51602

605-665-4491

Gurney Seed & Nursery Company
Second and Capitol Streets
Yankton, SD 57079

605-665-4451

Mellinger's, Inc.
2310 South Range Road
North Lima, OH 44451-9731

216-549-9861

Thompson & Morgan, Inc.
P. O. Box 1308
Jackson, NJ 08527

201-363-2225

CHAPTER 29

SPECIAL FOOD GIFTS

Cooks always enjoy giving and receiving gifts of beautiful and well-prepared foods, no matter what the occasion. Food and equipment from any of the suppliers in the preceding chapters would make wonderful gifts (most will be delighted to put together gift selections at your request), and here are a few more sources for special presents that say, "Bon appétit!"

Baskets with treats from New England and beyond—

Baskets from the Old Cider Mill
1287 Main Street
Glastonbury, CT 06033

203-633-4880

In addition to baskets filled with New England regional specialties, you can send a Baker's Delight selection, Chocolate Lover's Basket, College Survival Kit, Get-Well Basket, Welcome Baby Basket, and more. Custom selections also available.

Free illustrated brochure
Phone and mail orders, gift orders
AMEX, MC, VISA

Gifts from a California restaurant—

Café Beaujolais Bakery
Box 730
Mendocino, CA 95460

800-332-3446
707-964-0292

Panforte (the bakery's first and still most popular item), dried fruit fruitcakes, cookies, sweets, jam, chutney, herb blends, and more. Gift samplers, too.

Free illustrated catalog
Phone and mail orders, gift orders, and gift certificates
MC, VISA

Soups from a Florida inn—

Chalet Suzanne
P. O. Box AC
Lake Wales, FL 33859

800-288-6011
Fax: 813-676-1814

Soups made from traditional recipes have been served to guests of the Hinshaw family for more than fifty years. Choose from almost 20 flavors of soup plus aspics, glazes, and sauces, all with recipes. Gift certificates for meals and accommodations at the inn are also available.

Free color brochure
Phone, fax, and mail orders, gift orders
AMEX, DISC, DC, MC, VISA

Classic fruitcakes—

Collin Street Bakery
401 West Seventh Avenue
Corsicana, TX 75110

800-248-3366
214-872-8111

Fruitcakes baked from the same
German recipe since the 1890s.

Free color brochure
Phone and mail orders, gift orders
AMEX, DC, MC, VISA

Fruit treats from the Northwest—

Cranberry Sweets
P. O. Box 501
Bandon, OR 97411

503-347-9475
503-888-9824

Original Cranberry Sweets plus a
variety of cranberry-nut candies and
chocolate-dipped cranberry treats. Also
pâtés de fruit made from berries and
fruit.

Free color catalog
Phone and mail orders, gift orders
AMEX, MC, VISA

Baked specialties—

Cryer Creek Kitchens
P. O. Box 5079
Corsicana, TX 75110

800-468-0088
214-872-8411

Pecan pie, fudge pecan pie, cheesecake,
rum cake, fruitcake, pineapple

macadamia cake, cookies, and nut
confections.

Free color catalog
Phone and mail orders, gift orders
AMEX, MC, VISA

Hand-decorated petits fours—

Divine Delights
1125 Magnolia Avenue
Larkspur, CA 94939

800-4-HEAVEN
415-461-2999

Pretty hand-decorated petits fours
available in chocolate, fresh strawberry,
lemon, white chocolate, marzipan, and
more. Also walnut fudge brownies,
butter tea cakes, and, for the holidays,
stollen and plum pudding.

Free brochure
Phone and mail orders, gift orders, and
gift certificates
MC, VISA

Gifts of meat, game, and salmon—

Dutchess Farms
Old Indian Road
Milton, NY 12547

914-795-2175

Gifts of meat and game, game birds and
poultry; many selections are available
smoked. Also smoked salmon and fresh
kosher salmon, lox and bagels,
fruitcakes and specialty cakes.

Free color brochure
Mail orders, gift orders
No credit cards

Baking since 1898—

Eilenberger's Butter Nut Baking Company
P. O. Box 710
Palestine, TX 75802-9987

214-729-2253
Fax: 214-723-2915

Old-fashioned cakes, including fruitcake, apricot cake, pecan cake, chocolate Amaretto cake, and Australian apple cake.

Free color brochure
Phone, fax, and mail orders, gift orders
AMEX, DC, MC, VISA

Traditional holiday favorites—

The Epicure's Club
107 F. Corporate Boulevard
P. O. Box 271
South Plainfield, NJ 07080

201-753-1220

Gift boxes and baskets featuring fruit, smoked meats, cheese, petits fours, cakes, nuts, and confections.

Free color catalog
Phone and mail orders, gift orders
AMEX, MC, VISA

Fruit and nut pâté—

The Flour Arts Pantry, Inc.
5668 Oak Grove
Oakland, CA 94618

415-652-7044

Nutty Fruit Confection, a fruit and nut pâté with a misting of Amaretto, but with no candied fruit, added sweeteners, fats, or salt.

Free color brochure
Mail orders, gift orders
No credit cards

Classic holiday favorites—

Goodies from Goodman
12102 Inwood Road
Dallas, TX 75244

800-535-3136
214-387-4804
Fax: 214-387-9984

Fruit baskets and boxes; selections with cheese, meats, preserves, nuts, confections. Also, smoked meats and floral selections.

Free color catalog
Phone, fax, and mail orders, gift orders
AMEX, MC, VISA

Gifts of foods for over fifty years—

Harry and David
Medford, OR 97501-0703

800-547-3033

Lavish fruit baskets and gift boxes that include confections, nuts, dried fruits, preserves, cheeses, and baked goods. The Fruit-of-the-Month Club® delivers fresh fruit year-round

Free color catalog
Phone and mail orders, gift orders
AMEX, MC, VISA

Hawaiian favorites—

Hawaiian Holiday Macadamia Nut Company
P. O. Box 707
Honokaa, HI 96727

800-444-6887

Macadamia nuts, plain and flavored, plus confections and cookies made with macadamias. Also coconut chips and Kona coffee.

Free color catalog
Phone and mail orders, gift orders
AMEX, MC, VISA

Gift baskets for cooks and food lovers—

Improv Gourmet Food Gift Baskets
17320 Germantown Road
Germantown, MD 20874

301-428-1010

Pretty gift baskets filled with a variety
of foods. Choose from Gourmet
Cooking Kits (ingredients for a French
or Italian dinner), Pasta Feast,
Chocolate Decadence, the College Care
Package, International Great Tastes, and
more.

Free color brochure
Phone and mail orders, gift orders
AMEX, MC, VISA

Your purchases benefit this nonprofit
group—

Lambs Farm
P. O. Box 520
Libertyville, IL 60048

800-52-LAMBS
312-362-4636

Baskets and boxes of meats and
cheeses, preserves and jellies, plus
confections, cakes, nuts, and greeting
cards. Purchases benefit a community
of mentally retarded adults.

Free color catalog
Phone and mail orders, gift orders
AMEX, MC, VISA

Aplets and Cotlets—

Liberty Orchards Company, Inc.
Cashmere, WA 98815

800-888-5696
Fax: 509-782-1487

Aplets and Cotlets are all-natural
confections made from the fruits and
nuts of the Pacific Northwest. With low
sodium and low cholesterol, they may
be ideal confections for friends with diet
restrictions.

Free color catalog
Phone, fax, and mail orders, gift orders
MC, VISA

Well-seasoned gifts—

McSteven's
P. O. Box 293
Clackamus, OR 97015-0293

800-547-2803
503-657-3055

Gift baskets packed with your selection
of mulling spices, spiced cocoas,
flavorings for popcorn, herbal
seasonings, baking mixes, and teas.

Free illustrated catalog
Phone and mail orders, gift orders
MC, VISA

For wine lovers on your list—

Marin Wine Cellar
2138-2140 Fourth Street
San Rafael, CA 94901

415-459-3823
Fax: 415-456-8858

Imported and California wines,
champagnes, madeira, and port
available in all price ranges and shipped
worldwide.

Free illustrated price list
Phone, fax, and mail orders, gift orders
AMEX, MC, VISA

Homemade cakes from a historic house—

Matthews 1812 House
Box 15, Whitcomb Hill Road
Cornwall Bridge, CT 06754

800-666-1812

Homemade, all-natural cakes including brandied apricot cake, fruit and nut cake, lemon rum sunshine cake; and confections—chocolates, chocolate-dipped apricots, old-fashioned hard candy. Also condiments, jams and jellies, and smoked meats.

Free color catalog
Phone and mail orders, gift orders
AMEX, MC, VISA

Easy gift giving—

Nationwide Gift Service
P. O. Box 32070
Phoenix, AZ 85064

800-243-3787
602-957-4923

Send champagne, wines, liqueurs, and spirits, as well as such food items as pâté, steaks, smoked salmon, and confections; also attractive boxes and baskets of food specialties. Nonfood gifts, too.

Free color catalog
Phone orders, gift orders
AMEX, DC, CB, MC, VISA

Authentic Danish kringle—

O & H Danish Bakery
1841 Douglas Avenue
Racine, WI 53402

800-227-6665
414-637-8895

Freshly baked pastries with nut and fruit fillings shipped fresh from the oven.

Free illustrated brochure
Phone and mail orders, gift orders
MC, VISA

Popcorn presents—

Panhandler Popcorn
P. O. Drawer 878
1300 South I-27
Plainview, TX 79072

800-332-1365

Plain and flavored popcorn packed in decorative tins to please all ages. Also candy and nuts and a selection of Tex-Mex food gifts.

Free color catalog
Phone and mail orders, gift orders
MC, VISA

Cookies and more—

Pepperidge Farm Mail Order Company
P. O. Box 917
Route 145
Clinton, CT 06413

203-669-4438

Many cookie selections, other baked goods (fruitcake, cheesecakes, tea cakes, muffins, stollen), confections, nuts, preserves, and soups.

Free color catalog
Phone and mail orders, gift orders
AMEX, DC, CB, MC, VISA

Real English plum puddings—

Proper Puddings, Inc.
RD 3, Box 455
Pine Bush, NY 12566

914-733-1324

These authentic plum puddings, made
by hand in small batches and matured
in brandy for three months, are packed
in English glazed crocks.

Free price list
Mail orders, gift orders
No credit cards

Gift baskets for all occasions—

Provender
3883 Main Road
Tiverton, RI 02878

401-624-8096

Gift baskets packed especially for a
hearty breakfast, morning tea, the
cocktail hour. For cooks, a basket with
olive oil, balsamic vinegar, fresh garlic,
and a garlic press. Other selections
include a chocolate lover's basket, one
filled with penny candy, and more.

Free illustrated brochure
Phone and mail orders, gift orders
AMEX, MC, VISA

For peanut butter enthusiasts—

Trombly's Peanut Butter Fantasies
64 Cummings Park
Woburn, MA 01801

800-422-1322
617-935-6460

Flavored peanut butters—honey
cinnamon, chocolate, banana crunch,
and chocolate raspberry. Also
confections: peanut butter truffles and
peanut butter with dark and white
chocolate. Peanut sauce (for everything
from stir frying to making a tasty
milkshake), too.

Free color brochure
Phone and mail orders, gift orders
MC, VISA

Gifts to please peanut lovers—

Virginia Diner
Route 460, Box 310
Wakefield, VA 23888-0310

800-868-NUTS
Fax: 804-899-2281

Gifts of peanuts and peanut confections
plus baskets packed with peanut
products (oil, butter, flour, soup mix);
also peanut pie, peanut wreaths, and a
Perpetual Peanut Club that delivers
gifts year-round.

Free color catalog
Phone, fax, and mail orders, gift orders
MC, VISA

CHAPTER 30

SUPPLIES FOR MAKING BEER AND WINE

If you've ever been faced with a bumper crop of strawberries or seen bushels of beautiful and inexpensive plums at a farmers' market, you may have wondered if this fruit might make some interesting wine. And if you're a beer enthusiast you might relish the idea of making your own hearty brew at home. Well, here's where to begin! The sources in this chapter offer catalogs that provide enjoyable and instructive introductions to the art of making beer and wine, and include everything you'll need to get started. Most companies put together kits of basic supplies and ingredients that make it especially easy and offer free and friendly advice to help you along.

It's quite legal to make your own wine and beer for personal use, and no registration is required. You may make 100 gallons of each per year for a one-person household, and 200 gallons of each per year for a household of more than one member.

Everything for making beer, wine, and liqueurs—

Beer & Wine Hobby
P. O. Box 3104
Wakefield, MA 01880

800-523-5423 (orders)
617-933-8818 (advice line)
Fax: 617-662-0872

This company offers everything you'll need for beer making—imported dry and liquid malt extracts, grains, hops, sugars, and yeasts, plus equipment. There are several kits that contain everything necessary to make your first batch. Wine-making supplies include concentrates for fruit wines, Italian and California grape concentrates, dried fruits, and yeasts. Fresh grapes are available by special order. All kinds of equipment, including oak barrels and grape presses, are offered. Noirot cordial extracts in over 20 flavors will let you make inexpensive liqueurs at home. Also supplies for making soft drinks and wine and malt vinegars.

Free catalog
Phone, fax, and mail orders
MC, VISA

Make German lager and English ale at home—

Bellinghausen Brewery Company
P. O. Box 257
Westwood, MA 02090

617-329-9099

Hazelnut Liqueur

from Beer & Wine Hobby

Put into blender:
  1 bottle Noirot hazelnut extract
  2 cups sugar

Fill to 32-ounce line with vodka.
Blend on medium speed until sugar dissolves. For extra smoothness, add 2 tablespoons glycerine. This makes a rich, nutty liqueur similar to Frangelico.

To make a heavenly fresh cream cordial:
Pour equal amounts of light cream and finished hazelnut liqueur into a serving glass. Mix well and serve immediately.

According to Steve Bellinghausen, it is surprisingly easy to brew truly world-class beers and ales at home. His company has assembled a "Basic Brewery" that supplies everything you need to make a case of Classic German Lager and a case of smooth English Amber Ale. Both will be ready to enjoy in under 30 days, and ingredient packages are available for future batches.

Free illustrated brochure
Phone and mail orders
MC, VISA

Supplies and step-by-step instructions—

The Cellar
14411 Greenwood North
Box 33525
Seattle, WA 98133

206-365-7660
Fax: 206-365-7677

For beermaking, this company offers various imported and domestic malts, hops, and a full line of equipment. Malted grains are also available, and you may have them ground at no extra charge. Grape and fruit concentrates, yeasts and additives for wine are available, as well as fermentation equipment, barrels, crushers, and presses. This catalog also contains illustrated step-by-step brewing and wine-making instructions and recipes, and a line of beer and wine glasses and corkscrews. The Cellar is pleased to offer expert advice to both the novice and the experienced beer and wine maker.

Free illustrated catalog
Phone, fax, and mail orders
MC, VISA

Make beer, wine, vinegar, and soft drinks—

Great Fermentations of Marin
87 Larkspur Street
San Rafael, CA 94901

800-542-2520 (orders)
415-459-2520 (advice line)

Equipment and ingredient kits from Great Fermentations will get you started easily. Everything for making beers, wines, vinegars, soft drinks, and liqueurs is available individually, too, including fresh grapes in season. There's also a press for cider making and a very complete selection of books about brewing and wine making, including books about making cider and mead; even a video about making wine from fruit.

Free illustrated catalog
Phone and mail orders
AMEX, MC, VISA

Make beer and wine—or cheese, bread, and vinegar—

Home Brew International, Inc.
1126 South Federal Highway, Suite 182
Fort Lauderdale, FL 33316

305-764-1527

For beginners, Home Brew recommends one of its foolproof kits containing everything you'll need including *The New Brewer's Handbook*, an informative guide with recipes. (The wine-making kit comes with *Enjoy Home Winemaking, A Guide for the Beginner*.) All equipment and ingredients can also be ordered separately. In addition, you'll find supplies for cheese making, bottling your own red, white, or malt vinegar, and baking sourdough bread.

Free illustrated catalog
Mail orders
No credit cards

Try some uncommon fruit wines—

Joe and Sons
P. O. Box 11276
Cincinnati, OH 45211

513-662-2326

Joe and Sons are a complete source of equipment and supplies for making wine and beer at home. Among their hundreds of items you'll find imported beer ingredients from England, Germany, Holland, and Australia. Over a dozen fruit wine concentrates from Oregon include some unusual flavors— gooseberry, boysenberry, loganberry, and marionberry. Joe and Sons also have ingredients for homemade soft drinks—try some old-fashioned sarsaparilla, cream soda, or birch beer.

Free illustrated catalog
Phone and mail orders, gift orders
MC, VISA

Supplies, advice, and recipes—

E. C. Kraus
Box 7850
Independence, MO 64053

816-254-7448

Another fine source of ingredients and equipment for making wine, beer, soda pop, and cordials, E. C. Kraus also offers dried wine-making ingredients— elderberries, elderflowers, dandelions, rose hips shells, ginger root, sarsaparilla, and woodruff herb. Here is some advice from Kraus: using white oak chips in the wine-making process will speed up the aging process and give you about the same benefits as using a new oak keg. Recipes from the company's customers are included in the catalog.

Free illustrated catalog
Phone and mail orders
MC, VISA

Several kits to get you started—

Mayer's Cider Mill
P. O. Box 204
Webster, NY 14580

800-876-2937
716-671-1955
Fax: 716-671-5269

You can order from a complete list of equipment and supplies, or get started by choosing from Mayer's several kits for making beer, wine, cold duck, or champagne. There's also a good selection of books and supplies, including decorative labels for your finished products. At Mayer's you'll also find kits for making brandied fruit and perfumes.

Free catalog
Phone, fax, and mail orders
AMEX, MC, VISA

Helpful descriptions of equipment and books—

O'Brien's Cellar Supplies
Box 284V
Wayne, IL 60184

708-289-7169

All the equipment and supplies in the well-prepared O'Brien's catalog include clear descriptions of what they are and how and why they are used. Among the wine concentrates you'll find some fast-maturing varieties that are ready in just three weeks. The full range of supplies includes a line of inexpensive equipment for corking champagne bottles. The wine- and beermaking books from O'Brien's are also well described, making it easy to choose one appropriate to your level of interest and expertise.

Free illustrated catalog
Phone and mail orders
MC, VISA

Supplies from a Minneapolis store—

Semplex of U.S.A.
P. O. Box 11476
Minneapolis, MN 55411

612-522-0500

Since 1962, Semplex has served amateur oenologists and brewers through its large Minneapolis store and mail order service. The catalog, helpfully indexed, supplies all the equipment and supplies you'll need, either individually or in the kits that are recommended for beginners. A complete line of Noirot extracts, from Amaretto to verbena, is offered, as well as a selection of British and American books. Semplex recommends *Growing Grapes in Minnesota* for anyone interested in growing wine grapes in a cold climate. A get-acquainted offer brings you a free introductory beer- or wine-making book with your first order.

Free illustrated catalog
Phone and mail orders
DC, CB, MC, VISA

A complete guide to beermaking—and equipment, too—

Specialty Products International, Ltd.
Box 784
Chapel Hill, NC 27514

919-929-4277

When you write or call Leigh P. Beadle of Specialty Products International you'll receive a copy of his *Home Beermakers' Guide*, a booklet that introduces you to the equipment, ingredients, and procedures for making flavorful beers at home. You can order a complete beermaking kit from Leigh or individual ingredients to make fine beer for about 50¢ a six-pack.

Free illustrated catalog
Phone and mail orders
MC, VISA

A newsy, informative beermaking catalog—

William's Brewing
P. O. Box 2195
San Leandro, CA 94577

415-895-2739

Bill Moore's catalog is more like a newsletter with lots of helpful advice and time-tested recipes from satisfied customers. You can order the William's brewery kit with everything you'll need (including a siphonless fermenter) and choose from ingredients for over a dozen kinds of beer from light lager to stout. Or order items individually. You'll also find everything from home draft systems to a selection of old-fashioned wall-mounted bottle openers that are rugged and inexpensive.

Free illustrated catalog
Phone and mail orders, gift orders
MC, VISA

From a large Miami supplier—

Wine & Brew by You, Inc.
5760 Bird Road
Miami, FL 33155

800-451-5414
305-666-5757

Sandy Morgan started making wine and beer at home twenty-five years ago and opened her store in 1972 to turn her hobby into a business. Now the Florida store she runs with partner Craig McTyre is one of the largest in the country, and the mail order department supplies home beer and wine makers all over the country with equipment and supplies. You'll find everything to make beer, wine, soft drinks, and liqueurs, and you can order from a selection of books, including two written by Sandy and Craig.

Free illustrated catalog
Phone and mail orders
MC, VISA

A complete selection for wine and beer making—

Wine Art
5890 North Keystone Avenue
Indianapolis, IN 46220

317-546-9940

Wine Art, a well-stocked shop in Indianapolis, can mail order everything you need for making wine or beer. The selection of wine concentrates is vast and includes more than a dozen fruit varieties. Among the beer malts you're sure to find one to make your favorite kind of brew. There's a good selection of yeasts, additives, bottling equipment, and barrels. Wine Art also stocks racks, glassware, corkscrews, and additional wine serving accessories.

Free price list
Phone and mail orders
AMEX, MC, VISA

GLOSSARY

Adzuki beans: flavorful red-maroon beans with a white stripe, often used for desserts in Japan.

Agar-agar: a type of unflavored vegetable gelatin in flake form.

Aïoli: Strongly flavored garlic mayonnaise.

Amaranth seed: a high-protein grain (about 16% protein) that makes a nutritious hot breakfast cereal and can be ground into low-gluten amaranth flour.

Anasazi beans: all-purpose beans that combine the flavors and textures of pinto and kidney beans; named for the Anasazi cliff dwellers of the Southwest.

Andouille: smoked, seasoned pork French sausage used in Cajun cooking such as gumbos and jambalaya.

Annatto seeds (also called achiote seeds): deep red-orange seeds with a subtle flavor; they turn rice a saffron color.

Antipasto: Italian for hors d'oeuvre; a first course.

Arborio rice: short-grained white Italian rice; ideal for risotto and paella.

Atole: roasted cornmeal; mix with milk and sugar for a traditional New Mexico breakfast.

Baklava: Middle Eastern sweet pastry made with tissue-thin layers of phyllo pastry and spiced ground nuts and soaked in syrup.

Balsamic vinegar: well-aged Italian vinegar with a distinctive flavor (more information on page 159).

Basmati rice: long-grained Indian rice with wonderful aroma and nutlike taste; excellent with curries.

Beignet: French for fritter or doughnut; a traditional New Orleans treat.

Berbere: blend of hot spices for Ethiopian dishes.

Biscotti: crisp Italian cookies or biscuits; means twice baked.

Bok choy: a variety of Chinese cabbage; also called Chinese white cabbage.

Boniato: tropical white sweet potato popular in Cuba and Latin America.

Bouquet garni: bundle of herbs (often parsley, thyme, marjoram, and bay leaf) used to flavor soups, stews, and similar dishes; sometimes the herbs are tied in a small cheesecloth bag.

Buckwheat groats (also called *Kasha*): buckwheat kernels; makes a tasty hot cereal.

Bulgur: cracked-wheat kernels; a staple grain of the Middle East; use as a cereal or in place of rice in pilafs.

Calamari: Italian for squid.

Cassia buds: small, clove-like dried flower buds of the Chinese cassia tree; used to flavor preserved fruits and vegetables; can also be simmered to give the house an aromatic cinnamon fragrance.

Cassoulet: a French stew made with white beans.

Cellophane noodles: translucent noodles made from mung beans; used in oriental cooking.

Charcuterie: French name for a delicatessen selling prepared meats; also, the products sold.

Charnuska: black cumin or Russian caraway seeds.

Chèvre: cheese made from goats' milk.

Chicory: salad green with curly leaves, also called curly endive. The roots of another variety of chicory are dried, roasted, and ground and used to flavor coffee.

Chile con queso: spicy Mexican dip made with cheese, green chilies, tomatoes, and seasonings.

Chilies: See page 203 for a description of various types of chilies.

Chorizo: Spanish or Mexican pork sausage seasoned with garlic, chili powder, spices, and herbs.

Chutney: relish made with fruit and vegetables preserved with sugar, vinegar, and spices; although traditionally served with curry, chutneys complement many foods and are flavorful accompaniments or ingredients.

Clarified butter: butter that has been melted, skimmed, and strained; ideal for sautéing because it can withstand higher temperatures without burning.

Coriander (also called *cilantro* or *Chinese parsley*): aromatic herb with flat leaves and stronger, more distinctive flavor than regular parsley. Also, a spice sold whole or ground.

Cornichons: small gherkin pickles from France; typical garnish with pâté.

Couscous: granular semolina, a staple of African cuisine; also, the name for the cooked dish.

Crème fraîche: cultured fresh cream (more information and cooking suggestions on page 32).

Cumin (also called *comino*): strongly aromatic seed that is an essential ingredient in curry powder and chili powder.

Daikon: Japanese white radish.

Dolma: Greek appetizer of grape leaves stuffed with rice and/or meat and seasonings.

Epazote: pungent herb used in Mexican dishes, especially to flavor beans.

Extra-virgin olive oil: olive oil with an acidity level below one percent (more information on page 159).

Falafel: Middle Eastern vegetarian dish of deep-fried balls made from beans or chick-peas, garlic, and spices.

Fava beans: small fava beans are used in casseroles and Middle Eastern dishes such as falafel; large fava beans are also known as broad beans.

Fenugreek seeds: small red-brown seeds with a distinctive burnt sugar taste; frequently used in curry powder, chutneys, and spice blends.

Fermented black beans: preserved black soybeans with a strong and distinctive flavor; used in Chinese cooking.

Feta cheese: Greek cheese made from sheep's or goat's milk; crumbly, white, and strong-flavored.

Fiddleheads: curled tips of young fern fronds gathered in the spring; many ferns are poisonous so it's wise to purchase fiddleheads from a produce dealer.

Filberts: another name for hazelnuts.

Fish sauce (also called fish gravy or fish soy)*:* distinctively flavored sauce made from fermented fish or seafood; a savory flavor essential in Thai cooking.

Five spice powder: a combination of anise seed, fennel, clove, cinnamon, and Szechwan pepper used in Chinese cooking.

Flageolets: small, oval French green kidney beans; available in U.S. either canned or dried.

Focaccia: round, flat Italian bread, often flavored with pesto, cheese, and herbs.

Foie gras: liver of a goose or duck that has been fattened by force-feeding.

Frittata: Italian open-faced omelet; fillings may include cheese, vegetables, ham, and herbs.

Fromage blanc: light cheese made from skimmed cow's milk (more information on page 32).

Galanga (also called *galangal)*: aromatic root, similar in appearance to ginger root, essential to Thai cooking.

Garam masala: aromatic Indian seasoning blend, which may contain cardamom, black pepper, coriander, cumin, cinnamon, cloves, ginger, and other spices.

Garbanzo beans (also known as *chick-peas):* cream-colored round dried beans with a nutty flavor; a staple in Middle Eastern, Latin American, and Indian cooking.

Garlic: see page 193 for a glossary of these types: elephant, silverskin, rocambole, red Italian.

Grenadine: red, sweet, non-alcoholic flavoring syrup used for making cocktails and as a cooking ingredient.

Gumbo filé: powdered sassafras leaves used to flavor and thicken Creole gumbos.

Hazelnuts (also known as *filberts):* flavorful round nut grown extensively in Oregon (more information on page 151).

Hoisin sauce: sweet, brownish-red Chinese sauce made with soybeans, sugar, garlic, and spices.

Hummus: a Middle Eastern dip made from chick-peas pureed with seasonings such as sesame tahini, garlic, lemon juice.

Juniper berries: Deep-purple berries with bittersweet flavor; ideal for flavoring game and poultry.

Krupuk: Asian wafer chips or snacks (more information on page 216).

Lavosh: Armenian flatbread.

Lemon grass: tropical grass with citrus flavor; essential to Thai and Vietnamese cooking.

Lotus root: long, potatolike root used in Chinese cooking.

Mahleb: seed of wild cherry used to flavor Armenian, Greek, and Arabic breads.

Malossol caviar: fresh caviar processed with reduced salt (more information in the caviar glossary on page 24).

Maple sugar: granulated maple product produced by boiling all the liquid from maple syrup.

Marron: French for chestnut.

    Crème de marrons: sweetened puree of chestnuts.

    Marrons en sirop: whole chestnuts in vanilla syrup.

    Marrons glacés: preserved chestnuts in sugar.

Mascarpone: rich, fresh Italian cheese (more information and serving suggestions on page 32).

Maskal Teff: staple grain of Ethiopia.

Melba sauce: raspberry sauce traditionally used with peaches and ice cream for Peach Melba.

Mesclun: French salad mixture of lettuces and other greens.

Miso: soybean paste made from fermented cooked soybeans; used in Japanese cooking to flavor soups and in dressings for vegetables.

Mole: Mexican sauce of spices, chili peppers, nuts, seeds, and chocolate for poultry.

Mortadella: Italian spiced pork sausage.

Mushrooms:

    Cèpes/Porcini: Cèpes are imported from France; porcini are the same variety imported from Italy; they have a rich, woodsy flavor that complements chicken, omelets, pasta, risotto.

    Chanterelles: reddish-yellow mushroom with a pretty cup shape.

    Morels: distinctively flavored wild mushroom with elongated caps and spongelike surface.

Shiitake: Japanese mushrooms with large, meaty caps (Chinese call them Tonku or Black Chinese Mushrooms); cultivated and readily available fresh in the U.S.A.

Orzo: tiny Greek pasta shaped like grains of rice.

Paella: classic Spanish dish of saffron-flavored rice with a variety of meats and seafood.

Pancetta: unsmoked, cured Italian bacon.

Panettone: traditional yeast-leavened Italian cakelike bread made with raisins and candied fruit.

Parchment paper: paper for a variety of cooking purposes, including lining pans, wrapping food, and forming pastry tubes; food cooked and served in parchment paper is called *en papillote.*

Pecan rice: long-grain rice with a nutty flavor grown in southern Louisiana.

Pectin: natural fruit product that gels jam and jellies.

Pepitas: pumpkin seeds.

Peppercorns:

> *Black:* pungent flavor and aroma. Tellicherry black peppercorns are considered the best.
>
> *Green:* zesty flavor and color bonus.
>
> *Pink:* bright color and biting flavor.
>
> *White:* pungent; appropriate for light-colored dishes.

Pesto: zesty Italian sauce made from basil, cheese, garlic, pine nuts, and olive oil.

Phyllo (also called *filo*): tissue-thin sheets of pastry for Middle Eastern sweet and savory pastries.

Pignoli (also called *piñon* and *pine nuts*): small oval nuts; a Mediterranean staple indispenable for pesto, stuffings, salads, and cookies.

Piloncillo: raw brown sugar pressed into small cones; used in Mexican cooking.

Poi: traditional Hawaiian dish made from taro, a staple root vegetable in Hawaii and Polynesian countries.

Polpo: Italian for octopus.

Posole: a Mexican dish of fresh hominy combined with spices and pork.

Praline: crunchy mixture of nuts and crystallized sugar used in desserts and candy or for topping ice cream.

Psyllium: high-fiber seed that is a natural laxative; try it sprinkled on cereal, yogurt, or cottage cheese.

Quatre épices: blend of four spices, usually black pepper, cloves, ginger, and nutmeg.

Quinoa: high-protein, gluten-free grain; quick-cooking and versatile as a rice substitute and in main dishes and desserts.

Ristra: decorative hanging arrangement of dried onions, garlic, or chili peppers.

Rose water: flavoring distilled from fresh rose petals.

Saffron: highly valued seasoning made from the stigmas of the *Crocus sativus;* imparts distinctive flavor and vivid yellow color.

St. John's bread: sweet, starchy pods from the carob tree; said to have been the "locust" that sustained John the Baptist in the wilderness.

Salpicão: Portuguese smoked ham roll.

Sambal: a paste of chili peppers and other seasonings used to flavor Indonesian dishes (more information on page 216).

Sea vegetables (or seaweed): see page 192 for descriptions of alaria, nori (amanori), kelp, and dulse.

Soba: Japanese thin buckwheat-flour noodles.

Star anise: star-shaped pod from a Chinese evergreen tree; intense licoricelike flavor and aroma.

Sumac berry: red berries from a special variety of sumac tree with a tart, lemony flavor; used in Middle Eastern cooking.

Tahini: paste made from crushed sesame seeds.

Tasso: highly seasoned smoked pork strips that add Cajun flavor to rice dishes, beans, casseroles, and other dishes.

Tofu: soybean curd.

Truffles: highly prized fungi, either black or white; the most famous come from Périgord in southwestern France.

Turbinado sugar: pure, unrefined raw sugar.

Vanilla bean: podlike seed capsule of the Vanilla *planifolia,* usually 5 to 8 inches long.

Wasabi: Japanese green horseradish; available canned or in powdered form to mix with water.

Wehani rice: California-grown rice developed from basmati; turns russet when cooked and has a nutty aroma.

Yucca root: a basic Latin American food, often used in the U.S. for making tapioca.

Zahter: Middle Eastern spice of ground sumac and thyme.

INDEXES

INGREDIENTS AND SUPPLIES

SUPPLIERS

RECIPES